IMAGINING
EGYPT

IMAGINING EGYPT

A LIVING PORTRAIT OF THE TIME OF THE PHARAOHS

Written and Illustrated by Mark Millmore

BLACK DOG
& LEVENTHAL
PUBLISHERS
NEW YORK

Imagining Egypt
Copyright © 2007 by Eyelid Productions, Ltd.

ISBN-10: 1-57912-547-6
ISBN-13: 978-1-57912-547-9

Library of Congress Cataloging-in-Publication Data

Millmore, Mark.
  Imagining Egypt: a living portrait of the land of the pharaohs/written and illustrated by Mark Millmore.
  p. cm.
  Includies bibliographical references and index.
  Contents: In the beginning – The kings and queens – The pyriamids – The temples – The hieroglyphs – The gods and goddesses – Daily life in ancient Egypt – The land of the dead – The dynasties
    ISBN-13: 978-157912-547-9 (alk. paper)
    ISBN-10: 1-57912-547-6 (alk. paper)
    l. Egypt—CivilizationTo 332 B.C. 2. Egypt—Civilization—332 B.C.-638 A.D. I. Title.

DT61.M5526 2007
932—dc22   2007042979

Cover and Interior Design: Sheila Hart Design

Manufactured in China

Published by
Black Dog & Leventhal Publishers, Inc.
151 West 19th Street
New York, New York 10011

Distributed by
Workman Publishing Company
225 Varick Street
New York, New York 10014-4381

g f e d c b a

ACKNOWLEDGMENTS
I would like to thank Paul Kendrick for his contributions to my Egyptian projects, Gregg Gillespie for opening the door of opportunity, and especially Parti Patiyem for her help, support, and encouragement during the production of this book. I would like to thank J.P. Leventhal for giving me the opportunity to create this book; Laura Ross, my editor, who endured my artistic temperament; and Sheila Hart, whose designs enhanced my art—I've learned a lot about making a book from Sheila. I'd also like to thank Dana Trombley, editorial assistant; True Sims, production director; Iris Bass, copyeditor; Claire Petrie and Fiorella deLima, proofreaders; and the rest of the staff of Black Dog & Leventhal. Finally, I would like to thank Bruce Leavitt, who is a fan of my web site and gave me one of his Sandblaze Systems, Inc., computers, which I used to render all the temple reconstructions. www.sandblaze.com

Dedicated to the memory of
Lionel Miskin and Vivian Stanshall,
who were my artistic mentors,
and Jean-François Champollion,
who unlocked the hieroglyphic
code and rediscovered
the Egyptians for the world.

Contents

Welcome to the Land of the Pharaohs

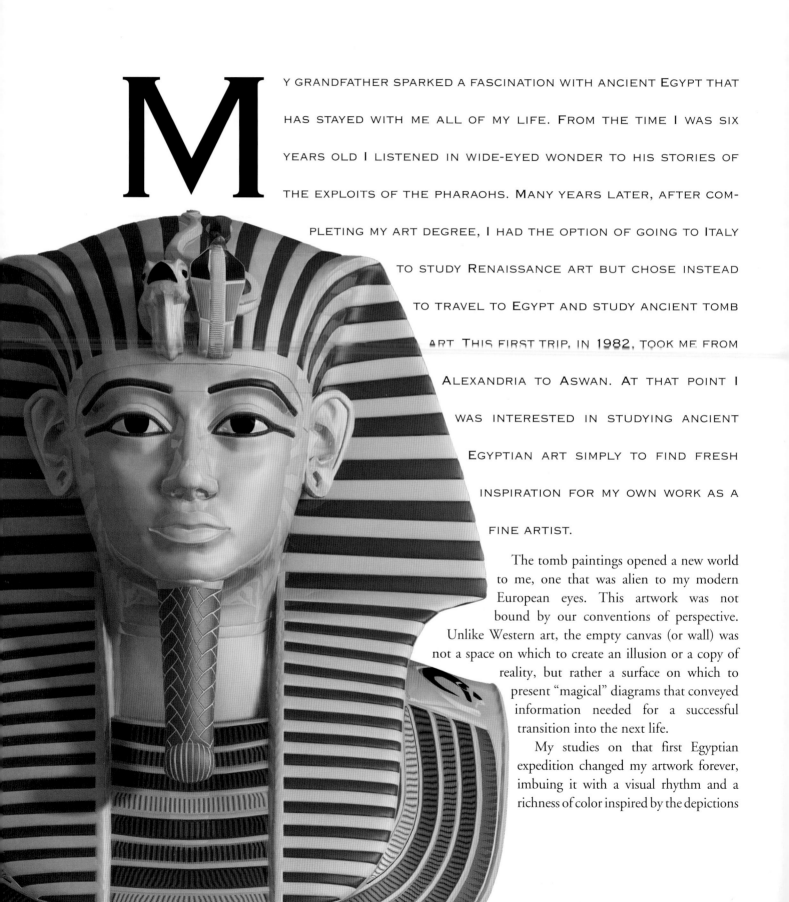

MY GRANDFATHER SPARKED A FASCINATION WITH ANCIENT EGYPT THAT HAS STAYED WITH ME ALL OF MY LIFE. FROM THE TIME I WAS SIX YEARS OLD I LISTENED IN WIDE-EYED WONDER TO HIS STORIES OF THE EXPLOITS OF THE PHARAOHS. MANY YEARS LATER, AFTER COMPLETING MY ART DEGREE, I HAD THE OPTION OF GOING TO ITALY TO STUDY RENAISSANCE ART BUT CHOSE INSTEAD TO TRAVEL TO EGYPT AND STUDY ANCIENT TOMB ART. THIS FIRST TRIP, IN 1982, TOOK ME FROM ALEXANDRIA TO ASWAN. AT THAT POINT I WAS INTERESTED IN STUDYING ANCIENT EGYPTIAN ART SIMPLY TO FIND FRESH INSPIRATION FOR MY OWN WORK AS A FINE ARTIST.

The tomb paintings opened a new world to me, one that was alien to my modern European eyes. This artwork was not bound by our conventions of perspective. Unlike Western art, the empty canvas (or wall) was not a space on which to create an illusion or a copy of reality, but rather a surface on which to present "magical" diagrams that conveyed information needed for a successful transition into the next life.

My studies on that first Egyptian expedition changed my artwork forever, imbuing it with a visual rhythm and a richness of color inspired by the depictions of the creatures of air, river, and desert. It also left me with a keen curiosity to find out more about those ancient people and their way of life. I bought many books on the subject, most of which were made up of academic descriptions of artifacts accompanied by wonderful photographic illustrations. Some of these books were so esoteric that they were virtually unreadable. At the opposite extreme were books that ignored or twisted material evidence to support ridiculous and outlandish speculations. (All of these I chucked into the rubbish bin.)

I found few scholars willing to come off the fence and present a personal vision based on their knowledge, something that might make the ancient world meaningful to us today.

Then, in the mid-1980s, I discovered John Romer. He became a sort of hero to me because his books and films evoked the human dimension of ancient Egyptian society. The BBC and Channel 4-TV series *Romer's Egypt* and *Ancient Lives* are intimate and moving portrayals of actual ancient people. At last I had found a doorway into the world of the ancient Egyptians and could begin to gather clues as to the nature and values of their civilization.

Inspired by Romer's works, and for my own amusement, I published a Web site in 1996 and called it "Mark Millmore's Ancient Egypt" (www.discoveringegypt.com). It features my drawings, paintings, etchings, and photos, along with my rather personal and opinionated writings about the ancient peoples of the Nile. Having been involved in the computer business I was quite familiar with computer-generated imagery and began to recreate some of the ancient temples, showing them as they might have appeared when new. To my surprise the website has become very popular, currently receiving around 15,000 visitors per day. It has also generated lots of e-mail from kids, schoolteachers, and adults who ask all sorts of questions about the ancient Egyptians.

From this correspondence I began to realize that there are vast numbers of people all over the world who would like to learn about ancient Egyptian history (and perhaps history in general), but who might be put off by the complex and impenetrable writings of academia. I have often spent an hour a day answering people's questions, checking the answers in Egyptology books and rephrasing the information so that it might be understood by any curious person.

This book owes a great deal to that process of answering questions from my online visitors, and is for all those people who marvel at the achievements of ancient Egypt and want an introduction to its history and its people. The artwork and recreations of the ancient monuments are my personal vision, based on many years of Egyptian travel and observation. The temple reconstructions are an attempt to show how these wonderful buildings might have appeared in ancient times. (I emphasize the word "might" because it is important to remember that we cannot ever know exactly how they looked in their own time—but we can speculate intelligently, based on all of the information we have.)

Finally, there is some disagreement among historians over the ancient Egyptian chronology—and there are even some claims for an entirely new chronology—but as yet there is no conclusive material evidence to support a radical new view. So, for consistency, I've used the basic chronology found in the *British Museum Dictionary of Ancient Egypt.*

And now, let's travel back in time to the lost world of the ancients. I hope you enjoy this journey, and that it will inspire you to dig deeper into the riches that history has to offer us. I think you'll agree that there is much to learn from the great works and words of an early civilization that was, in many ways, as sophisticated as our own.

MARK MILLMORE

In the Beginning
Unlocking the Wonders of Ancient Egypt

ANCIENT PEOPLES REVERED EGYPT AS A BEACON OF WISDOM AND CIVILIZATION. FOR THE EGYPTIANS THEMSELVES, THE LAND WAS SACRED: IT BELONGED TO THE GODS, AND WAS THE CLOSEST PLACE TO PARADISE ON EARTH. WHILE OTHER PEOPLES LIVED AS SCATTERED TRIBES, EGYPT WAS A COUNTRY—INDEED, IT WAS THE FIRST AND ONLY NATION STATE OF THE ANCIENT WORLD. THE SUMERIANS, THE BABYLONIANS, THE TROJANS, AND THE GREEKS HAD ALL FORMED CITY STATES, BUT NOT NATION STATES AS WE UNDERSTAND THEM TODAY. THESE LITTLE CITY STATES GREW, FLOURISHED, WERE CONQUERED, AND SOME DISAPPEARED INTO OBLIVION, LEAVING LITTLE TRACE OF THEIR EXISTENCE. BUT THE EGYPTIANS THRIVED AND THEIR CULTURE BLOSSOMED FOR MORE THAN THREE THOUSAND YEARS. THEY CAME TO TOWER ABOVE ALL OTHER CIVILIZATIONS AND LEFT BEHIND A WEALTH OF INFORMATION ABOUT THEIR WAY OF LIFE.

During its long history, Egypt influenced the development of other civilizations in the ancient Mediterranean world. Even when it was conquered by the Persians, ruled by the Greeks, and finally incorporated into the Roman Empire, its culture continued to spark people's imaginations. But after three thousand years, the world outside Egypt changed so radically that eventually it came to bear on Egypt itself. The decline of its traditions began during the Roman occupation: as a province of the Roman Empire, Egypt had no god-king pharaoh to focus the religious beliefs of its people, to maintain the

temples, and to carry out the ritual festivals. Gradually, the traditions that had characterized the Egyptian nation began to fade away and the last vestiges of the living culture ceased to exist in AD 391, when the Christian Byzantine emperor Theodosius I closed all pagan temples throughout the Roman Empire.

It was the spread of Christianity in Egypt during the first century AD that finally turned the Egyptians away from their traditions for good. They had always been a deeply religious people and the Christian message embodied themes that they recognized from their own ancient religion. The death and resurrection of Jesus was reminiscent of the story of Osiris; and the Christian story of Mary, the sacred mother of god, filled the place of the Isis myth. The Christian idea that the dead are judged before their souls can enter paradise was in keeping with Egyptian religious beliefs as well. Even the Christian symbol of the cross resembled the ankh, the Egyptian symbol for eternal life. What's more, the belief that God had chosen Egypt as a safe place for his infant son was a great source of pride to Egyptian Christians. The new religion filled the vacuum created by the loss of their ancient traditions and the Egyptians soon converted their temples into churches.

The descendants of those early Egyptian Christians are known as Copts, and the Coptic language was the last incarnation of ancient Egyptian. The sacred hieroglyphs were soon forgotten because Coptic was written using the Greek alphabet. Without knowledge of their own ancient

The word "Copt" comes from the Greek word "Aigyptos" or Egypt. The Coptic Church is founded on the teachings of Saint Mark, who brought Christianity to Egypt during the reign of the Roman emperor Nero in the first century AD.

A RECREATION OF MEDIEVAL CAIRO BASED ON ANTIQUE ENGRAVINGS.

OSIRIS, RULER OF THE DEAD, SITS ON HIS THRONE.

language the Copts lost touch with their history, and the culture and achievements of the ancient Egyptians became shrouded in the mists of myth and fable. Egypt's great legacy was all but forgotten—and, all too soon, Christians came to ridicule those ancient people as godless pagans. By the Middle Ages, our knowledge of the ancient Egyptians was limited to references in Greek and Roman literature and stories from the Old Testament Bible.

The great monuments were used as quarries and destroyed—much of medieval Cairo was built using the facing stones from the pyramids. There was also a huge trade in mummies for medicine and tombs up and down the Nile were ransacked. Many thousands of mummies were ground into powder and exported to Europe by the ton, to be used as cures for stomach ailments and other illnesses.

Luckily, all was not lost forever. In 1798 AD, Napoleon invaded Egypt, taking with him 167 of France's scientific elite. In 1802, the Imperial Press published a record of their observations in a book called *Description de l' Egypte*, which detailed the wonderful artifacts of the ancient Egyptians. At that point, the magnificent civilization of ancient Egypt began to awaken from its long slumber, and Egyptology was born.

The Beginnings of Egyptian Civilization

The land of Egypt is in a part of North Africa that is surrounded by the Sahara, the world's largest desert. This inhospitable wilderness contains only a few oases in addition to the Nile—the world's longest river. To the north is the Mediterranean Sea and to the east the Red Sea and the Sinai desert, which connects Egypt to the Eurasian continent. From the south, the White Nile flows through the Sudan where it connects with the Blue Nile and continues out of Africa through Egypt and into the Mediterranean Sea.

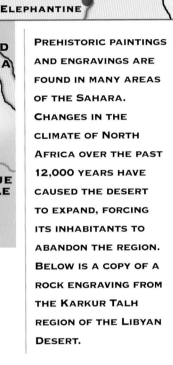

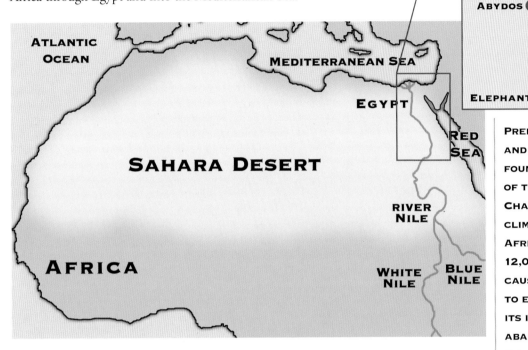

There would have been no ancient Egypt without the Nile. Each year, after the monsoon rains fall in the Ethiopian Highlands, the Blue Nile floods. Before the Aswan Dam was built in the 1960s this flood deposited a rich black soil in Egypt that nourished the land and made it perfect for growing crops.

The environment in the region was not always as it is now. More than ten thousand years ago, before recorded history, the area we now call the Sahara Desert was subtropical grassland supporting game animals such as antelope, buffalo, giraffe, elephant, rhinoceros, and warthog. Many stone artifacts and examples of rock art have been found revealing a human presence in regions that are now too dry for occupation. Between ten and five thousand years ago, the Sahara gradually became uninhabitable and the human population shifted east towards the fertile Nile River. It must have been during this period that the Paleolithic nomadic hunter-gatherers gave way to an agricultural way of life.

By around 5000 BC the population along the Nile began to farm the land and this led to the development of villages and towns. Some time before 3200 BC, these villages and towns had grown in population to an estimated 100,000

to 200,000. They had also developed into two separate but culturally similar kingdoms: a northern kingdom situated in the river delta and a southern one in the Nile valley.

Around 3200 BC there appears to have been a struggle to unite these two kingdoms. A mace head found at Hierakonpolis is inscribed with the earliest examples of hieroglyphic writing and refers to a king called the Scorpion. The Scorpion mace head commemorates this king's military victories over the peoples of the desert, the oases, and lower Egypt. It also shows the king digging a canal, which suggests they had the resources to carry out large building projects.

The Scorpion King's successor was Narmer, who completed the unification of the two kingdoms. We know this from the inscriptions on a large slate offering palette found in the temple of Hierakonpolis in 1897. The Narmer Palette is inscribed on both sides. On one side the king wears the white crown of upper Egypt and is shown holding a mace with which he is about to club the head of a kneeling enemy whom he grasps by the hair. The hieroglyphs refer to the king's victory over the people of the delta. The other side of the palette has an engraving of two animals whose long necks are entwined. This probably symbolizes the union of the Two Lands. The king is shown wearing the Red Crown as he inspects the decapitated

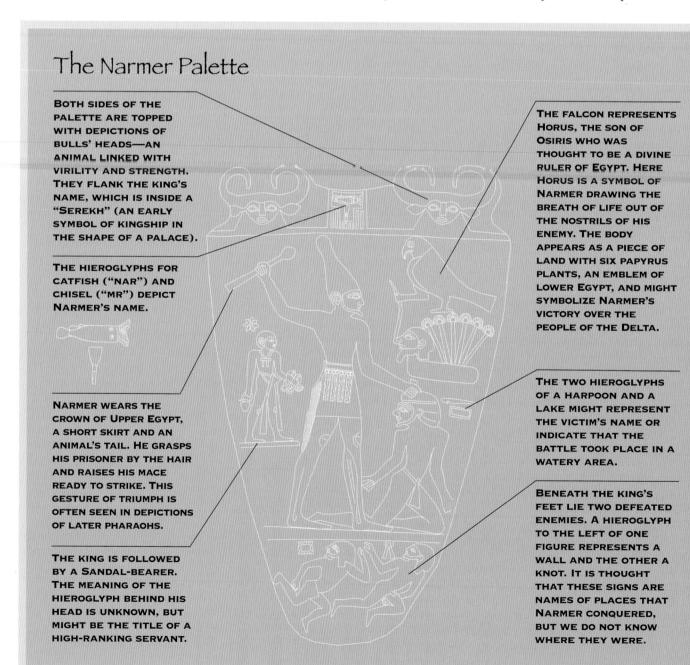

The Narmer Palette

BOTH SIDES OF THE PALETTE ARE TOPPED WITH DEPICTIONS OF BULLS' HEADS—AN ANIMAL LINKED WITH VIRILITY AND STRENGTH. THEY FLANK THE KING'S NAME, WHICH IS INSIDE A "SEREKH" (AN EARLY SYMBOL OF KINGSHIP IN THE SHAPE OF A PALACE).

THE HIEROGLYPHS FOR CATFISH ("NAR") AND CHISEL ("MR") DEPICT NARMER'S NAME.

NARMER WEARS THE CROWN OF UPPER EGYPT, A SHORT SKIRT AND AN ANIMAL'S TAIL. HE GRASPS HIS PRISONER BY THE HAIR AND RAISES HIS MACE READY TO STRIKE. THIS GESTURE OF TRIUMPH IS OFTEN SEEN IN DEPICTIONS OF LATER PHARAOHS.

THE KING IS FOLLOWED BY A SANDAL-BEARER. THE MEANING OF THE HIEROGLYPH BEHIND HIS HEAD IS UNKNOWN, BUT MIGHT BE THE TITLE OF A HIGH-RANKING SERVANT.

THE FALCON REPRESENTS HORUS, THE SON OF OSIRIS WHO WAS THOUGHT TO BE A DIVINE RULER OF EGYPT. HERE HORUS IS A SYMBOL OF NARMER DRAWING THE BREATH OF LIFE OUT OF THE NOSTRILS OF HIS ENEMY. THE BODY APPEARS AS A PIECE OF LAND WITH SIX PAPYRUS PLANTS, AN EMBLEM OF LOWER EGYPT, AND MIGHT SYMBOLIZE NARMER'S VICTORY OVER THE PEOPLE OF THE DELTA.

THE TWO HIEROGLYPHS OF A HARPOON AND A LAKE MIGHT REPRESENT THE VICTIM'S NAME OR INDICATE THAT THE BATTLE TOOK PLACE IN A WATERY AREA.

BENEATH THE KING'S FEET LIE TWO DEFEATED ENEMIES. A HIEROGLYPH TO THE LEFT OF ONE FIGURE REPRESENTS A WALL AND THE OTHER A KNOT. IT IS THOUGHT THAT THESE SIGNS ARE NAMES OF PLACES THAT NARMER CONQUERED, BUT WE DO NOT KNOW WHERE THEY WERE.

The Mace

The mace is a kind of club that is used as a weapon. It was commonly used by early ancient cultures that did not have the resources to produce sharp metal blades, and usually consisted of a heavy wooden shaft with a head made of stone. One of the earliest images of a mace is on the Narmer Palette.

A COPY OF THE INSCRIPTIONS ON THE SCORPION MACE

NARMER WEARS THE RED CROWN OF LOWER EGYPT AND HOLDS A MACE AND FLAIL. HE IS FOLLOWED BY HIS SANDAL-BEARER AND PRECEDED BY HIS VIZIER, OR HIGH PRIEST. THE TWO HIEROGLYPHS NEXT TO HIS HEAD SAY "TJET" BUT THE MEANING IS UNKNOWN. THE PARADE IS LED BY FOUR MEN CARRYING STANDARDS— THE FIRST IS AN ANIMAL SKIN OR THE ROYAL PLACENTA, FOLLOWED BY A JACKAL AND TWO FALCONS. THE EXACT MEANING OF THESE EMBLEMS IS UNKNOWN BUT THE FALCONS PROBABLY REPRESENT THE GOD HORUS.

A BULL SYMBOLIZING THE KING TRAMPLES HIS ENEMIES AND DESTROYS THE WALLS OF A CITY OR FORTRESS. ITS NAME IS WRITTEN WITHIN THE WALLS BUT THE MEANING IS UNKNOWN. THIS IS THE FIRST TIME A KING IS DESCRIBED AS "THE VICTORIOUS BULL," AN HONORIFIC COMMONLY USED BY LATER KINGS.

TEN DECAPITATED CORPSES ARE SHOWN LYING ON THE GROUND WITH THEIR HEADS BETWEEN THEIR LEGS. THEIR ARMS ARE BOUND, WHICH SUGGESTS THAT THEY WERE EXECUTED AFTER THE BATTLE.

THE HIEROGLYPHS OF THE SHIP, HARPOON, AND FALCON SAY "MAREOTIS," THOUGHT TO BE THE NAME OF THE CONQUERED REGION. IN FRONT OF THESE SYMBOLS IS THE WING OF A DOOR AND A SPARROW, MEANING "TO CREATE," SO IT IS POSSIBLE THAT THESE HIEROGLYPHS, WHEN WRITTEN TOGETHER, MEAN THAT NARMER FOUNDED A NEW PROVINCE FROM THE CONQUERED LAND.

TWO MEN TIE TOGETHER THE STRETCHED NECKS OF MYTHICAL BEASTS WITH BODIES AND HEADS OF LIONESSES. THIS IMAGE IS UNUSUAL IN EGYPTIAN ART AND HAS NO CLEAR EXPLANATION. IT COULD REPRESENT THE BINDING TOGETHER OF UPPER AND LOWER EGYPT, OR THE SYMBOLIC TAMING OF WILD ANIMALS BY THE KING. THE CIRCULAR AREA IS DEEPER THAN THE PALETTE'S SURFACE SO IT COULD JUST BE A CONVENIENT DEPRESSION FOR CONTAINING LIQUID.

corpses of his defeated enemies.

Historians identify Narmer with Menes (Meni in ancient Egyptian), whom the Egyptians believed was the first king of the first dynasty and founded the city of Memphis. But the ancient Egyptians also understood their origins through legends and the mythology of their religion.

The Mythological Origins of the Pharaohs

Kingship in the ancient world was essential: a people without a king was in great peril because only an anointed king could commune with the gods and only a king could intervene with the supernatural beings that controlled the destructive forces of nature. But, unlike other ancient kings, an Egyptian king was regarded as more than just an anointed messiah—he was seen as the actual living incarnation of god. Without him, society and indeed the world might collapse into chaos.

According to ancient legend, the first kings of Egypt were gods. We do not know if they were real people who were later deified or if they were mythical figures, but the authority and legitimacy of all the kings of Egypt rested on descent from this one mythical blood line of the gods. The most important myth, the one that legitimized the rule of the kings was that of Osiris, Isis, Seth and Horus. According to legend Osiris and Isis were the children of gods who became gods themselves. Osiris was originally a vegetation god linked with the growth of crops. He was thought to have been the first king of Egypt and became judge of the dead and ruler of the afterlife. To the Egyptians, Isis was the Mother of God (Horus). Her cult lasted well into Roman times and spread throughout the Roman Empire.

The Story of Osiris and Isis

Egypt flourished under the rule of Osiris because he was a wise and gentle king. He set himself the task of civilizing the people, who at that time indulged in cannibalism, human sacrifice, and other savage practices. [1]
Osiris gave them a code of laws, taught them the art of agriculture, and showed them the appropriate rites for worshipping the gods. Once he had succeeded in establishing law and order in Egypt, he left his beloved wife Isis to rule the country and traveled the world to continue his work of civilization.

However, all was not well at home. Osiris had an enemy, a very bitter one, and that was his brother Seth. [2] *Seth was jealous and determined to destroy his brother, but Isis was intelligent and ruled Egypt so well that his schemes to pervert and usurp its government came to naught.*

When the king returned from his travels, Seth hatched a plan to rid himself of Osiris. He secretly measured the king's body and made a marvelous chest, richly fashioned and adorned with gold and precious stones. He invited his fellow plotters and his brother to a great feast. During the banquet Seth had the beautiful chest brought into the hall and said, as though in jest, that if it fitted anyone there, he would give it to them. One by one, the guests lay down in the chest but it fitted none of them. When Osiris laid himself in the beautiful receptacle the conspirators quickly nailed down the lid, carried it out, and cast it into the Nile.

For many years Isis searched for the body of her husband and eventually, with the help of some demons, she discovered that the chest had been cast up on the shore of Byblos and that the waves had flung it into the branches of a magnificent tree, which had then grown around it and enclosed the coffin of Osiris within its trunk. [3]

Not knowing that the tree contained the body of Osiris, the king of Byblos cut it down and made it into a pillar to support the roof of his palace. [4] *So Isis went to Byblos and begged that the great pillar might be given to her. Of course, a goddess's wishes cannot be refused, so the king granted her request. Isis then cut open the tree and took the body of Osiris home to Egypt where she wept over the remains of her royal husband. Then she concealed the chest in a secret place and went to Horus, her young son, whom she had hidden from the wicked Seth.* [5]

Seth went out hunting and discovered the richly adorned coffin containing the dead Osiris. In his rage he tore the body into fourteen pieces, which he scattered all over the kingdom. [6] *Isis began her search all over again—but this time the*

other gods took pity on her and came to her aid. Nephthys left her evil husband Seth and came to help, and even Seth's son, Anubis, appalled by his father's deed, took on the form of a jackal to help in the search.

Piece by piece, Isis recovered the fragments of Osiris. And wherever she found one she formed, by magic, the likeness of his whole body and caused the priests to build a shrine and perform his funeral rites. Thus she made it harder for Seth to further defile the body of the dead god. She did not bury any of the pieces in the places where the tombs and shrines of Osiris stood, but gathered them together and rejoined them by magic. Then she had the body embalmed and hidden away in a place she alone knew of. It was only then that the spirit of Osiris was able to pass into Amenti and rule over the dead. [7]

1. The ancient Egyptians believed that Osiris taught mankind the arts of civilization. This could be interpreted as an allegory that marks the transition from a hunter-gatherer way of life to an agrarian life style.

2. The archetypal rivalries and jealousies between siblings appear in stories from many different cultures. Better known and much later tales are those of Cain and Abel from the Bible and Romulus and Remus from Roman mythology.

3. The tree that grows around Osiris' body establishes his credentials as a fertility god who nourishes the crops and ensures an abundant harvest.

4. The pillar represents the concept of stability, and the gods' power to support the balance that keeps chaos at bay.

5. Isis represents the ideal wife and mother—loving, devoted, and caring.

6. Seth stands for all that is dangerous, chaotic, and evil. He was generally reviled in ancient Egypt, but there were occasions when pharaoh took a Seth name, such as Seti, so as to embody the terrible incarnation of Seth in battle.

7. The ancient Egyptians believed that the corporeal body must be preserved after death in order to maintain its spirit, which might return and inhabit the body at will. It was essential that Osiris' body be made whole before it was magically resurrected. In some versions of the story Horus is conceived after this event. Osiris then enters the afterlife ("Amenti" or "Durat" in ancient Egyptian) and becomes its ruler and the judge of the dead.

The Pharaoh as God

Horus, the falcon god, succeeded his father as king of Egypt and conquered Seth, the evil god of turmoil and confusion. He then became the god of order and justice. By the fifth dynasty (2494–2345 BC), it was believed that all living pharaohs were an incarnation of the god Horus and that they magically transformed into Osiris after death.

In life, the god pharaoh protected his people, not only by carrying out the secular duties of a ruler but by performing the religious rituals necessary to maintain the balance of "Maat," or truth, and the elemental order of the universe. If he failed in this, chaos would envelop the world and all would suffer. The Egyptian people believed that the dead pharaoh would protect them in the afterlife as well. As the incarnation of Osiris, he offered salvation and eternal life to all true believers. These concepts are fundamental to understanding the ancient Egyptians. Their civilization revolved around the divine king, who was the focus of their nation and the symbol of their social and moral values.

By the fifth dynasty it was believed that all living that they magically transformed into Osiris after

The Story of Horus and Seth

While Horus was a boy his mother, Isis, protected him from his wicked uncle Seth.[1] His dead father, Osiris, would often visit him in the form of a spirit and teach him all the things a great warrior should know.[2]

When he'd grown to manhood, Horus prepared for war with Seth by gathering his forces and supplies. Even Ra, the shining king of the gods, came to lend a hand. But Seth was secretly watching, having taken the form of a black pig, and he struck Horus in the eyes with a blinding fire.[3] Ra used his healing powers and restored Horus's sight.

Seth had struck the first blow and Horus was impatient to strike back. Soon Horus was ready and he set out up the Nile at the head of his army. The war lasted for many years and there were many battles but neither side could defeat the other. Eventually the two armies clashed among the islands and rapids of the First Cataract of the Nile. It was here that Seth took the form of an evil red hippopotamus of gigantic size. He sprang up onto the island of Elephantine and uttered a great curse against Horus.

Then a great storm rose up, the wind roared, and the water was heaped into great mountainous waves that drove Horus and his army down the Nile to Edfu.[4] There Horus stood fast, his own boat a gleaming beacon in the darkness, its prow shining like a ray of the sun. Seth sensed victory and blocked the way by straddling the Nile, but Horus was unafraid. He transformed himself into the shape of a handsome young man 100 feet tall, with golden skin. In his hand he held a mighty harpoon thirty feet long with a blade six feet wide.

Seth opened his immense jaws with the intention of crushing Horus and his army. But at that moment Horus cast his harpoon and it struck deep into the head of that vile red hippopotamus. The point of the blade penetrated deep into the creature's brain and the wicked Seth fell to the earth dead.

Horus became king of Egypt and all the pharaohs thereafter were descended from him. When he passed from the earth, he and the spirit of Seth appeared before the assembly of the gods and they debated for the rule of the world—but even Thoth the Wise could not pass judgment. So Horus and Seth still battle for the souls of men and the rule of the earth.[5]

1. As the mother of Horus, Isis was the house in which he came into being and represented the earth mother from whom all life originates. Her womb is the source of the feminine creative power that conceives and brings forth every living creature.

2. The ancient Egyptians believed that the spirits of the dead could return to the land of the living. Indeed, statues were often made so that their dead owners could enter them and see through the sculpted eyes—and they were sometimes defaced to prevent the spirit of the dead person from inhabiting them.

3. The Eye of Horus, or *wadjet*, has the eye markings of a falcon, the bird linked with Horus the sky god. Injury to the eye and its healing were believed to represent the waxing and waning of the moon and in some stories, the eye was healed by the god Thoth or Horus used it to restore Osiris to life. It was also a symbol of the sun god Ra, and as an amulet it gave protection against the evil eye.

4. It was believed that the temple of Edfu was built on the site of the great battle and its walls are carved with images showing the defeat of Seth. In ancient times there was an annual festival called the Triumph of Horus which ended with the ritual slaying of a hippopotamus, the symbol of Seth.

5. The ancient Egyptians believed that the last battle was still to come, and that Seth would finally be destroyed by Horus. Then Osiris would rise from death and return to earth, bringing with him all of his faithful followers.

pharaohs were an incarnation of Horus and death.

II

KINGS AND QUEENS

THE EGYPTIANS' TITLE FOR THEIR KINGS WAS "NISU" OR "ITY," NOT "PHARAOH"—WHICH IS A HEBREW PRONUNCIATION OF THE EGYPTIAN WORD "PER-AA," MEANING GREAT HOUSE.

Traditionally, the royal succession was not as simple as the king's oldest son automatically succeeding his father. A pharaoh could have many wives but there was only one "great wife" or queen. It was from the great wife's children that the heir to the throne was usually chosen. There were occasions when a co-regency in which two rulers, an elder king and his junior partner (normally his son and heir), governed jointly. An example of this is Amenemhat I (1985–1955 BC), who made his son Sesostris co-regent.

If the great wife had only daughters, a son from one of Pharaoh's lesser wives could become king—but only if he married a daughter of the great wife: his half sister. In some circumstances, a commoner could become king if he married a daughter of the great wife. An example of this was the succession to the throne of Snefru, in 2613 BC who married princess Hetep-Heres, the daughter of Huni, and thus founded the fourth dynasty.

So, succession in ancient Egypt was not handed down by birth but by marriage, and a pharaoh could only legitimize his rule if he married a royal princess, a daughter of a previous pharaoh's great wife. Under normal conditions all pharaohs were male but there were three rulers of ancient Egypt who were women: Hatshepsut (1473–1458 BC), Twosret (1188–1186 BC), and Cleopatra (51–30 BC).

The most important task of a new king was to carry out the burial of his predecessor. After that, his primary duty was to safeguard the country by maintaining law and order, administering justice, protecting his people from foreign invasion, and presiding over all of the necessary annual religious festivals believed to make the River Nile flood, thus ensuring a good harvest and prosperity for all.

Crowns and Regalia

When the king sat on his throne wearing all of his symbols of office—the crowns, scepters, and other ceremonial items—the spirit of the great god Horus spoke through him. These symbols of authority included a crook and a flail. The crook was a short stick curved at the top, much like a shepherd's crook. The flail was a long handle with three strings of beads. The king wore various crowns: the White Crown represented Upper Egypt and the Red Crown, Lower Egypt (the area around the Nile Delta). Sometimes these crowns were worn together and called the Double Crown, and were the symbol of a united Egypt. There was also a third crown, worn by the kings of the New Kingdom, called the Blue Crown or war helmet.

CROWNS AND HEADDRESSES WERE MOSTLY MADE OF ORGANIC MATERIALS AND HAVE NOT SURVIVED, BUT WE KNOW WHAT THEY LOOKED LIKE FROM MANY PICTURES AND STATUES. THE BEST KNOWN CROWN IS FROM TUTANKHAMUN'S GOLDEN DEATH MASK. THIS WAS CALLED THE NEMES CROWN (SHOWN ABOVE) AND WAS MADE OF STRIPED CLOTH. IT WAS TIED AROUND THE HEAD, COVERED THE NECK AND SHOULDERS, AND WAS KNOTTED INTO A TAIL AT THE BACK. THE BROW WAS DECORATED WITH THE "URAEUS," A COBRA AND VULTURE.

THE BLUE CROWN OR "WAR CROWN" (LEFT) WAS WORN FROM THE EIGHTEENTH DYNASTY ONWARD; IT WAS A TALL HELMET ADORNED WITH THE URAEUS ON THE BROW.

(OPPOSITE) THE NEMES CROWN. (LEFT TO RIGHT) THE RED CROWN OF LOWER EGYPT, THE WHITE CROWN OF UPPER EGYPT AND THE DOUBLE CROWN OF UPPER AND LOWER EGYPT.

The Crook and Flail

(RIGHT) THE CROOK (HEKA) IS SIMILAR TO A SHEPHERD'S CROOK AND SYMBOLIZED THAT PHARAOH WAS THE SHEPHERD OF HIS PEOPLE. A CROOK IS ALSO THE HIEROGLYPH FOR THE WORD "RULE" OR "RULER." THE FLAIL (NEKHAKHA) IS A KIND OF WHIP SYMBOLIZING PHARAOH'S POWER.

The Cobra and the Vulture

THE URAEUS IS A COBRA SPITTING VENOM, AND REPRESENTED WEDJAT, THE GODDESS OF LOWER EGYPT. IT WAS ALSO CALLED THE FIERY EYE OF RA AND WAS THOUGHT TO PROTECT FROM EVIL.

THE VULTURE REPRESENTED NEKHBET, THE VULTURE GODDESS OF UPPER EGYPT. SHE WAS THE GUARDIAN OF MOTHERS, CHILDREN, AND THE PHARAOH.

TOGETHER THEY WERE KNOWN AS NEBTY, THE TWO LADIES, AND COMPRISED ONE OF THE TITLES THAT FORMED THE KING'S NAME—KNOWN AS THE NEBTY NAME.

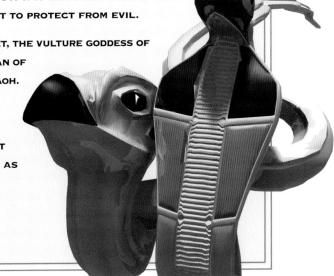

The names of the pharaohs were deeply spiritual.

While today, we tend to think of names as simple labels, chosen for their sound or to honor a family member or tradition, to the Egyptians, a name was an essential, living aspect of the individual. What someone was called was important for the survival of his or her spirit, and sometimes a name was a declarative statement; for example, Rahotep means "Ra is satisfied."

The king's name said something about what he stood for. Amenemhat's Horus Name translates as "Repeater of Births," which was probably chosen to mark his inauguration of a new dynasty.

Each king had five names, and each had an accompanying title.

- **THE HORUS NAME** was written together with the hieroglyph meaning Horus, and was first used during the Old Kingdom 2686–2181 BC. It was a public statement that the king was a manifestation of the falcon god Horus.
- **THE NEBTI NAME**, or "Two Ladies," was written together with the hieroglyph meaning "He of the Two Ladies," the cobra representing the goddess Wedjat of Lower Egypt and the vulture goddess Nekhbet of Upper Egypt. Although this title was used in earlier times, it did not become a standard until the twelfth dynasty, around 1985 BC.
- **THE GOLDEN HORUS NAME** was written together with the hieroglyph meaning "Golden Horus." This title became a standard from the Middle Kingdom 2055 BC onward and conveyed the meaning that, like gold, the king was eternal and could not be destroyed.

- **THE THRONE NAME**, or Prenomen, was written together with the hieroglyph meaning "King of Upper and Lower Egypt" and was chosen by the king on his coronation. It often contained the name of the god Ra, as in "Satisfied Is the Heart of Ra" (Amenemhat I) or "The Lord of Strength Is Ra" (Ahmose I).
- **THE BIRTH NAME**, or Nomen, was given to the king's son and heir. It was a name favored by the family of a ruling dynasty. For example, all the kings of the twelfth dynasty were called either Amenemhat or Sesostris, and most of the kings of the eighteenth dynasty were called Amenhotep or Thutmose. The birth name was written together with the hieroglyph meaning "Son of Ra."

To the Egyptians, a name was an essential, living aspect of the individual.

The Name of Rameses II

The Horus Name of Rameses II (right) translates as "Horus strong bull loved by Maat." Maat was the goddess of truth.

His full name is:
Horus the strong bull loved by Maat,
He of the two mistresses, and protector of Egypt who strikes foreign countries.
He is the Golden Horus who is powerful by his years of victory.
The king of Upper and Lower Egypt, in whom the justice of Ra is powerful, chosen by Ra.
The Son of Ra, it is Ra who gave birth to him and he is beloved of Amun, ruler of truth.

(LEFT) THE NAME OF KING PTOLEMY SET WITHIN A ROYAL CARTOUCHE. (BELOW) THE FIVE NAMES OF TUTANKHAMUN. (FROM THE TOP) THE HORUS NAME, THE NEBTI NAME, THE GOLDEN HORUS NAME, THE THRONE NAME, AND THE BIRTH NAME.

OFFICIALS CALLED "VIZIERS" (PRIME MINISTERS) HELPED THE KING GOVERN. OTHER OFFICIALS INCLUDED A TREASURER AND AN ARMY COMMANDER.

EGYPT WAS DIVIDED INTO FORTY-TWO PROVINCES OR "NOMES" THAT WERE RUN BY LOCAL GOVERNORS.

NOT ALL HIGH-RANKING OFFICIALS CAME FROM THE NOBLE CLASS—IT WAS POSSIBLE TO RISE THROUGH THE RANKS.

THE VIZIER PTAHHOTEP (AROUND 2200 BC) WROTE, "IF YOU ARE POOR, SERVE A WORTHY MAN. DO BE ARROGANT TOWARDS HIM IF HE WAS ONCE POOR BUT RESPECT HIM FOR WHAT HE HAS ACHIEVED BY HIS OWN EFFORTS."

Horus Kanakht tut mesut
Horus strong bull fitting of created forms.

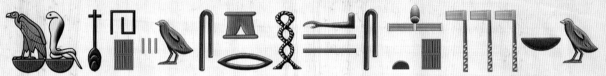

Nebty nefer-hepu segereh-tawy sehetep-netjeru nebu
He of the Two Ladies Dynamic Of laws, who calms the two lands, who regains the favor of all the gods.

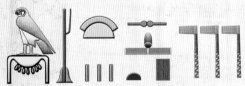

Wetjes-khau sehrtep-netjeru
Who displays the regalia, who gains the favor of the gods.

Nesu bity
King of Upper and Lower Egypt

NebKheperuRa
The lordly manifestations of Ra.

Sa Ra
Son of Ra

Tutankhamun
The living image of Amun

A lot can happen to a country in 3,000 years and it's impossible to say how many kings ruled in ancient Egypt. There were periods when the country was united and prosperous and there were eras when it sank into economic decline and civil disorder. Sometimes there was even more than one king at a time. We do know of around 170 pharaohs.

We know about some of these kings through their monuments but others left us actual information about their reign. They usually depicted themselves as mighty and victorious warrior kings but some of the details that survive provide us with a more intimate picture of their lives.

Pepi II

The Longest Ruling King in History
2278–2184 BC

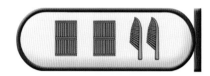

BIRTH NAME: PEPI

THRONE NAME: NEFER-KA-RA "BEAUTIFUL IS THE SOUL OF RA"

Pepi II lived to the age of one hundred years and ruled for ninety four of them. His older brother, the pharaoh Merenra, reigned for only a few years and died suddenly, so Pepi became king while still a child.

Many inscriptions survive from this period, recording trading expeditions to the south. One of the most interesting of these concerns the caravan leader, Harkhuf. He made many journeys into Nubia, and on one occasion wrote to the nine-year-old Pepi II, describing a dancing dwarf he was bringing back to Egypt. The excitement of the little king is palpable in the letter he wrote back to Harkhuf. He was clearly a normal boy, unable to contain his joy and forgetting his royal dignity.

The Letter of Pepi II

YOU HAVE SAID IN YOUR LETTER THAT YOU HAVE COME DOWN IN SAFETY FROM YAM WITH THE ARMY AND BROUGHT MANY BEAUTIFUL GIFTS WHICH HATHOR, LADY OF YAMU, HAS GIVEN TO THE KING OF UPPER AND LOWER EGYPT.

YOU ALSO SAY IN THIS LETTER THAT YOU HAVE BROUGHT A DWARF OF DIVINE DANCES FROM THE LAND OF THE HORIZON-DWELLERS. LIKE THE DWARF WHOM THE TREASURER OF THE GOD, BAURDED, BROUGHT FROM PUNT IN THE TIME OF KING ISESI.

YOU SAY TO MY MAJESTY, NEVER BEFORE HAS ONE LIKE HIM BEEN BROUGHT BY ANY OTHER WHO HAS VISITED YAM.

EACH YEAR YOU DO WHAT YOUR LORD DESIRES—SPENDING DAY AND NIGHT WITH THE CARAVAN. NOW COME NORTHWARD AT ONCE TO THE COURT. YOU MUST BRING THE DWARF, ALIVE, SOUND, AND WELL TO REJOICE AND GLADDEN THE HEART OF THE KING OF UPPER AND LOWER EGYPT.

(ABOVE) THE SOUTHEAST CORNER OF PEPI II'S PYRAMID
SHOWS SOME OF THE WHITE LIMESTONE CASING BLOCKS.
PEPI'S PYRAMID WAS THE LAST OF THE OLD KINGDOM
PYRAMIDS. (TOP BACKGROUND) A RECONSTRUCTION
SHOWING TWO OF THE THREE SMALLER PYRAMIDS BUILT
FOR PEPI'S WIVES.

Nubia

*Nubia was an ancient region in
northeastern Africa roughly corresponding to modern Sudan.
In ancient times it extended from
the southern border of Egypt,
near the first cataract, eastward
to the shores of the Red Sea,
southward to modern Khartoum,
and westward to the Libyan
Desert. It was called Kush by the
Egyptians and Ethiopia by the
ancient Greeks.*

WHEN HE COMES DOWN WITH YOU INTO THE SHIP,
APPOINT RELIABLE PEOPLE WHO SHALL BE BESIDE HIM
ON EACH SIDE OF THE VESSEL AND TAKE CARE LEST HE
SHOULD FALL INTO THE WATER!

WHEN HE SLEEPS AT NIGHT, APPOINT TRUSTWORTHY PEOPLE WHO SHALL SLEEP BESIDE HIM. INSPECT HIM TEN
TIMES A NIGHT BECAUSE MY MAJESTY DESIRES TO SEE THIS DWARF MORE THAN THE ALL PRODUCTS OF SINAI
AND PUNT.

IF YOU ARRIVE AT THE COURT AND THE DWARF IS WITH YOU, ALIVE AND WELL, MY MAJESTY WILL MAKE
YOU MANY EXCELLENT HONORS TO BE AN ORNAMENT FOR THE SON OF YOUR SON FOREVER. ALL THE
PEOPLE WILL SAY WHEN THEY HEAR WHAT MY MAJESTY DOES FOR YOU: "IS THERE ANYTHING LIKE THIS
WHICH WAS DONE FOR THE PRIVY COUNSELOR HARKHUF, WHEN HE CAME DOWN FROM YAM?"

Amenemhat I *Founder of the Twelfth Dynasty 1985–1955 BC.*

BIRTH NAME: AMENEMHAT

**THRONE NAME: SEHETEP-IB-RA
"SATIFIED IS THE HEART OF RA"**

Amenemhat I was a southerner, a commoner by birth, the son of one Sesostris and a woman from Nubia. He had no legal claim to be king, but was the vizier to King Mentuhotep IV. As such, his position was the highest office a non-royal person could achieve in ancient Egypt.

Amenemhat first distinguished himself in the second year of Mentuhotep IV's reign, when he led an expedition near the Red Sea to obtain stone for the king's sarcophagus. A strange incident occurred during this mission:

"There came a gazelle heavy with young, going with her face before her while her eyes looked backward. She did not turn back but rested on the block of stone intended for the king's sarcophagus and dropped her young while the king's army looked on."

They sacrificed her upon the block as a good omen.

Mentuhotep IV's reign ended in chaos and civil war. He had been a weak king, in power for only six years, and his name doesn't even appear in many contemporary records. It's not clear how Amenemhat succeeded him. As Mentuhotep lacked a son, he may have nominated Amenemhat his successor—but, judging by what happened after, it is more likely that Amenemhat seized the throne by force.

Amenemhat was a strong man, an experienced administrator with an excellent understanding of politics. He probably made allies of the governors and the army, who then supported him in the takeover. The country was in a state of despair and many powerful people must have been convinced that Amenemhat was the man who might lead them back to prosperity and strength.

With the help of the provincial governors, Amenemhat restored unity to Egypt. His first act was to move the capital from Thebes to a more central location, at Itj-towy, just south of Memphis. From there, he could more easily keep an eye on the whole country. He also strengthened his position in the delta by building fortresses along the eastern

paign against the Libyans in the Western Desert. When the son received news of his father's murder, he hurried back to the capital and quickly crushed any opposition to his own succession. The story of the assassination was recorded as though Amenemhat was speaking posthumously to his son:

> "I took an hour of rest after the evening meal, when night had come. Feeling weary I lay on my bed and as I began to fall asleep the weapons that were intended for my protection were turned against me. I awoke at the commotion to find I was under attack by my own bodyguard. Had I been able to seize a weapon I would have made the cowards flee, but no one is strong at night, and no one can succeed alone with no helper."

Two fine works of literature have survived from Amenemhat's reign: "The Instruction of Amenemhat" is a political thesis for his son Sesostris, offering advice concerning government to the new king. "The Story of Sinuhe," a popular work at the time it was written, describes Sesostris's reaction to the news of his father's murder. It relates how Sinuhe, one of his officers,

and western frontiers. Then, with his supporters, he sailed up the Nile and crushed all opposition to his rule.

During this period, Amenemhat probably made a number of enemies among the nobility, who would have viewed him as an upstart with no legitimate claim on the throne. Amenemhat was wise enough to take precautions against possible conspiracies, and introduced a number of changes that strengthened the government and brought long-lasting political stability to Egypt.

To put an end to any lingering uncertainty over his succession, he made his son, Sesostris, co-regent in his twentieth year. Sesostris assumed the task of extending Egyptian control into Nubia to the south, advancing as far as the Second Cataract of the Nile and building fortifications at strategic points. Meanwhile, Amenemhat opened copper and turquoise mines in Sinai and inaugurated a new program of building in Egypt, that included a pyramid for himself at Lisht.

Amenemhat reigned for thirty years but eventually some of his many enemies succeeded in assassinating him. It happened while Sesostris was returning from a cam-

Libya

The word Libya was used by the Greeks to describe the land west of Egypt and north of the Sahara Desert.

The Romans, after defeating the Carthaginians, gave the name Africa to this region. Africa was eventually used to describe the whole continent.

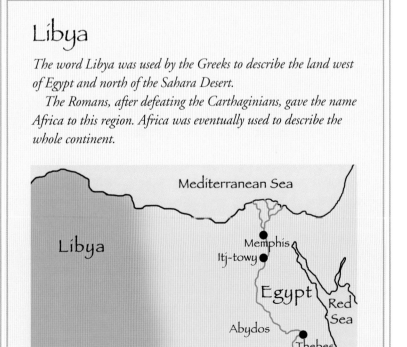

overheard the message and ran away into exile because of his involvement in the plot. In the end all is forgiven and Sinuhe returns home to die an old man in his homeland.

(RIGHT) THE INNER SANCTUARY AT HATSHEPSUT'S TEMPLE. (BOTTOM RIGHT) THE ENTRANCE TO THE TEMPLE.

Amenemhat was buried in his pyramid at el-Lisht; now a pile of rubble, the burial chamber has not been entered during modern times because of the rise in the water table.

Amenemhat was a great king who vigorously reorganized the government even while he made many political enemies. He was a common man who succeeded against all the odds to set the foundations of a prosperous Egypt. His successors maintained his policies, and the result was a unified nation that lasted throughout the Middle Kingdom.

Hatshepsut

The Woman Who Was King 1473–1458 BC.

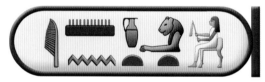

BIRTH NAME: HATSHEPSUT

**THRONE NAME: MAAT-KA-RA
"TRUTH IS THE SOUL OF RA"**

Although the status of women in ancient Egypt was higher than in any other ancient civilization, the notion that a woman could be king was abhorrent to the Egyptians. Yet, a woman did become king—and not just an ordinary king. She became the first great woman in recorded history, the forerunner of such figures as Cleopatra, Elizabeth I, and Catherine the Great. Her name was Hatshepsut and she ruled as pharaoh for fifteen years. Sadly, after her death the Egyptians, who were a deeply conservative people, obliterated her memory so that later pharaohs such as Rameses II and Cleopatra would have been ignorant of her existence.

Hatshepsut's grandfather was King Ahmose I. He is notable for having completed the expulsion of the Hyksos, who had invaded Lower Egypt and occupied it for more than one hundred years during the Second Intermediate Period. It was he who inaugurated the New Kingdom and the eighteenth dynasty, giving rise to some of the most extraordinary characters in ancient Egyptian history.

Hatshepsut was also descended from a number of strong women, including Aahotep, the mother of Ahmose, who is thought to have been a military leader and received the "Golden Flies" awarded to soldiers who fought courageously.

The Hyksos

The Hyksos were a group of mixed Semitic-Asiatic peoples who settled in northern Egypt during the eighteenth century BC. In about 1630 BC, they seized power and ruled Egypt as the fifteenth dynasty.

They were finally expelled by the Theban king and founder of the eighteenth dynasty, Ahmose, in about 1521 BC. Although much maligned by later Egyptians, the Hyksos did not harm Egyptian culture. Indeed they introduced the horse, the chariot, and the compound bow, along with many other technological innovations.

When Ahmose died, his son Amenhotep became pharaoh—but he left no male heirs. Thutmose I, a commoner and army general, became king by marrying Amenhotep's sister, the daughter of King Ahmose and Queen Ahimose Nefertiri.

Thutmose I was a strong pharaoh and, with his large professional army, made conquests south into Nubia and north as far as the Euphrates River—the farthest any pharaoh had gone up to that time. He erected two large obelisks at Karnak Temple and began the tradition of royal burials in the Valley of the Kings.

Although Thutmose had three sons and two daughters by his great wife, only one of these children was alive when Thutmose died: the twelve-year-old Hatshepsut. Thutmose did have a son by a minor wife, also called Thutmose, and to strengthen his claim to the throne, this son was married to Hatshepsut. Thutmose II did ascend the throne but he suffered from poor health and reigned for only fourteen years. He left a daughter by Hatshepsut and a son, again called Thutmose, by Isis, a harem girl.

It is possible that Thutmose II realized Hatshepsut was ambitious for power because he proclaimed the young Thutmose his successor. But when he died Thutmose III was still a small child, and his aunt and stepmother, Hatshepsut, acted as regent for him. Not content to be the power behind the child king, Hatshepsut soon proclaimed herself pharaoh, and the boy was kept away from the court. He was sent off to join the army where he grew up.

To support her cause, Hatshepsut claimed that the god Amun had taken the form of her father and visited her mother, and she herself was the result of this divine union. As the self-proclaimed daughter of God, she further justified her right to the throne by declaring that the god Amun-Ra had spoken to her, saying,

> *"Welcome my sweet daughter, my favorite, t he king of Upper and Lower Egypt, Maatkare, Hatshepsut. Thou art the king, taking possession of the Two Lands."*

Hatshepsut dressed as a king, even affecting a false beard, but it was never her intention to pass herself off as a man; rather, she referred to herself as the "female falcon."

Her success was due, at least in part, to the respect of the people for her father's memory and the loyal support of influential officials who controlled all the key positions of government. During her rule, the Egyptian economy flourished; she expanded trading relations and dispatched a major sea-borne expedition to the land of Punt, on the African coast at the southernmost end of the Red Sea.

(LEFT) HATSHEPSUT IN THE FORM OF OSIRIS. SHE WEARS A FALSE BEARD AND THE DOUBLE CROWN OF UPPER AND LOWER EGYPT.

(BOTTOM) A FESTIVAL SCENE FROM HATSHEPSUT'S TEMPLE, SHOWING SOLDIERS CARRYING THEIR AXES AND THE BRANCHES OF TREES.

Hatshepsut launched an extensive building program, repairing the damage wrought by the Hyksos and building magnificent temples. She renovated her father's hall in the Temple of Karnak, erecting four great obelisks nearly 100 feet (30 m) tall, and added a chapel. But her greatest achievement was her mortuary temple at Deir el Bahri, one of the most beautiful temples in Egypt. She called it the Most Sacred of Sacred Places. The walls were illustrated with a colorful account of the trading expedition to Punt, featuring images of ships and of the marching army led by her general, Nehsi. From the drawings we can see that the expedition brought back many wonderful things including gold, ebony, animal skins, baboons, and refined myrrh, as well as living myrrh trees that were then planted around the temple. The walls at Deir el Bahri also depict the houses of the people of Punt and an image of its obese queen.

The man responsible for the construction of this temple was Senenmut, Hatshepsut's closest adviser, overseer of the Royal Palace, the Granaries of Amun, and the Works, and tutor to her daughter. There is strong evidence that he was Hatshepsut's lover as well: he remained unmarried and she gave him one of her own royal sarcophagi for his tomb. (Senenmut never used this tomb because Hatshepsut had a second tomb made for him within the precincts of her mortuary temple, one that is aligned with her own.) Even more telling, in a cave above the temple there is some graffiti left by workmen showing a female pharaoh making love to the overseer of the Works.

As Hatshepsut and her political allies aged, her hold on the throne weakened. The early death of her daughter, whom she had married to Thutmose III, may have contributed to her decline. Eventually, her nephew took his rightful place as pharaoh, though the circumstances of this event are unknown and what became of Hatshepsut is a mystery. Whether she died naturally or was deposed and eliminated is uncertain. What we do know is that about twenty years after her death, Thutmose had her name removed from nearly all the monuments, carved out and replaced with either the name of her father, her husband, or Thutmose III himself. Ironically, some of the best-preserved obelisks in Egypt are those of Hatshepsut. Thutmose III had stone walls built around them to hide them from public view, thus also protecting them from the elements.

Thutmose III inherited an economically strong Egypt from Hatshepsut, the foundation on which the greatness of the New Kingdom was built. With his military education, Thutmose III was able to bring unimagined wealth into Egypt and make it the first ancient superpower.

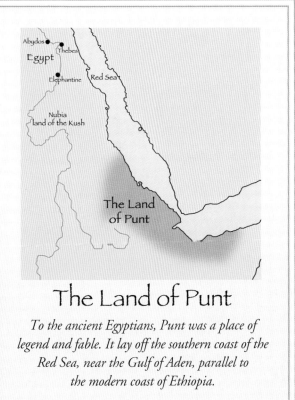

The Land of Punt

To the ancient Egyptians, Punt was a place of legend and fable. It lay off the southern coast of the Red Sea, near the Gulf of Aden, parallel to the modern coast of Ethiopia.

Thutmose III *The Napoleon of Ancient Egypt 1479–1425 BC.*

BIRTH NAME: THUTMOSE

THRONE NAME: MEN-KHEPER-RA
"LASTING IS THE MANIFESTATION OF RA"

Thutmose III possessed the archetypal qualities of a great ruler. A brilliant general who never lost a battle, he also excelled as an administrator and statesman. He was an accomplished horseman, archer, athlete, and discriminating patron of the arts. Thutmose had no time for pompous, self-indulgent bombast and his reign, with the exception of his uncharacteristic spite against the memory of Hatshepsut, shows him to have been a sincere and fair-minded man.

Thutmose III had spent the long years of his aunt Hatshepsut's reign training in the army. This kept him away from court politics but nevertheless prepared him well for his own role as pharaoh because great ability in war was considered a virtue and a strength in the ancient world. Egyptian pharaohs were expected to lead their armies into foreign lands and demonstrate their bravery on the field in person. After a few victorious battles, a king might return home in triumph, loaded with plunder and a promise of annual tribute from the defeated cities. But during Hatshepsut's reign, there were no wars and Egypt's soldiers had little practice in warfare. The result was that Egypt's neighbors were gradually becoming independent—and when this new, unknown pharaoh came to the throne, these other kings were inclined to test his resolve.

In the second year of his reign, Thutmose found himself faced with a coalition of the princes from Kadesh and Megiddo, who had mobilized a large army. What's more, the Mesopotamians and their kinsmen living in Syria refused to pay tribute and declared themselves free of Egypt. Undaunted, Thutmose immediately set out with his army. He crossed the Sinai Desert and marched to the city of Gaza, which had remained loyal to Egypt. The events of the campaign are well documented because Thutmose's private secretary, Tjaneni, kept a record which was later copied and engraved onto the walls of the Temple of Karnak.

This first campaign revealed Thutmose to be the military genius of his time. He understood the value of logistics and lines of supply, the necessity of rapid movement, and the sudden surprise attack. He led by example and was probably the first person in history to take full advantage of sea power to support his campaigns.

Megiddo was Thutmose's first objective because it was a key point strategically. It had to be taken at all costs. When he reached Aruna, Thutmose held a council with all his generals. There were three routes to Megiddo: two long, easy, and level roads around the hills, which the enemy expected Thutmose to take, and a narrow, difficult route that cut through the hills. His generals advised him to go the easy way, saying of the alternative, "Horse must follow behind horse and man behind man also, and our vanguard will be engaged while our rearguard is at Aruna

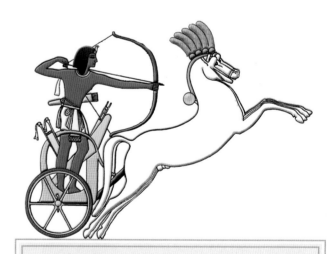

Megiddo lies about eighteen miles (29 km) southeast of modern Haifa, in northern Israel. In ancient times, Megiddo was of vital importance because it was the crossroad of military and trade routes.

Megiddo controlled the trading route between Egypt and Mesopotamia, standing along the northwest-southeast route that connected the Phoenician cities with the Jordan River valley.

(LEFT) THUTMOSE III SMITING HIS ENEMIES, TEMPLE OF KARNAK. (BELOW) PAINTINGS MADE FROM STATUES AND CARVINGS OF THE KING.

When the soldiers heard this bold speech they shouted in one voice, "We follow thy Majesty whithersoever thy Majesty goes."

Thutmose led his men on foot through the hills "horse behind Horse and man behind man, his Majesty showing the way by his own footsteps." It took about twelve hours for the vanguard to reach the valley on the other side, and another seven hours before the last troops emerged. Thutmose, himself, waited at the head of the pass till the last man was safely through. The sudden and unexpected appearance of Egyptians at their rear forced the allies to make a hasty redeployment of their troops. There were said to have been over three hundred

without fighting." But Thutmose's reply to this was, "As I live, as I am the beloved of Ra and praised by my father Amun, I will go on the narrow road. Let those who will, go on the roads you have mentioned; and let anyone who will, follow my Majesty."

THE BATTLE OF MEGIDDO WAS FOUGHT IN MAY 1482 BC. THE CANAANITE COALITION, HAD GATHERED ON THE PLAINS OF MEGIDDO IN ORDER TO INVADE EGYPT. TO PREEMPT THEIR STRATEGY, THUTMOSE RAPIDLY MARCHED TO ARUNA, TAKING THE COALITION BY SURPRISE. ALTHOUGH THE CANAANITE FORCES STILL HELD A STRONG POSITION, THEY WERE FORCED TO SPLIT THEIR ARMIES IN ORDER TO COVER THE TWO POSSIBLE ROUTES THEY BELIEVED THUTMOSE WOULD TAKE.

THUTMOSE REALIZED THAT THE ENEMY WOULD EXPECT HIM TO TAKE THE SAFE ROUTE AND THERE WAS AN OPPORTUNITY TO TAKE THE CANAANITE CO-ALITION BY SURPRISE, SO HE MARCHED HIS ARMY SINGLE-FILE THROUGH THE ARUNA PASS.

NORTHERN COALITION FORCE

SOUTHERN COALITION FORCE

MEDITERRANEAN SEA

ARUNA

MEGIDDO

EGYPT

SINAI DESERT

allied kings, each with his own army, an immense force. However, Thutmose was determined and when the allies saw him at the head of his men leading them forward, they lost heart for the fight and fled for the city of Megiddo, "as if terrified by spirits: they left their horse and chariots of silver and gold."

The Egyptian army, being young and inexperienced, simply lacked the control to take the city immediately. Thutmose was angry. He said to them,

"If only the troops of his Majesty had not given their hearts to spoiling the things of the enemy, they would have taken Megiddo at that moment. For the ruler of every northern country is in Megiddo and its capture is as the capture of a thousand cities."

Megiddo was besieged. A moat was dug around the city walls and a strong wooden palisade erected. The king gave orders to let nobody through except those who signaled at the gate that they wished to give themselves up. Eventually the vanquished kings sent out their sons and daughters to negotiate peace. According to Thutmose,

"All those things with which they had come to fight against my Majesty, now they brought them as tribute to my Majesty, while they themselves stood upon their walls giving praise to my Majesty, and begging that the Breath of Life be given to their nostrils."

They received good terms for surrender. An oath of allegiance was imposed upon them:

Thoutii Rahotep –How Thoutii took the town of Joppa.

Fragments of this story can be found on the Harris papyrus, which was discovered in 1874. The plot bears a resemblance to "Ali Baba and the Forty Thieves." General Thoutii's tomb was discovered in 1824 by Bernardino Drovetti at Saqqara, intact with all of its funeral equipment. Unfortunately, the contents were dispersed without any scientific record being made, and the tomb was lost.

•

During the reign of Thutmose III, the Prince of Joppa rose in rebellion and slaughtered all the Egyptian soldiers that were billeted in his city. When the news reached Pharaoh he became enraged and was determined that this act of blatant treachery against his men would not go unpunished.

The walls of Joppa were strong and Pharaoh did not care for a long and costly siege, so he called together all his nobles and generals to see what could be done, but none came up with any ideas. Finally I stepped forward and said, "My king. Life, Health, Strength be to you, if you give me your magic cane, a regiment of infantry and some charioteers I will kill the Prince of Joppa and take the city." Pharaoh smiled and granted my request and gave me his magic cane, which made its owner invincible.

The very next day, at the head of my men, I marched to Joppa. When we arrived there, I had four hundred wine jars made, each of them large enough to hold a man. Two of the jars I filled with treasure and in the remainder I concealed my best men.

I then sent a message to the Prince of Joppa, saying, "I am Thoutii, the Egyptian infantry officer. King Thutmose is jealous of my bravery and has sought to kill me—but I managed to escape. I have stolen his magic cane and will give it to you if you will let me join forces with you."

Now, I knew that the Prince of Joppa was a greedy man and had heard of my courageous exploits in the wars. He was delighted that such a brave fighter as myself would wish to join forces with him against Pharaoh. Believing me to be a new and powerful ally, he sent back a message accepting my offer. He also promised me a share of his territories and then he set up camp outside the city to welcome me. He invited me inside his camp to dine, and during the course of our conversation he asked about the magic cane; the prince was impatient to see it with his own eyes. So I told him that it was hidden in the baggage with which my horses were laden, and I requested that my men and horses be brought into the camp to be rested. After

"We will not again do evil against Men-kheper Ra, our good Lord, in our lifetime, for we have seen his might, and he has deigned to give us breath."

Thutmose III is compared to Napoleon, but unlike Napoleon he never lost a battle. He conducted sixteen campaigns in Palestine, Syria and Nubia and his treatment of the conquered was always humane. He established a sort of "Pax Egyptica" over his empire. Syria and Palestine were obliged to keep the peace and the region as a whole experienced an unprecedented degree of prosperity.

His impact upon Egyptian culture was profound. He was a national hero, revered long after his time. Indeed, his name was held in awe even to the last days of ancient Egyptian history. His military achievements brought fabulous wealth and his family resided over a golden age that was never surpassed. He was also a cultured man who demonstrated a curiosity about the lands he conquered; many of his building works at Karnak are covered with carvings of the plants and flowers he saw on his campaigns. He also set up a number of obelisks in Egypt, one of which, erroneously called Cleopatra's Needle, now stands on the Embankment in London. Its twin is in Central Park in New York. Another is near the Lateran, in Rome, and yet another stands in Istanbul. In this way, Thutmose III maintains a presence in some of the most powerful nations of the last two thousand years.

they arrived I fetched the magic cane and I could see the prince was impressed—but he still had some doubts "If I let you into my city what is to stop you from betraying me? Your army is still encamped outside and, although leaderless, they remain a threat."

To this I replied "I do not ask you to trust me, we both know that men break their word when it suits them. I will give you something to ensure the loyalty of myself and my army."

I took the prince to my baggage train and showed him the two jars of treasure. I told him that the other jars were all filled with gold and jewels to pay the army while on campaign and that they would be loyal to whoever possessed this treasure. Finally, I said to him, "I will give you all this treasure as a gesture of good will. Therefore, you will not only have myself but also my men."

The Prince of Joppa was delighted and immediately ordered that the jars be taken into the city. So my men loaded the jars containing my best soldiers onto ox-drawn carts and took them into city. There, they released their companions and a great cry was heard from within the city walls. The Prince of Joppa exclaimed, "What is that terrible sound?"

"That," I replied, "Is the sound of my men taking your city." Then I seized the Prince by his clothes and said, "Behold, here is good King Thutmose's magic cane, which you were so eager to possess!" With that I raised the cane and struck the Prince a mortal blow on his forehead. After my men had rested I sent a message to Pharaoh saying, "My king Life, Health, Strength be to you, I have killed the Prince of Joppa and all the people of Joppa are prisoners. Let them be sent for and brought to Egypt, that your house may be filled with male and female slaves who will be yours forever. And let Amun-Ra, thy father, the god of gods, be glorified."

Amenhotep III *The Magnificent King 1390–1352 BC.*

Amenhotep III was the great grandson of Thutmose III. He reigned for almost forty years at a time when Egypt was at the peak of her glory. He lived a life of pleasure, building huge temples and statues. He was incredibly rich and his palace at Thebes was the most opulent of the ancient world.

With stable international trade and a plentiful supply of gold from the mines, the economy of Egypt was booming. This great wealth led to an outpouring of artistic talent and Amenhotep was the driving force behind this activity. Much credit must also go to the king's scribe, overseer, and architect, Amenhotep, son of Hapu, who was so highly thought of by the king that he was rewarded with his own mortuary temple.

Amenhotep's patronage of the arts set new standards of quality and realism in representation. His building works can be found all over Egypt. Many of the finest statues in Egyptian art, attributed to Rameses II, were actually made by Amenhotep III. (Rameses II simply removed Amenhotep's name and replaced it with his own.) One of Amenhotep's greatest surviving achievements is the Temple of Luxor on the east bank of the river.

Unfortunately, his mortuary temple, the largest of its kind ever built, was destroyed when Rameses II used it as a quarry for his own temple. Only the two colossal statues that stood at the entrance survive.

In the early years of his reign, Amenhotep was a vigorous young man who enjoyed sport and hunting. In his fifth year as king, he led an expedition to Nubia to put down a rebellion, but there was no need for military activity for the remainder of his reign. Amenhotep favored peaceful pursuits over war—although he wasn't averse to adopting grandiose names, at one point describing himself as "Great of strength who smites the Asiatics."

Indulging himself in all the pleasures, extravagances, and luxuries of life were

(ABOVE BACKGROUND) THE COURTYARD OF AMENHOTEP III AT LUXOR TEMPLE. (LEFT ABOVE) THE FIGURE OF QUEEN TIY IS CARVED INTO THE THRONE. (LEFT BELOW) PORTRAIT OF TIY. (LEFT) AMENHOTEP WEARS THE DOUBLE CROWN OF EGYPT.

his priorities. He had a large harem that included foreign princesses, though the great love of his life was his queen, Tiy, whom he had married before becoming king. She was a commoner, which was unusual for a chief wife. While most royal marriages were politically motivated, Amenhotep's marriage to Tiy seems to have been motivated by genuine feeling. He made her a lake 3,600 cubits long by 600 cubits wide (about a one mile 1.6 km in length) in her town of T'aru. He then held a festival on the lake, during which he and Tiy sailed a boat called the *Disk of Beauties*.

Tiy gave birth to six children: four daughters and two sons. The eldest boy, Thutmose, became a priest and is thought to have begun the tradition of burying the mummified Apis bull, which was believed to be the incarnation of the god Ptah. Unfortunately, Prince Thutmose died, and his brother, the future Akhenaton, ascended the throne.

As he aged, Amenhotep grew fat and suffered ill health. His mummy shows that he endured painful dental problems. There is even a record of one of his allies, King Tushratta of Mitanni, sending him a statue of the goddess Ishtar for its healing properties.

Amenhotep began restricting the power of the priests of Amun by recognizing other cults. One of these was a special form of the god Ra known as the Aten. It was this deity which Amenhotep's son, Akhenaton, was to promote as the one and only true god, causing trouble within Egyptian society over the next generation.

Amenhotep, son of Hapu
1430–1350 BC

A government official under Amenhotep III, he was greatly honored by the king in his own lifetime and was eventually deified one thousand years after his death. He began as a scribe who, through his own talents, advanced to become, a military officer and later supervised the construction of Amenhotep III's mortuary temple at Thebes, as well as other temples. The king honored him by sponsoring building works in Athribis, his native city, and even had a small funerary temple made for him next to his own temple.

Amenhotep's greatest legacy was his high standard of artistic and architectural achievement. This sophisticated and refined taste in art permeated Egyptian society and is manifest in the tombs of high officials such as Ramose and Khaemhet. He set the stage for Akhenaton's unique style and left some of the finest monuments in Egypt. Amenhotep truly deserves the title "the Magnificent."

The Colossi of Memnon

THE TWO MASSIVE 60 FT (18 M) HIGH STATUES OF AMENHOTEP III ONCE STOOD GUARD AT THE ENTRANCE OF HIS MORTUARY TEMPLE, THE LARGEST OF ITS KIND EVER BUILT. THE GREEK HISTORIAN STRABO TELLS OF AN EARTHQUAKE IN 27 BC THAT DAMAGED ONE OF THE COLOSSI, AND THEREAFTER IT "SANG" EVERY MORNING AT DAWN. THE SOUND WAS PROBABLY CAUSED BY THE EVAPORATION OF DEW INSIDE THE CRACKED STONE. THE GREEKS IDENTIFIED THE STATUE WITH HOMER'S MEMNON, SINGING TO HIS MOTHER EOS. IN AD 199 THE ROMAN EMPEROR SEPTIMIUS SEVERUS HAD THE STATUES RESTORED AND THE MYSTERIOUS SINGING CEASED.

Akhenaten

The Heretic 1352–1336 BC.

**ADOPTED NAME: AKH-EN-ATEN
"SERVANT OF THE ATEN"**

Amenhotep IV changed his name to Akhenaten and defied tradition by establishing a new monotheistic cult dedicated to the god Aten.

The eighteenth-dynasty royal line had been kept as pure as possible by marrying the heirs to princesses of the king's own family. Amenhotep III, Akhenaten's father, defied this custom by marrying a commoner named Tiy. She was Akhenaten's mother and enjoyed unusual power. By the time Akhenaten took the throne, his family had been ruling Egypt for nearly two hundred years and had established a huge empire dominating Palestine, Phoenicia, and Nubia.

A century before, Thutmose III had swept all before him, conquering the Middle East and Nubia and establishing a military priesthood which now controlled the empire. At the center was the god Amun of Thebes. His priests had become powerful, possibly more powerful than pharaoh himself. The imperial elegance of Egypt was supreme. It was rich and confident, with soldiers and officials established in foreign countries. Of course foreigners, in turn, came to live in Egypt, bringing new customs and ideas. The young prince and future king grew up in this new and changing Egypt.

The religion of ancient Egypt was a traditional institution and at the beginning of his reign, the young pharaoh still worshiped the old gods, especially Amun of Thebes and the sun god, Re-Harakhte. However, within a few years there were changes. He abandoned work on a temple dedicated to Re-Harakhte and began to build a place to worship a new form of the sun god, called the Aten.

The Aten was never shown in human or animal form, but was represented as the sun disk with extended rays ending in hands. Aten was the life-giving and life-sustaining power of the sun. Unlike the old gods, he had no carved image hidden in a dark room deep within a temple but was worshipped out in the light of day.

The king also encouraged artistic inventiveness and realism in visual representation. Among the surviving works of this period are the colossal statues of Akhenaten, the paintings from his private residence, the bust of his wife Nefertiti, and that of his mother, Queen Tiy. These works are unique in Egyptian art, as they do not flatter the king and his family but reveal them as real people, in all their beauty and decay. They demonstrate a revolutionary sophistication and creative freedom.

Nefertiti, famous from her portrait bust, is thought to have been an Asian princess from Mitanni. She encouraged and supported her husband in his revolutionary ideas and together they took on the religious establishment. In the

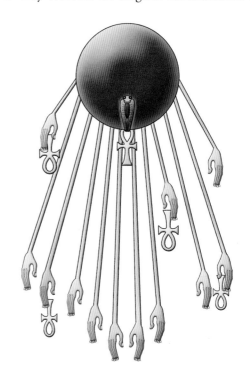

fifth year of his reign, the king changed his name from Amenhotep ("Amun is Pleased") to Akhenaten, or "Servant of the Aten"—thus formally declaring his new religion. He moved his capital from Thebes to a place now called Tell el-Amarna or Amarna, more than 200 miles (300 km) north, on a desert bay on the east side of the Nile River. Here he began to build a new city, which he called Akhetaten, "Horizon of Aten." The new city had many spacious villas with trees, pools, and gardens. Indoors, the walls were painted in the eccentric new style.

(LEFT) THE SUN DISK OF THE ATEN RADIATES BEAMS OF LIGHT ENDING IN HANDS, WHICH HOLD THE "ANKH," THE HIEROGLYPH FOR LIFE. (ABOVE LEFT) THE HEAD OF AKHENATEN AND (RIGHT) HIS WIFE NEFERTITI. THE ART OF THE AMARNA PERIOD IS RECOGNIZABLY DIFFERENT FROM ALL OTHER EGYPTIAN ART. IT RANGES FROM BRILLIANTLY NATURALISTIC TO WONDERFULLY

BIZARRE CARICATURES OF THE ROYAL FAMILY. (BACKGROUND ABOVE) A RECONSTRUCTION OF THE TEMPLE OF THE ATEN IN AKHENATEN'S NEW CITY. "AKHETATEN" MEANS "THE HORIZON OF THE ATEN" BECAUSE OF A NATURAL CUT IN THE HILLS WHERE THE MORNING SUN DISK ROSE AND LOOKED LIKE THE HIEROGLYPH FOR "HORIZON."

The religion of the Aten is not completely understood today. We do know that Akhenaten and his wife Nefertiti worshipped only the sun god, and the names of other gods and goddesses were removed from view. The funerary religion of Osiris was dropped, and Akhenaten became the source of blessings for people after death.

Monotheistic
The doctrine or belief that there is but one God.

The philosophy of the Aten had an intellectual basis featuring a godhead that was both monotheistic and abstract. It is possible the Hebrew prophets' concept of a universal god was derived in part from this cult. But this religious and artistic renaissance was short lived; Akhenaten made himself unpopular by closing the old temples, and his lack of enthusiasm for the practical duties of kingship was detrimental to Egypt's Imperial interests. Surviving documents show that Akhenaten paid little attention to the army and navy, foreign trade began to fall off, and internal taxes began to disappear into the pockets of local officials.

Letters to the king discovered in the ruins of Tell el-Amarna, known as the Amarna Letters, show the discontent of the army commanders and high commissioners in Palestine and Syria. The local princes, who had been loyal to Egypt, no longer saw any advantage in trading with Egypt. The Hittites from the north began to make gains and this led to a general disintegration of the empire. Eventually, a dissatisfied priesthood and civil officials combined with the army to discredit the new religion.

There is some evidence that at the urging of Tiy, the queen mother, Akhenaten made compromises to placate the different factions growing within Egyptian society. He also became estranged from Nefertiti.

When Akhenaten died, he was succeeded briefly by Smenkhkare, his favorite, and then by Tutankhaten who changed his name to Tutankhamun, dropping the Aten and embracing Amun. Tutankhamun eventually returned Egypt to its traditional values and Akhenaten's memory was erased. Later Egyptian historians would refer to him only as "the heretic king."

The city of Akhenaten was abandoned and the court returned to Thebes. Later, Horemheb razed the city to the ground and Rameses II reused the stone blocks of its temples for his work at nearby Hermopolis.

The Amarna Letters

The Amarna Letters were written on 350 clay tablets and found in the ruins of Akhenaten's capital city. They are in Akkadian cuneiform characters which was the international diplomatic language of the day. Most of the letters are dated to the reigns of Amenhotep III (1390–1352) and Akhenaten (1352–1336) and consist of correspondence between the Egyptian government and its representatives in Canaan and Amurru. They give us a unique insight into the international affairs of Egypt and the major powers of the Middle East: Babylonia, Mitanni, and Assyria.

For more information about the Amarna Letters go to the Imagining Egypt Resources page at **WWW.DISCOVERINGEGYPT.COM**

Akhenaten was an intellectual and philosophical revolutionary who had the power and wealth to indulge his ideas. However, the ancient Egyptians were a deeply religious people who loved their ancient traditions and were not ready to embrace such radical changes. It would not be until the Christian era that the Egyptians would finally reject the old gods in favor of a single universal deity.

(ABOVE) PART OF A WALL FROM THE TEMPLE OF AKHENATEN AT KARNAK. THE FRAGMENTS WERE REMOVED FROM THE INTERIOR OF THE NINTH PYLON, WHERE THE BLOCKS HAD BEEN USED AS A RUBBLE CORE. (ABOVE RIGHT) A RECONSTRUCTION OF AKHENATEN'S TEMPLE. WORSHIP WAS CARRIED OUT IN THE OPEN, SURROUNDED BY HUNDREDS OF OFFERING TABLES, WHICH CAUGHT THE RAYS OF THE SUN GOD.

Akhenaten made himself unpopular by closing the old temples, and his lack of enthusiasm for the practical duties of kingship was detrimental to Egypt's Imperial interests.

Letter from Yapahu of Gezru

TO THE KING, MY LORD, MY GOD, MY SUN. THUS SAYS YAPAHU, THE RULER OF GAZRU—YOUR SERVANT. I PROSTRATE MYSELF BOTH UPON THE BELLY AND BACK. AND TO ALL THAT THE KING, MY LORD, HAS TOLD ME I HAVE PAID CLOSE ATTENTION. I AM THE KING'S SERVANT AND THE DUST OF YOUR TWO FEET.

LET THE KING, MY LORD, BE AWARE THAT MY YOUNGER BROTHER, HAS REBELLED AGAINST ME AND HAS ENTERED MUHHAZU. HE HAS GIVEN OVER HIS TWO HANDS TO THE LEADER OF THE BRIGANDS AND IS AT WAR WITH ME.

Tutankhamun

The Boy King 1336–1327 BC.

BIRTH NAME: TUT-ANKH-ATEN
"LIVING IMAGE OF THE ATEN"

ADOPTED NAME: TUT-ANKH-AMUN
"LIVING IMAGE OF AMUN"

THRONE NAME: NEB-KHEPERU-RA
"LORD OF MANIFESTATIONS IS RA"

| A STATUE OF THE GOD AMUN AT KARNAK WITH THE FEATURES TUTANKH-AMUN. | (TOP RIGHT) A SOLID GOLD COFFIN THAT CONTAINED TUTANKH-AMUN'S MUMMY. |

It is ironic that the Egyptian king who is most famous today was in fact a little known and unimportant pharaoh in his own time. He had no real power, his impact on Egyptian history was trivial, and the modest works carried out during his short reign were plagiarized by his successors.

We are fortunate enough to be able to examine many of the objects he owned—and yet we know almost nothing about what sort of person he was. What we do know is fragmentary, and until material evidence is found we can only speculate on the story of his life. We know that he was born and lived his early life in the city of Akhetaten. It is possible that he was the son of Lady Kiya, who is thought to be a Mitannian princess and wife of Akhenaten. It is likely that she died giving birth to him. He might also have been the brother or half brother of Smenkhkara, his immediate predecessor.

Toward the end of Akhenaten's reign, senior court officials like the civil servant Ay and the commander of the army Horemheb realized that the empire, and indeed Egyptian society, was disintegrating. Akhenaten's co-regent, Smenkhkara, probably made an attempt to rescue the situation. He left the new city of Akhetaten and moved the administration back to Memphis. He may even have been in contact with members of the old outlawed priests of Amun. But he died unexpectedly.

Soon after Akhenaten's death Tutankhaten, as he was then called, was crowned at Memphis. He was only nine years old at the time, and had few close relatives left. His wife, Ankhesenpaaten, was older, and he was probably the political puppet of Ay and Horemheb. Under their tutelage, he changed his name to Tutankhamun; restored Amenhotep III's Theban palace; issued a decree restoring the temples, images, and privileges of the old gods; and admitted the errors of Akhenaten's political and religious policies.

During Tutankhamun's ninth year, Horemheb marched the army into Syria to assist Egypt's old ally, the Mitannian kingdom of northern Syria, which was embroiled in hostilities with vassals of the Hittites. It was around this time that Tutankhamun died. He was eighteen, and modern medical analysis of his mummy shows that he may have received a blow to the head—but we can only speculate as to whether he was murdered or the victim of an accident such as a fall from his chariot. A number of well-preserved chariots were found in Tutankhamun's tomb and, like most Egyptian kings, it seems he was a keen charioteer.

There is an interesting postscript to the story of Tutankhamun, involving his succession and providing insight into the struggles among the key players of the time. Ankhesenamun, Tutankhamun's wife, was left a widow and

in a difficult position. She found herself surrounded by older, ambitious men, such as Ay and Horemheb, who were competing for power. In order for one of them to legitimize his claim to the throne, he would have to marry young Ankhesenamun, the only surviving member of her dynasty.

It is easy to sympathize with this young widow's predicament. From letters found in the Hittite archive, we know that she had no particular affection for her aged Egyptian suitors; in fact, she wrote to Suppiluliumas I, the Hittite king, asking him to send one of his sons for her to marry, promising that she would make him pharaoh of Egypt. The Hittites, being old enemies of Egypt, were at first suspicious of this offer. In Egypt, Ankhesenamun's behavior was considered nothing short of treason. Suppiluliumas eventually sent prince Zannanza, but it seems that the prince got no further than the Egyptian border, where he was murdered.

Ankhesenamun was then forced to marry Ay, who, eight months after the death of Tutankhamun, became king. Traditionally a king was buried seventy days after his death, but it is possible that Tutankhamun lay unburied for eight months while all these political maneuverings were going on.

Ankhesenamun rapidly disappears from the records; indeed there is a monument where her name has been hacked out. One can only imagine her fate after failing in her attempt to bring a foreigner to rule Egypt.

Ay was king for only four years, and was succeeded by Horemheb. Although the records state the eighteenth dynasty ended with Horemheb, Tutankhamun was really the last member of his family to rule Egypt.

It was a sad end for a family that produced such a great cast of characters: king Hatshepsut, who was actually a woman dressed in men's clothes; Thutmose III, the Napoleon of Egypt; Thutmose IV, the young man who dreamt of the sphinx and became king; and Amenhotep III, the sophisticated, refined king who brought forth a crazy, flamboyant genius of a son, Akhenaten.

Tutankhamun's tomb was entered twice by robbers but they were caught before they could do very much damage. During the nineteenth dynasty, Akhenaten, Smenkhkara, Tutankhamun, and Ay were removed from the royal lists and publicly condemned. During the twentieth dynasty, the entrance to the young king's tomb was covered in rubble when Rameses VI had his tomb cut immediately above it. Then Tutankhamun was forgotten for 3,200 years—until Howard Carter, an English Egyptologist, discovered his intact burial chamber in 1922.

A PAINTING OF A LIFE-SIZED STATUE OF TUTANKHAMUN. THIS STATUE WAS FOUND AT THE ENTRANCE TO HIS BURIAL CHAMBER.

The Hittites

The Hittites were an ancient Indo-European people who probably originated in an area beyond the Black Sea. They settled in the region roughly corresponding to modern Turkey at the beginning of the second millennium BC.
By 1340 BC, they had become one of the great powers in the Middle East and a serious rival to Egyptian power in the region.

Rameses II *The Great 1279–1213 BC.*

BIRTH NAME: RA-MESSES, MERY-AMUN

**THRONE NAME: USR-MAAT-RA SETEP-EN-RA
"THE JUSTICE OF RA IS POWERFUL, CHOSEN OF RA"**

(ABOVE) A MASSIVE STATUE OF RAMESES II AT LUXOR TEMPLE. (OPPOSITE PAGE) THE EGYPTIAN ARMY ON THE MARCH.

Rameses II, son of Seti I, was about thirty years old when he became king of Egypt, and he reigned for sixty-seven years. Among his many wives were some of his own immediate relatives, and he's said to have fathered 111 sons and 51 daughters.

As was usual in those days, the threat of foreign aggression against Egypt was always at its greatest on the ascension of a new pharaoh. Subject kings no doubt saw it as their duty to test the strength of a new king of Egypt. Likewise, it was incumbent on the new pharaoh to make a display of force if he was to keep peace during his reign. In his fourth year as pharaoh, Rameses was fighting a series of campaigns in Syria against the Hittites and their allies. The Hittites proved to be a strong foe and the war lasted for twenty years.

On the second campaign, Rameses found himself in some difficulties when attacking "the deceitful city of Kadesh." This action nearly cost him his life.

In the end neither side was victorious. And finally, after many years of war, Rameses was obliged to make a treaty with the king of the Hittites.

The Chariot

The Hyksos introduced the chariot into Egypt during the Second Intermediate period. Egyptian chariots were pulled by two horses. They were lightly constructed and highly maneuverable. The chariot revolutionized warfare and there are many depictions from the New Kingdom of Pharaoh riding his chariot and slaying his enemies.

The Battle of Kadesh

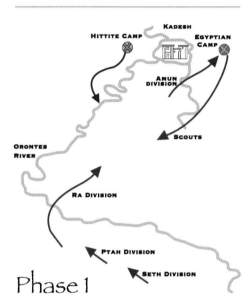

Phase 1

RAMESES DIVIDES HIS ARMY INTO FOUR: THE AMUN, RA, PTAH, AND SETH DIVISIONS. RAMESES, HIMSELF, IS IN THE VANGUARD, LEADING THE AMUN DIVISION, WITH THE RA DIVISION ABOUT A MILE AND A HALF BEHIND. HE CAMPS OUTSIDE THE CITY, BUT UNKNOWN TO HIM, THE HITTITE ARMY IS HIDDEN AND WAITING. WHEN HE REALIZES THE DANGER, HE SENDS ONE OF HIS VIZIERS WITH SOME SCOUTS TO BRING UP THE DIVISIONS OF PTAH AND SETH. THE RA DIVISION CONTINUES TO MARCH DOWN THE PLAIN TOWARD HIS CAMP.

Phase 2

THE HITTITES ATTACK AND ROUTE THE RA DIVISION AS IT IS CROSSING A FORD. WITH THE CHARIOTS OF THE HITTITES IN PURSUIT, RA FLEES IN DISORDER, SPREADING PANIC. RA RUNS STRAIGHT INTO THE UNSUSPECTING AMUN DIVISION. WITH HALF HIS ARMY IN FLIGHT, RAMESES FINDS HIMSELF ALONE WITH ONLY HIS BODYGUARD TO ASSIST HIM. RAMESES IS NOW SURROUNDED BY 2,500 HITTITE CHARIOTS.

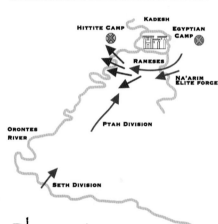

Phase 4

THE BATTLE CONTINUES FOR FOUR HOURS, WITH RAMESES AND HIS ELITE FORCE PUSHING THE HITTITES BACK ACROSS THE ORONTES AS THE PTAH AND SETH DIVISIONS ARRIVE. AT THE END OF THE BATTLE BOTH SIDES ARE EXHAUSTED.

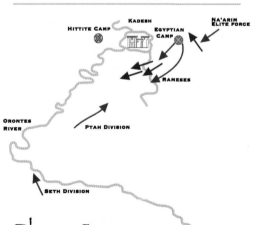

Phase 3

RAMESES CHARGES THE ENEMY WITH HIS SMALL BAND OF MEN. AT THIS POINT, THE HITTITES STOP TO PLUNDER THE EGYPTIAN CAMP, GIVING THE EGYPTIANS TIME TO REGROUP WITH THEIR OTHER TWO DIVISIONS. THE NA'ARIM ELITE FORCE ALSO ARRIVES IN TIME TO SUPPORT THE COUNTER ATTACK.

It was agreed that Egypt would not invade Hittite territory, and likewise the Hittites would not invade Egyptian territory. They also agreed on a defense alliance to deter common enemies, mutual help in suppressing rebellions in Syria, and an extradition treaty.

Thirteen years after the establishment of this treaty, in the thirty-fourth year of his reign, Rameses married the daughter of the Hittite king. Her Egyptian name was *Ueret-ma-a-neferu-Ra*, meaning "Great One Who sees the Beauties of Ra."

Although brave in battle, Rameses was an inept general—and one can't help wondering how Thutmose III would have dealt with the Hittites. Maybe Rameses also pondered this: he spent the rest of his life bolstering his image with huge building projects. His name is found everywhere on monuments and buildings in Egypt, and he frequently usurped the works of his predecessors and inscribed his own name on statues that don't represent him. The smallest repair of a sanctuary was sufficient excuse for him to have his name inscribed on every prominent part of the building. His greatest works were the rock-hewn temple of Abu Simbel, dedicated to Amun, Ra-Harmachis, and Ptah. Its length is 185 feet, its height 90 feet, and the four colossal statues of the king in front of it—cut from the living rock—are 60 feet high. He also added to the temple of Amenhotep III at Luxor and completed the hall of columns at Karnak, still the largest columned room of any religious building in the world.

Although Rameses is probably the most famous king in Egyptian history, his actual deeds and achievements cannot be compared with the great kings of the eighteenth dynasty. Whereas kings such as Thutmose III left a stronger and more dynamic Egypt, after Rameses'

(TOP) THE ENTRANCE TO THE ROCK-HEWN TEMPLE OF ABU SIMBEL AND (ABOVE) THE SMALLER TEMPLE AT ABU SIMBEL DEDICATED TO QUEEN NEFERTARI AND THE GODDESS HATHOR. THESE MAGNIFICENT MONUMENTS WERE SAVED FROM THE RISING WATERS OF LAKE NASSER IN THE 1960S. AN INTERNATIONAL CAMPAIGN LEAD BY UNESCO RESULTED IN THE WHOLE MOUNTAINSIDE BEING CUT INTO MASSIVE BLOCKS AND RECONSTRUCTED ON HIGHER GROUND ABOVE THE FLOOD WATERS. BEFORE THE RELOCATION, TWICE EACH YEAR, ON FEBRUARY 20 AND OCTOBER 20, THE RAYS OF THE SUN PENETRATED INSIDE THE SANCTUARY AND STRUCK THE FOUR SEATED STATUES OF RA-HORAKHTY, PTAH, AMUN, AND RAMESES. BECAUSE THE TEMPLE IS NOW ON HIGHER GROUND, THIS OCCURS A DAY LATER.

death Egypt fell into decline. Luckily for the country, its prestige and preeminence as a world superpower were such that this process took a long time. Only one other king, Rameses III (1184–1153 BC), was able to temporarily halt this process.

Rameses II's greatest works were the rock-hewn temple of Abu Simbel, dedicated to Amun, Ra-Harmachis, and Ptah. Its length is 185 feet, its height 90 feet, and the four colossal statues of the king in front of it—cut from the living rock—are 60 feet high.

Queen Nefertari

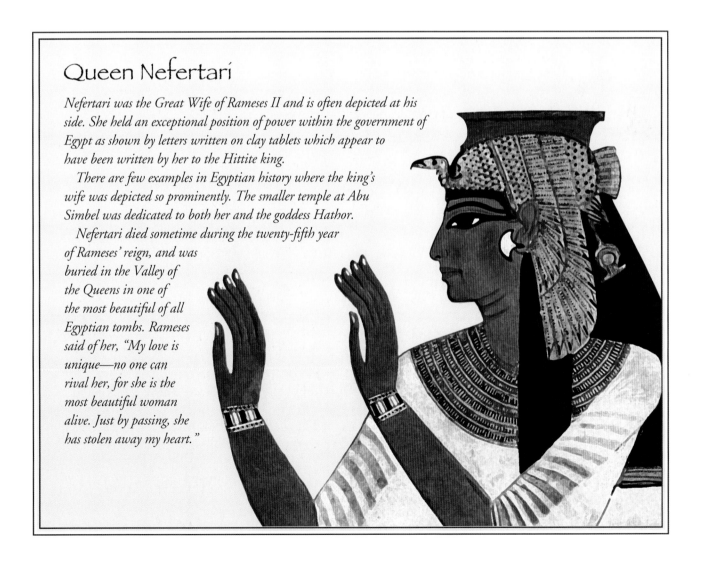

Nefertari was the Great Wife of Rameses II and is often depicted at his side. She held an exceptional position of power within the government of Egypt as shown by letters written on clay tablets which appear to have been written by her to the Hittite king.

There are few examples in Egyptian history where the king's wife was depicted so prominently. The smaller temple at Abu Simbel was dedicated to both her and the goddess Hathor.

Nefertari died sometime during the twenty-fifth year of Rameses' reign, and was buried in the Valley of the Queens in one of the most beautiful of all Egyptian tombs. Rameses said of her, "My love is unique—no one can rival her, for she is the most beautiful woman alive. Just by passing, she has stolen away my heart."

Rameses III *The Last Great Pharaoh 1184–1153 BC.*

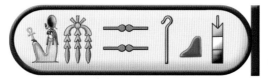

BIRTH NAME: RA-MESSES, HEQAIUNU

THRONE NAME: USER-MAAT-RA MERY-AMUN
"POWERFUL IS THE JUSTICE OF RA, BELOVED OF AMUN"

For two thousand years, Egypt had enjoyed prestige throughout the known world. By the time of Rameses III, however, the world was going through great upheavals. The long period of Middle Eastern stability established by Thutmose III and continued through Rameses II's treaties with the Hittites was about to come to an end. This was the time of the Trojan Wars and the fall of Mycenae, a time when age-old empires were weakened by complacent rulers and failed harvests.

The longest known papyrus scroll, the Great Harris Papyrus, records that many people throughout the region became homeless: "The foreign countries plotted on their Islands and the people were scattered by battle all at one time and no land could stand before their arms." This great body of people without countries was well armed and desperate. Known as the Sea Peoples, they obliterated the Hittite Empire and for a while threatened Egypt with extinction. But Egypt was not about to give up and sink into oblivion, not yet anyway. There was still one more moment of glory for these most ancient of ancients.

(BELOW) THE IMAGE OF RAMESES III FROM HIS MORTUARY TEMPLE AT MEDINET HABU. (BELOW RIGHT) RAMESES' ARMY ON THE MARCH FROM MEDINET HABU.

During the first few years of his reign, Rameses III consolidated the work of his father, Setnakhte, by bringing unity to the country. In his fifth year, when the Libyans attacked, Egypt was well prepared. It had been twenty-seven years since Rameses II's son, Merenptah, had repulsed the Libyans last offensive. This time, an organized and efficient Egyptian army easily defeated them. But this was nothing compared to the second and much greater threat, which came three years later. The Sea Peoples were on the move. They had desolated much of the late Bronze Age civilizations and were ready to make a move on Egypt. A vast horde was marching south with a huge fleet at sea supporting the progress on land.

To counter this threat, Rameses acted quickly. He established a defensive line in southern Palestine and requisitioned every available ship to secure the mouth of the Nile. Dispatches were sent to frontier posts with orders to stand firm until the main army could be brought into action. The clash, when it came, was a complete success for the Egyptians. The Sea Peoples were defeated and scattered on land, but their navy continued toward the eastern Nile delta, their new aim to defeat the Egyptian navy and force an entry up the river. Although the Egyptians had a poor reputation as seamen, they fought with the tenacity

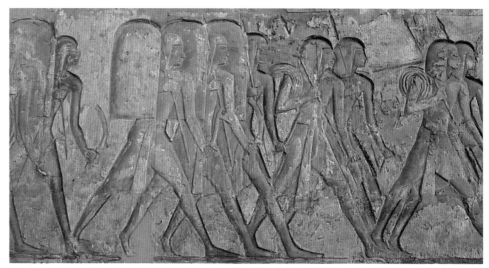

of those defending their homes. Rameses lined the shores with ranks of archers who kept up continuous volleys into the enemy ships when they attempted to land. Then the Egyptian navy attacked, using grappling hooks to haul in the enemy ships. In the brutal hand-to-hand fighting that ensued, the Sea Peoples were utterly defeated.

The power of the Sea Peoples was broken in the Nile Delta but some, the biblical Philistines, settled in Palestine, which is named after them. With the exception of one more conflict with the Libyans, the rest of Rameses III's long reign was peaceful. Trading contacts were revived with the Land of Punt while law and order was reestablished throughout the country. There was a major program of tree-planting and building, the finest example of which is the temple at Medinet Habu.

Rameses III had two principal wives plus a number of minor ones. It was one of these minor wives, Tiye, who caused his destruction. She hatched a plot to kill him with the aim of placing her son, Prince Pentaweret, on the throne. She and her confederates stirred up a rebellion and used magic wax images and poison as their weapons. The conspiracy failed and the traitors were arrested, but not before Rameses was mortally wounded. Fourteen officials sat in judgment and all of the accused but one were found guilty and condemned to commit suicide. Rameses died before the trial was over.

Rameses III's death marked the end of an era. He had ruled for thirty-one years and was the last of the great pharaohs. Egypt began to suffer economic problems and was unable to exploit the innovations of the Iron Age that began a round 1200 BC because she had no source of ore. But the most important factor in Egypt's decline was a breakdown in the fabric of its society. There were disputes between officials and governors and infighting between the north and south. The priesthood became excessively powerful and eventually took control of the government. From that time on, others would determine the destiny of the Mediterranean world. The Assyrians, Persians, Greeks, and eventually the Romans were to become the leading players on the international political stage.

The Sea Peoples

The Sea Peoples were a loose confederation of people originating in the eastern Mediterranean who invaded eastern Anatolia, Syria, Cyprus, and Egypt around the end of the Bronze Age. They destroyed many of the old powers, including the Hittite Empire, but they were defeated by Ramses III, who saved Egypt from destruction.

Rameses III said, "I prepared the river mouth like a strong wall with warships, galleys, and skiffs. They were completely equipped both fore and aft with brave fighters carrying their weapons and the pick of Egypt's infantry all being like roaring lions upon the mountains. On land were chariots with able warriors and goodly officers whose hands were competent. Their horses quivered in all their limbs, prepared to crush the foreign countries under their hoofs."

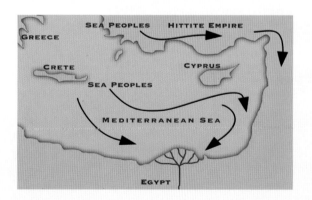

Cleopatra VII Thea Philopator

The Last Pharaoh 51–30 BC.

**BIRTH NAME: CLEOPATRA NETJERET MER-IT-ES
"GODDESS BELOVED OF HER FATHER"**

Cleopatra's fame has endured for over two thousand years, her story an enduring subject of literature from Plutarch to Shakespeare to George Bernard Shaw. The powerful queen has been depicted in successful films and on television.

Historical accounts of Cleopatra tell of a beautiful, highly educated woman who was schooled in physics, alchemy, and astronomy, and could speak many languages. Her voice, said the Greek biographer Plutarch,

"was like an instrument of many strings, which could pass from one language to another."

Cleopatra VII Thea Philopator was of Macedonian descent, not a native Egyptian. She was the second daughter of King Ptolemy XII and the last sovereign of her dynasty, which had been founded by Alexander's general, Ptolemy, in 326 BC. She came to power in 51 BC, at the age of seventeen, and was married to her eldest brother, Ptolemy XIII. He attempted to murder her and seize power for himself but she escaped safely into Syria and later returned with an army. In the end, neither Cleopatra nor her brother was strong enough to gain a decisive advantage.

At this point the Romans entered the scene. Julius Caesar was pursuing his enemy, Pompey, after the battle of Pharsalus, and Pompey was seeking sanctuary in Egypt with Ptolemy XIII. Hoping to please Caesar, Ptolemy had Pompey killed but, unluckily for Ptolemy, Caesar was sickened by the manner of his old adversary's death.

Egypt was the largest supplier of grain for Rome at this time, and it was vital that the country be settled. Caesar set about promoting political stability and favored Cleopatra over Ptolemy.

Ptolemy then attacked the small Roman garrison on the Island of Pharos, intending to drive Caesar out of Egypt. Caesar ordered his men to set fire to the Egyptian fleet in the harbor. Unfortunately, the flames spread to the city and the great library, which held over a million unique books—the largest collection in the ancient world—was destroyed. Ptolemy drowned during the battle and Cleopatra became the undisputed ruler of Egypt.

Caesar was the strong man, the dictator of Rome, and although Egypt was rich, Rome was the world power. This fact wasn't lost on Cleopatra, so she pursued the great man. For his part, Caesar needed money and Egypt could supply his needs. So, out of both a strong personal attraction and mutual interests, the two became lovers. Together, they sailed up the Nile visiting the ancient monuments, and Caesar was fascinated by the long history of the ancient land. At Phelae, Cleopatra and Caesar were honored by the Egyptians as gods. Eventually, Caesar returned to Rome leaving Cleopatra pregnant. She gave birth, in 46 BC, to a boy whom she called Caesarion.

As soon as Caesar returned to Rome he marked his triumph with a lavish, four-day celebration. In 45 BC, Cleopatra visited Rome and took up residence in a villa owned by Caesar. Her wealth and sophistication caused jealousy among the nobility and the Roman Senate became suspicious of Caesar's intentions, believing that he wanted to make himself a king. Soon enough, they murdered him.

Cleopatra's hopes of influence and power were dashed when Caesar was assassinated. She returned to Egypt

Alexandria

Alexandria was founded by Alexander the Great in 332 BC, on the Mediterranean coast of Egypt. It was the richest and most opulent city of its time, with a thriving cosmopolitan community of about half a million people. By 320 BC it had replaced Memphis as the capital of Egypt and had become the intellectual center of the Hellenistic world. The most famous buildings in the city were the Library and the Museum, which housed a unique collection of literature comprising the knowledge of the ancient world. Alexandria's Pharos lighthouse was one of the wonders of the ancient world. Little excavation has taken place because the ancient city lies below the modern city.

(FAR LEFT) THE IMAGE OF CLEOPATRA FROM DENDARA TEMPLE. (LEFT) JULIUS CAESAR. (BACKGROUND) A RECONSTRUCTION OF THE GREAT HARBOR AT ALEXANDRIA, SHOWING THE PHAROS LIGHTHOUSE BUILT BY PTOLEMY SOTER 250 YEARS BEFORE CLEOPATRA.

where she concentrated on building up the economy and consolidating her power. Her first act was to have her younger brother poisoned so that she could elevate her son, Caesarion, in his place.

In 42 BC, at the Battle of Philippi, Caesar's assassins were routed and the Roman Empire was divided between Mark Antony and Caesar's great-nephew and personal heir, Octavian. Mark Antony took charge of the Eastern Empire and Octavian ruled the Western. Antony planned an invasion of Persia but he needed money for the venture. He saw the wealth of Egypt as the key and sent a message for Cleopatra to meet with him at the city of Tarsus in Asia Minor.

She was delighted: Here was a second chance to achieve her ambition of making Egypt a great power again. She had known Mark Antony when he'd been a young staff officer in Egypt. She was now twenty-eight and completely confident in her powers. Still, she delayed her departure and took her time, sailing to Tarsus in a great golden barge loaded with gifts.

Cleopatra sailed up the river and entered the city in an extravagant show of style. Antony was so captivated by her that he decided to put off his Persian campaign; he returned to Alexandria with Cleopatra, where he lived a life of pleasure.

In 40 BC, Antony left Alexandria to return to Italy, where he concluded a temporary agreement with Octavian. As part of this settlement he married Octavian's sister, Octavia. But three years later, Antony was convinced that he and Octavian could never come to terms. He needed money for his postponed Parthian campaign so once again he went to Cleopatra to get her to finance the invasion; the campaign went ahead but was, in the end, a costly failure.

Meanwhile, Octavian regarded Antony and his Egyptian power base as a threat to Rome's dominance of the Medi-terranean world. He waged a propaganda campaign against Antony from Rome, and Antony made what was to prove a fatal step: he married Cleopatra. The union was an insult to his wife Octavia and to her brother Octavian, but even worse, the marriage united all of Rome against him.

During Antony's absence, Cleopatra had made a critical mistake in her foreign policy toward Herod of Judea. Herod and Antony were old friends but Cleopatra tried, unsuccessfully, to seduce Herod on his way through Egypt. Her vanity got the better of her and she never forgave him for the rejection.

She later persuaded Antony to give her large portions of Syria and Lebanon and even tried to get the rich balsam groves of Jericho, part of Herod's own kingdom. However, Antony refused to give her Jericho, which only inflamed her hatred of Herod. She then interfered in Herod's unhappy family affairs by conspiring against him with the women in his household. This act was to come back to haunt her: When she needed Herod's help against Rome, he would not give it.

In 34 AD, Antony celebrated a great triumph in Alexandria. The crowds saw Antony and Cleopatra seated on golden thrones with their own three children and Julius

Caesar's son, Caesarion. Antony proclaimed Caesarion to be Caesar's son, thus diminishing Octavian's status as Caesar's adopted heir. Octavian responded by confiscating Antony's will from the temple of the Vestal Virgins, to whom it had been entrusted. He then leaked its contents to the Roman people, who were outraged at Antony's plans to bequeath his Roman possessions to this foreign woman and to transfer the capital from Rome to Alexandria.

The Roman Senate finally declared war against Cleopatra and on September 2, 31 BC, at the naval Battle of Actium, Octavian defeated the combined forces of Antony and Cleopatra.

Cleopatra fled with her forces at the height of the battle. When it really mattered, her judgment was questionable—and this fact, along with Antony's reckless, drunken behavior, doomed them to failure against the cold, calculating Octavian. Cleopatra retreated to her mausoleum and had a message sent to Antony saying she was dead. He was so devastated he committed suicide by falling on his sword.

Octavian eventually entered Egypt, and Cleopatra tried once again to captivate the most important Roman—but Octavian was not moved. He wanted to embellish his

triumph by having her and her children dragged through the streets of Rome in chains. Rather than suffer such humiliation she sent him a letter asking that she might be buried with Antony, and then committed suicide by allowing an asp to bite her. This snake is the symbol of Egyptian divine royalty. Plutarch describes the scene, saying that she was found "stone dead, lying upon a bed of gold, set out in all her royal ornaments."

Cleopatra was thirty-nine when she died in 30 BC. She'd been a queen for twenty-two years and was buried with her lover, Antony. Her high ambitions together with her arrogance ruined Egypt's future prospects of independence. While she might have of achieved client status for Egypt within the Roman Empire, her utter failure condemned her country to becoming a mere province of Rome. And yet, this extraordinary woman is one of the most famous in history. Together with Caesar, Antony, and Octavian (who later became Emperor Augustus), she played a crucial part in shaping the affairs of Western civilization and the course of history. The Greek historian Dio Cassius said of Cleopatra, "She captivated the two greatest Romans of her day, and because of the third she destroyed herself."

(LEFT) THE IMAGE OF MARC ANTONY. (ABOVE) A STATUE OF OCTAVIAN WHO LATER BECAME THE FIRST ROMAN EMPEROR AUGUSTUS. THE MONTHS OF JULY AND AUGUST ARE NAMED AFTER JULIUS CAESAR AND AUGUSTUS CAESAR.

III

THE PYRAMIDS

PYRAMIDS ARE THE OLDEST AND MOST DURABLE OF HUMANITY'S GREAT ACHIEVEMENTS.

STANDING AT THE FOOT OF ONE OF THE GREAT PYRAMIDS, LOOKING UP INTO THE SKY AND CONTEMPLATING THIS MANMADE MOUNTAIN, YOU CAN'T FAIL TO BE AWED BY THE ACHIEVEMENT OF THE EGYPTIANS. TO PUT THIS WONDER OF THE ANCIENT WORLD INTO PERSPECTIVE, CONSIDER THE GREAT PYRAMID AT GIZA. IT WAS BUILT OVER FOUR-AND-A-HALF THOUSAND YEARS AGO AND REMAINED THE TALLEST MANMADE STRUCTURE IN THE WORLD UNTIL THE EIFFEL TOWER WAS BUILT IN 1889.

There are a lot of far-fetched speculations about the pyramids as well as the Great Sphinx. Some people even believe they were built by aliens from other worlds! All of the material evidence, though, proves conclusively that they were made by the ancient Egyptians as gigantic burial structures. Most of the pyramids in Egypt were built in the span of a few hundred years, from the third to the sixth dynasties (2667–2181 BC).

The largest and most sophisticated pyramids were created during the Old Kingdom. They evolved from simple tombs made to protect the dead from jackals and other wild animals. The earliest graves were pits cut into the bedrock and covered in stones—but soon they developed into more elaborate structures made from mud brick and stone, featuring rooms designed so that people could enter and pay their respects to the dead. These structures became known as mastabas, from the Arabic word for "bench." All of the early pharaohs of the first two dynasties were buried in mastabas.

(TOP) THE PYRAMID OF SAHURE 2487–2475 BC. THE COLONNADED COURTS OF THE MORTUARY TEMPLE HAD RELIEFS DESCRIBING HIS NAVAL EXPEDITIONS. (BOTTOM) A RECONSTRUCTION OF FOUR MASTABA TOMBS. THEY USUALLY COMPRISED OF A PIT DUG INTO THE GROUND FOR THE BURIAL CHAMBER AND ABOVEGROUND ROOMS AND OFFERING CHAMBERS. THEY WERE THE STANDARD DESIGN OF TOMBS FOR NOBLES AND MINOR ROYALTY DURING THE PYRAMID AGE. (BELOW) A RECONSTRUCTION OF THE GIZA PYRAMIDS.

Saqqara

During the third dynasty, King Djoser (2667–2648 BC) began work on his mastaba tomb at Saqqara. The man responsible for carrying out the project was Djoser's Prime Minister, Imhotep.

Djoser and Imhotep decided to build an enormous mastaba of stone, but at some point during construction they built another mastaba on top of the first—and then another on top of the second. They continued this process until they had enlarged the structure into the world's first pyramid. It was what we now call a "step pyramid," consisting of six terraces some 200 feet (60 m) high.

But the king and his inventive architect did not stop there. Next they encased the surface in smooth white limestone, which must have caught the sunlight and reflected its rays. They built chapels around the base, and a vast courtyard for the king's festivals. Finally, the whole complex was enclosed by a wall.

Saqqara is also the site of many tombs of minor royalty and court officials. These are known as "the tombs of the nobles." The limestone walls of these structures are delicately incised with images showing all kinds of animals, fish, birds, insects, vegetation, and people hunting, herding, and farming. Some of the pictures still retain their original paint after 4,500 years. The quality of these compositions is proof that the ancient Egyptians quickly attained an artistic culture of a very high order. The sophistication and excellence of their artistry and architectural craftsmanship reached their apotheosis in the development of the pyramids.

PYRAMID OF UNAS
2375–2345 BC

SERAPEUM
UNDERGROUND TOMBS OF TH[E]
APIS BULLS WHICH WERE
SACRED TO THE GOD PTAH.

STOREROOMS

THE SED
FESTIVAL COURT
AND CHAPELS

MASTABA OF
PTAH-HOTEP
AND AKHET-
HOTEP

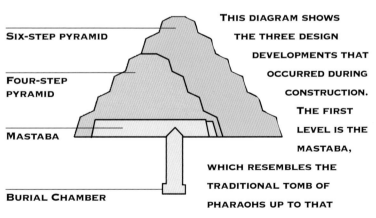

SIX-STEP PYRAMID

FOUR-STEP PYRAMID

MASTABA

BURIAL CHAMBER

THIS DIAGRAM SHOWS THE THREE DESIGN DEVELOPMENTS THAT OCCURRED DURING CONSTRUCTION. THE FIRST LEVEL IS THE MASTABA, WHICH RESEMBLES THE TRADITIONAL TOMB OF PHARAOHS UP TO THAT TIME; NEXT COMES THE FOUR-STEP PYRAMID; AND FINALLY, THE STRUCTURE WAS ENLARGED TO BECOME A SIX-STEP PYRAMID.

Imhotep *is credited as the inventor of building in stone and was a man of many talents—architect, physician, master sculptor, scribe, and astronomer. He may be the first true genius in recorded history, and his impact on Egyptian life and custom was profound. He was later deified as the god of wisdom and medicine. For thousands of years the Egyptians made a pilgrimage to his tomb, but the exact location is now lost. He is thought to have been buried near his king—a chamber dedicated to him found at Saqqara seems to suggest this might be true. It is known as the Tomb of the Birds, and contains over a million mummified ibises.*

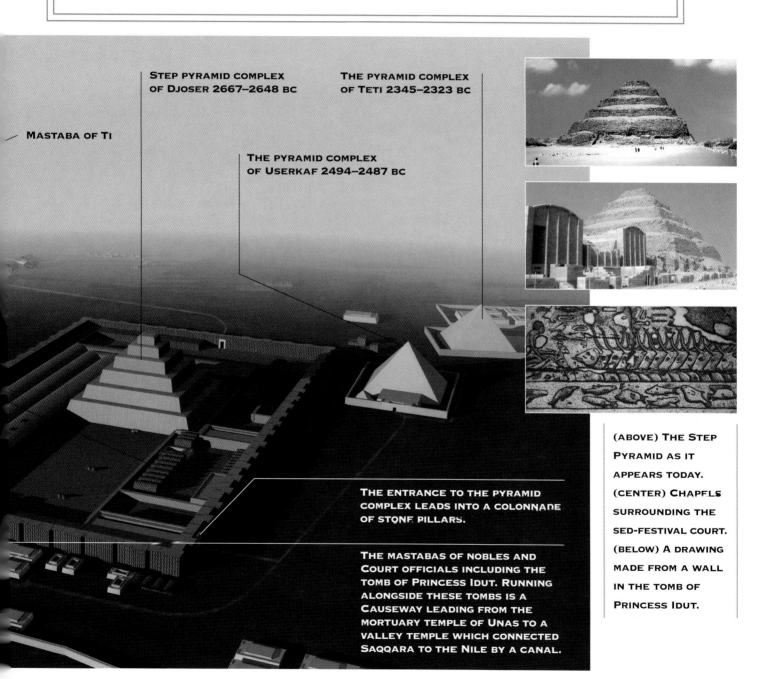

STEP PYRAMID COMPLEX
OF DJOSER 2667–2648 BC

THE PYRAMID COMPLEX
OF TETI 2345–2323 BC

MASTABA OF TI

THE PYRAMID COMPLEX
OF USERKAF 2494–2487 BC

THE ENTRANCE TO THE PYRAMID
COMPLEX LEADS INTO A COLONNADE
OF STONE PILLARS.

THE MASTABAS OF NOBLES AND
COURT OFFICIALS INCLUDING THE
TOMB OF PRINCESS IDUT. RUNNING
ALONGSIDE THESE TOMBS IS A
CAUSEWAY LEADING FROM THE
MORTUARY TEMPLE OF UNAS TO A
VALLEY TEMPLE WHICH CONNECTED
SAQQARA TO THE NILE BY A CANAL.

(ABOVE) THE STEP
PYRAMID AS IT
APPEARS TODAY.
(CENTER) CHAPELS
SURROUNDING THE
SED-FESTIVAL COURT.
(BELOW) A DRAWING
MADE FROM A WALL
IN THE TOMB OF
PRINCESS IDUT.

The fourth-dynasty king, Sneferu 2686–2667 BC, was the first to create the pyramid shape that we all recognize and associate with Egyptian architecture. He built three pyramids in all—but the first two were glorious failures! His first, the pyramid at Medum, began as a step pyramid and was then modified to form the first true pyramid. But it was unstable and the limestone blocks began to slip. Soon, work on it was abandoned. King Sneferu then moved to Dahshur and built a second pyramid, which we now know as the "Bent Pyramid" because its upper part rises at a shallower angle of incline than the lower part.

The Bent Pyramid was originally planned as a true pyramid, but the corners were built on unstable ground and the walls of the burial chambers inside began to crack and shift inward. Of necessity, the building's geometry was altered at a point just above half its height. The angle of incline was decreased from 54° 31' 13" to 43° 21'. This was probably done to alleviate the stresses in the lower part of the pyramid and make it stronger—but the bent pyramid was never used. Instead, Sneferu began a third pyramid about a mile way. This one is called the Red Pyramid because of the red limestone blocks used in its construction. It became the world's first successful true pyramid, at long last providing King Sneferu with a suitable burial place.

With the Red Pyramid, Sneferu set the standard for all true pyramids to come. He included aboveground burial chambers, a mortuary temple, and a causeway leading down to a valley temple. This was the model followed by his son, Khufu (later known as Cheops), who built the Great Pyramid at Giza.

(LEFT) THE STONE CORE OF THE PYRAMID AT MEDUM SURROUNDED BY RUBBLE. (CENTER) THE BENT PYRAMID STILL WITH MUCH OF ITS SMOOTH STONE SKIN. (RIGHT) SNEFERU'S FINAL AND SUCCESSFUL ATTEMPT—THE RED PYRAMID.

How Did They Do It?

WE KNOW VERY LITTLE ABOUT THE CONSTRUCTION METHODS USED IN THE BUILDING OF THE PYRAMIDS, THOUGH WE DO KNOW HOW THE STONE BLOCKS WERE QUARRIED. IN FACT, THE SAME METHODS ARE USED TODAY—BUT THE ANCIENT EGYPTIANS WORKED WITH MORE PRIMITIVE TOOLS.

FIRST, A LINE OF SLOTS WAS CUT INTO THE LIMESTONE WITH TOOLS OF COPPER AND A HARDER STONE CALLED DOLERITE. WOODEN WEDGES WERE THEN HAMMERED INTO THESE SLOTS AND SOAKED WITH WATER, WHICH MADE THE WOOD EXPAND AND SPLIT THE BLOCK AWAY FROM THE BEDROCK. FROM INSCRIPTIONS LEFT ON THESE BLOCKS, WE KNOW THAT THE QUARRYMEN WERE DIVIDED INTO GANGS WITH SUCH NAMES AS THE "VIGOROUS GANG" OR THE "BOAT GANG."

THE PYRAMIDS WERE PROBABLY BUILT USING MUD-BRICK RAMPS THAT SPIRALED AROUND THE SIDES, GREW IN HEIGHT WITH THE PYRAMID, AND WERE REMOVED WHEN THE PYRAMID WAS COMPLETE. BUT DESPITE MUCH SPECULATION, SOME OF IT FANCIFUL, WE STILL DO NOT UNDERSTAND ALL OF THE DETAILS INVOLVED IN ERECTING THE PYRAMIDS.

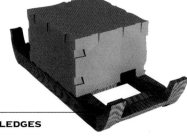

STONES WERE DRAGGED ON WOODEN SLEDGES

The Golden Lotus

Sneferu sent for his Chief Magician, Zazamankh, and said to him, "I'm bored. Devise something that will fill my heart with pleasure."

Zazamankh suggested that Pharaoh go sailing upon the lake below Memphis. "This will be no common voyage," he said, "because your rowers will be fair maidens from the Royal House and as you watch them rowing, your heart will grow glad."

All was done accordingly, and Sneferu was delighted at the sight of the beautiful rowers. But when an oar handle brushed accidentally against the head of one of the maidens, the golden lotus she wore was swept into the water. With a cry she leaned over and gazed after it as it sank.

"Why have you ceased to row?" asked Pharaoh.

"Forgive me, Pharaoh," she sobbed. "But the beautiful golden lotus that your majesty gave to me has fallen into the water."

"Row on as before, and I will give you another," said Sneferu. But the girl continued to weep. "I want my golden lotus back, and no other!"

Zazamankh was brought forward, and Pharaoh said to him, "Zazamankh, I wish to give back the golden lotus to the little one here, and see the joy return to her eyes."

Zazamankh began to chant great spells of power and the lake parted as if a piece had been cut out of it with a great sword. The water rose up and the Royal Boat slid gently down until it rested on the lake's bottom, next to the golden lotus.

With a cry of joy the maiden sprang over the side and picked it up and set it once more in her hair. When she had climbed back into the Royal Boat, it slid up the side of the water until it was level with the surface once more. Then the water slid back into place, and the evening breeze rippled the still surface of the lake as if nothing out of the ordinary had happened.

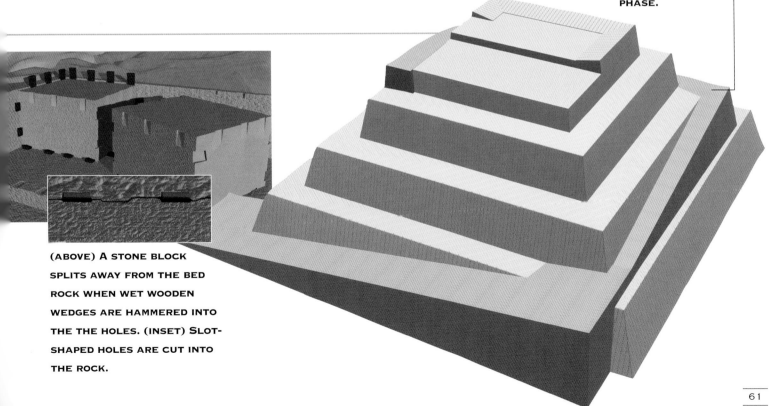

MUD-BRICK RAMPS FOR HAULING DRESSED STONES INTO POSITION. THESE WERE REMOVED AFTER THE CONSTUCTION PHASE.

(ABOVE) A STONE BLOCK SPLITS AWAY FROM THE BED ROCK WHEN WET WOODEN WEDGES ARE HAMMERED INTO THE THE HOLES. (INSET) SLOT-SHAPED HOLES ARE CUT INTO THE ROCK.

The Great Pyramid at Giza

When Khufu became pharaoh (2589–2566 BC), one of his first acts was to stem the increasing power of the priesthood. It is recorded that he shut all the temples and forbade sacrifices. As the priests' livelihoods depended on performing these rituals, it is not surprising that Khufu was unpopular with the religious orders.

Some believe that Khufu's pyramid at Giza was built by slaves—but this is not true. One hundred thousand people worked on the great structure for three months of each year, during the Nile's annual flood when it was impossible to farm the land and most of the population was unemployed. The pharaoh provided good food and

clothing for his workers and was kindly remembered in folktales for many centuries.

In all, three pyramids were built at Giza, each of which had an adjoining mortuary temple. A covered causeway attached to the mortuary temple descended down to a valley temple and landing stage that was connected to the Nile by a canal.

The largest of the three pyramids at Giza, known as the Great Pyramid, is truly an astonishing work of engineering. It was built over a twenty-year period, but unlike the Step Pyramid at Saqqara we do not know the name of the architect.

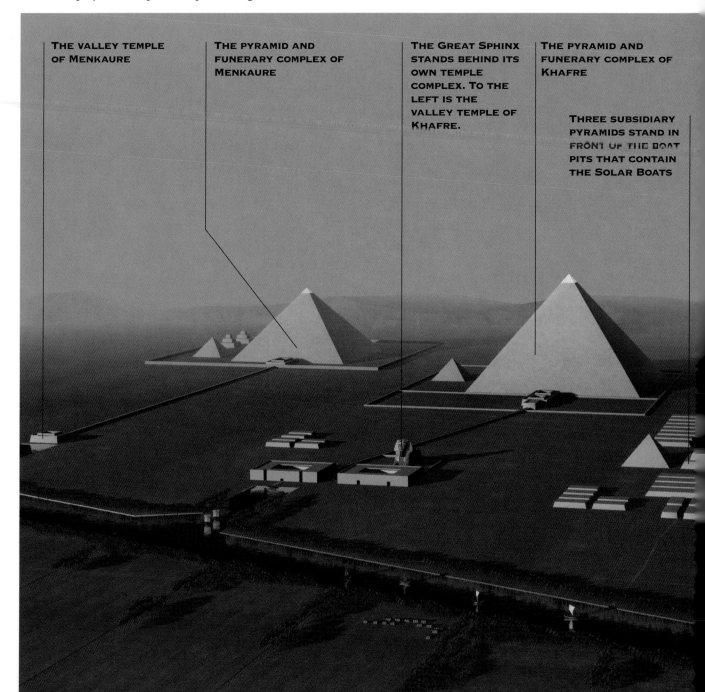

THE VALLEY TEMPLE OF MENKAURE

THE PYRAMID AND FUNERARY COMPLEX OF MENKAURE

THE GREAT SPHINX STANDS BEHIND ITS OWN TEMPLE COMPLEX. TO THE LEFT IS THE VALLEY TEMPLE OF KHAFRE.

THE PYRAMID AND FUNERARY COMPLEX OF KHAFRE

THREE SUBSIDIARY PYRAMIDS STAND IN FRONT OF THE BOAT PITS THAT CONTAIN THE SOLAR BOATS

THE GREAT PYRAMID OF
KHUFU AS IT APPEARS TODAY.

The sides are oriented to the four cardinal points of the compass and the length of each side at the base is 755 feet (230.4 m). The faces rise at an angle of 51° 52' and their original height was 481 feet (147 m). (They currently rise 451 feet [138 m].) It was constructed using around 2,300,000 limestone blocks, each weighing an average of 2.5 tons. Some blocks weigh as much as 16 tons! For centuries, the Great Pyramid was encased in smooth limestone, but this was plundered in our era to build Cairo.

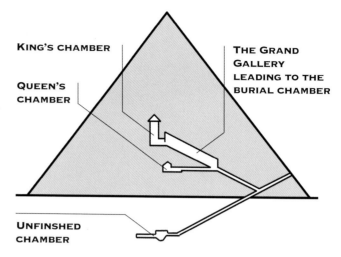

KING'S CHAMBER

QUEEN'S CHAMBER

THE GRAND GALLERY LEADING TO THE BURIAL CHAMBER

UNFINSHED CHAMBER

THE PYRAMID AND FUNERARY COMPLEX OF KHUFU

THE VALLEY TEMPLE WHICH IS CONNECTED TO KHUFU'S MORTUARY TEMPLE BY A COVERED CAUSEWAY

THE LAYOUT OF THE GIZA PLATEAU, SHOWING THE CANAL WHICH WAS CONNECTED TO THE NILE. IT WAS BUILT DURING THE CONSTRUCTION PHASE IN ORDER TO SUPPLY THE WORKFORCE AND BRING MATERIALS TO THE SITE.

Khufu's Solar Boat

In 1954, Kamal el-Mallakh found an enormous pit next to the Great Pyramid. It was sealed with forty-one stones, each weighing around 18 tons, and it contained the pieces of a magnificent boat made of cedar wood. The pit was 101 feet (30.8 m) long, too short for the boat which was 141 feet (43 m) long. So the ancient Egyptians had carefully dismantled the vessel. It took many years for the Egyptian Antiquities Organization to reassemble it, and it can now be seen in a museum next to the pyramid. Recent explorations suggest that there is another such boat nearby, but the authorities have decided to leave it where it is because the conservation technologies required to preserve such a fragile treasure have not yet been perfected.

The Second Pyramid at Giza

Khufu's son, Khafre (also known as Chephren), lived from 2558–2532 BC. His pyramid, on a nearby site at Giza, appears taller than his father's, but this is an illusion; it is built on higher ground and was in fact, originally 447.5 feet (136.4 m), 33.5 feet (10.2 m) shorter than the Great Pyramid. Khafre's pyramid retains some of its original limestone casing at the apex, so it is possible to imagine how the pyramids might have appeared in antiquity.

Khafre also built the Great Sphinx, which has become the elegant emblem of Egypt itself. The sphinx is 66 feet high (20 m) and 240 feet long (73 m) and is part of Khafre's pyramid complex. It represents Ra-Harakhte, the sun god, as he rises in the east at dawn—but the

(ABOVE) A RECONSTRUCTION OF THE SPHINX TEMPLE AND INSET AS IT APPEARS TODAY. (RIGHT) THE TIME WORN SPHINX AT GIZA WITHOUT ITS NOSE.

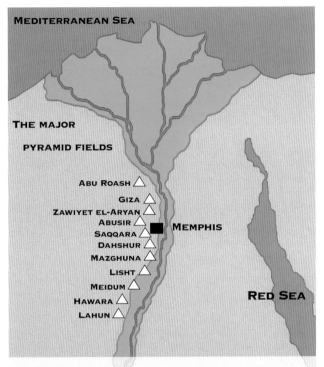

MEDITERRANEAN SEA

THE MAJOR

PYRAMID FIELDS

ABU ROASH △

GIZA △

ZAWIYET EL-ARYAN △

ABUSIR △ ◼ MEMPHIS

SAQQARA △

DAHSHUR △

MAZGHUNA △

LISHT △

MEIDUM △

HAWARA △ RED SEA

LAHUN △

face of the Sphinx is a portrait of Khafre himself, and is contemporary with his pyramid. It was carved from an outcropping of limestone left after quarrying the stone for his father's pyramid. Unfortunately, the Great Sphinx has deteriorated over the millennia and was extensively renovated in ancient times. More recently it was mutilated by the Sultan Mohammed an-Nasir in 1300 AD; and lost its nose in 1798, when Napoleon's soldiers used it for target practice. There have recently been a number of wild theories concerning the age of the Great Sphinx, but no material evidence exists to suggest that its history should be revised.

SAQQARA

DJOSER 2667-2648 BC

SEKHEMKHET 2648-2640 BC

TETI 2345-2323 BC

USERKAF 2494-2487 BC

DJEDKARA 2414-22375 BC

UNAS 2375-2345 BC

PEPY I 2321-2287 BC

MERENRA 2287-2278 BC

PEPY II 2278-2184 BC

KHENDJER 13TH DYNASTY

MEIDUM

SNEFERU 2613-2589 BC

SNEFERU'S FIRST PYRAMID

DAHSHUR

SNEFERU 2613-2589 BC

THE BENT PYRAMID &

THE RED PYRAMID

AMENEMHET II 1922-1878 BC

AMENEMHET II 1922-1878 BC

SENUSRET III 1874-1855 BC

AMENEMHET III 1855-1808 BC

ABU ROASH

DJEDEFRA 2566-2558 BC

GIZA

KHUFU 2589-2566 BC

KHAFRA 2558-2532 BC

MENKAURA 2532-2503 BC

ZAWIYET EL-ARYAN

TWO UNFINISHED PYRAMIDS

ABUSIR

SAHURA 2487-2475 BC

NEFERIRKARA 2475-2455 BC

RANEFEREF 2448-2445 BC

NYUSERRA 2445-2421 BC

MAZGHUNA

TWO PYRAMIDS - OWNERS

UNKNOWN

LISHT

AMENEMHAT I 1985-1955 BC

SENURSRET I 1965-1920 BC

HAWARA

AMENEMHAT III 1855-1808 BC

LAHUN

SENUSRET II 1880-1874 BC

The Third Pyramid at Giza

Khafre's son, Menkaura, who came to the throne in 2532 BC, built the third pyramid at the Giza necropolis (cemetery). With an original height of 228 feet (70 m), it is less than half the height and only one tenth of the mass of the pyramid built by his grandfather, Khufu. The lower layers consist of red granite from Aswan and the upper courses were originally made of gleaming white limestone.

The story of the Prince and the Sphinx demonstrates how the New Kingdom ancient Egyptians marveled at their predecessors' monuments, which were then well over a thousand year old.

There are over 100 recorded pyramids in Egypt, most of which belong to minor royalty or have no known owners. Although pyramid-building in stone continued until the end of the Old Kingdom, the pyramids of Giza were never surpassed in their size and the technical excellence of their construction.

Pyramids were built during the Middle Kingdom (2055–1650 BC) but these consisted of a mud-brick core with a stone skin and are now mere piles of rubble.

Pyramids required an enormous investment in resources and stood out in the landscape as easy pray to robbers. The last royal pyramid was built by the first king of the eighteenth dynasty Ahmose 1550–1525 BC but, after that, the Egyptians ceased building these majestic burial structures for all time.

What was the impact of pyramid-building on the peoples of the Nile? Is it conceivable that by bringing together so many people and giving them a common goal, that of making a mountain, a national identity was forged in their hearts. Disparate communities from upper and lower Egypt were united and grew to understand one another over the course of the great building projects. Egypt was the only nation state in the ancient world and it may be the only example in human history of a national identity forged not from war but from construction.

The Prince and the Sphinx

In 1926, some 3,230 years after Thutmose IV became Pharaoh of Egypt, Emile Baraize cleared the sand away from around the Great Sphinx at Giza and between its paws he found the remains of a shrine in which stood a red granite tablet fourteen feet high. This can still be seen there today. Inscribed on it in hieroglyphs is the story of the Prince and the Sphinx.

•

I am Prince Thutmose. My grandfather was Thutmose III, who conquered the world and gave the breath of life to those he defeated. My father is Pharaoh Amenhotep II, before whom all the kings of the world bow down. I have many brothers and half-brothers, and I fear for my life because they are jealous and forever plotting against me.

Yesterday, when the court was in residence at Memphis for the great festival of Ra, I escaped from the long and tedious ceremonies and I set off in my chariot to hunt. But the sun became too hot so I stopped to rest beneath the shade of a gigantic head rising out of the sand. It was a colossal carving of Ra-Harakht, the god of the rising sun, in the form of a lion. It had been made a thousand years ago by my ancestor Khafra and he had instructed his sculptors to shape the head and face of Ra-Harakht in his own likeness.

But since Khafra was laid to rest in his pyramid, the sands have blown against the sphinx until now it is almost buried. I could see no more than its head and shoulders, and for a long while I stood looking up into its majestic face praying to Ra-Harakht to help me in all my troubles, As I made my prayer the noonday sun beat mercilessly upon me and I began to feel drowsy. Suddenly I came to my senses and my heart leaped in shock because I could see the Great Sphinx heaving and struggling as if trying in vain to throw off the sand that buried its body. Its eyes shone with life and looked down upon me. Then the Great Sphinx spoke to me in a strong voice, like a kindly father speaks to his son.

"Look upon me, Thutmose, Prince of Egypt, and know that I am Ra-Harakht your father—the father of all Pharaohs of the Upper and Lower Lands. It rests with you to become Pharaoh and wear upon your head the Double Crown of

By giving them a common goal, a national identity was forged in their hearts.

South and North. It rests with you whether or not you sit upon the throne of Egypt, and whether the peoples of the world come and kneel before you in homage. If you become Pharaoh, whatever is produced by the Two Lands shall be yours, together with the tribute from all the countries of the world.

Thutmose, my face is turned toward you, my heart inclines to you to bring you good things, your spirit shall be wrapped in mine. But see how the sand has closed in around me on every side: it smothers me, it holds me down, and it hides me from your eyes. Promise me that you will do all that a good son should do for his father; prove to me that you are indeed my son and will help me. Draw near to me, and I will be with you always, I will guide you and make you great."

As I stepped forward the sun shimmered from the eyes of the Sphinx so brightly they dazzled me and the world went black and spun round me so that I fell insensible on the sand.

When I recovered, the sun was sinking toward the summit of Khafra's pyramid and the shadow of the Sphinx lay over me.

"Ra-Harakht, my father!" I cried, "I call upon you and all the gods of Egypt to bear witness to my oath. If I become Pharaoh, the first act of my reign shall be to free this, your image, from the sand and build a shrine to you and set in it a stone telling in the sacred writing of Khem of your command and how I fulfilled it."

I rode back to Memphis and my father commanded that I attend him in the great hall. I thought he would be angry with me for not attending the festival of Ra but to my surprise he publicly proclaimed me as heir to the throne. All those who had been against me now wanted to be my friend. I no longer feared for my life and when my father Amenhotep goes to join the gods I will indeed become King of Egypt.

THE TEMPLES

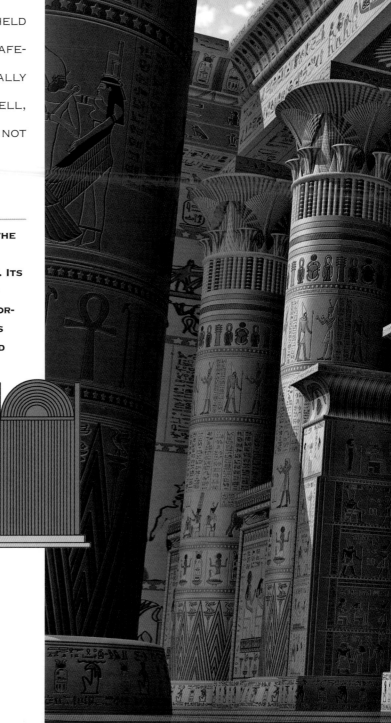

I N ANCIENT EGYPT, THE TEMPLES WERE THE LANDOWNERS, THE CENTERS OF ADMINISTRATION, AND THE POSSESS-ORS OF ALL WEALTH. FOR 3,000 YEARS THEY MAINTAINED CULTURAL CONTINUITY, UPHELD THE AUTHORITY OF THE RULERS, AND SAFE-GUARDED THE SOCIAL STRUCTURE. EVENTUALLY THEY BECAME POLITICAL POWERHOUSES AS WELL, THEIR HIGH PRIESTS WIELDING AS MUCH, IF NOT MORE, POWER THAN THE PHARAOH HIMSELF.

A RECONSTRUCTION OF A TEMPLE AT PHILEA. IT'S THE LAST EGYPTIAN TEMPLE TO HAVE BEEN BUILT AND OVER 3,000 YEARS SEPARATE IT FROM THE PER-NU. ITS PAINTED COLUMNS ARE BASED ON COLOR ILLUSTRA-TIONS MADE BY EARLY NINETEENTH-CENTURY EXPLOR-ERS. UNFORTUNATELY THE ORIGINAL PAINTWORK WAS DESTROYED BY THE RISING FLOODWATERS OF THE OLD ASWAN DAM, BUILT BETWEEN 1898 AND 1902 AD. (RIGHT) THE "HOUSE OF THE NORTH" AT SAQQARA WAS PROBABLY MADE FROM WOOD WITH REED MATS FOR THE ROOF AND WALLS. (BELOW) PER-NU THE PREDYNASTIC STATE SHRINE OF LOWER EGYPT. NO REMAINS EXIST AND THIS RECONSTRUCTION IS BASED ON ITS HIEROGLYPH.

Although temples were built during the Old Kingdom (2686–2181 BC), pyramids were the great accomplishment of that period. It was the rulers of the New Kingdom (1570–1070 BC) who used their wealth and resources to construct massive temple complexes.

The architects and craftsmen constructed these fabulous buildings using only natural raw materials—mud, stone, sand, wood, and water. Working with simple copper and stone tools, they created structures that have defied the ravages of time. They called these buildings "Houses of Millions of Years."

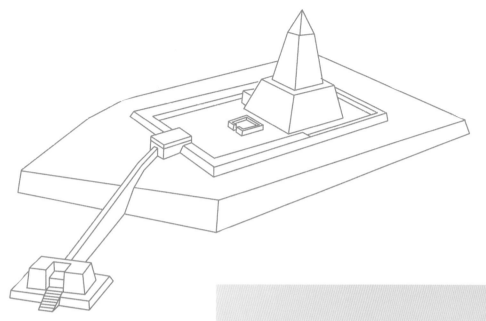

(LEFT) ABU GHURAB
(BETWEEN SAQQARA
AND GIZA) IS THE SITE
OF TWO SUN TEMPLES
DATING FROM APPROXI-
MATELY 2494–2345 BC.
THE EARLY PART OF THE
FIFTH DYNASTY IS
CHARACTERIZED BY THE
WORSHIP OF THE SUN
GOD RA, AND SIX SUN
TEMPLES WERE BUILT

(ABOVE) A RECON-
STRUCTION OF LUXOR
TEMPLE SHOWING THE
AVENUE OF SPHINXES.
(RIGHT) A RECON-
STRUCTION OF KING
NYUSERRA'S SUN
TEMPLE AT ABU
GHURAB.

Cult and Funerary Temples

The temples fell into two principal types: cult temples and funerary or mortuary temples. The cult temples housed images of the gods, while the mortuary temples were created as shrines to dead kings.

Cult Temples

Some of the earliest surviving cult temples are from the Old Kingdom. These are the sun temples of the fifth-dynasty kings at Abu Ghurab.

The layout consisted of a reception pavilion connected by a covered corridor on a causeway to the open court of the temple. Within stood a squat obelisk made of limestone and a huge alabaster altar. But these were modest structures when compared to the cult temples erected during the New Kingdom at Thebes.

The formula for the great New Kingdom temples involved a processional approach: an avenue of sphinxes that might be up to a mile long led to the great double-towered pylon entrance. This was fronted by a pair of huge obelisks, colossal statues of the king, and pennants flapping in the breeze from tall flagpoles. The pylon was covered in brightly painted scenes and led into an open courtyard of columns, which in turn formed the entrance to a pillared hypostyle hall. Beyond this was a smaller hall where offerings could be prepared. At the heart of the temple was the shrine for the god.

In addition there were storage chambers for temple equipment and sometimes a crypt. Outside the temple were service buildings and a lake or well for the water needed in the rituals. There would also be a birth house (*mammisi*) to celebrate the king's divine birth. The whole complex was contained inside a massive mud brick wall.

These temples were towns in there own right. The great precinct of the Temple of Karnak was a city, employing thousands of people.

Seti I (1294–1279 BC) of the 19th dynasty built an unusual cult temple at Abydos. It was dedicated to Osiris and contained seven chapels each glorifying a different deity, including the deified Seti himself. Remnants of these chapels exist today, featuring well-preserved ceilings and walls decorated with extraordinarily beautiful low-relief scenes still retaining much of their original color.

Of course the most remarkable monument of this type is that of Rameses II (1279–1213 BC) at Abu Simbel. It was literally cut from the natural rock, yet still follows the plan of a conventional Egyptian temple. Colossal seated statues emerge from cliff-face façade, and pillared halls lead to a vestibule and a shrine with four statues of divinities.

Funerary Temples

Most of the New Kingdom funerary temples were built along the desert edge in western Thebes. The most original and beautiful was Queen Hatshepsut's (1473–1458 BC) temple, designed and built by her steward (and, some say, her lover), Sennmut.

Three terraces lead up to the recess in the cliffs where the shrine was cut into the rock. Each terrace is fronted by colonnades of square pillars depicting reliefs of unusual subjects, including an expedition to Punt and the divine birth of Hatshepsut. Ramps lead from terrace to terrace, and the uppermost level opens into a large court with colonnades. Chapels of Hathor (the principal deity of the temple) and Anubis occupy the south and north ends of the colonnade of the second terrace.

The largest funerary temple was probably that of Amenhotep III (1390–1352 BC). Unfortunately, all that remains of it are the two huge quartzite statues, the Colossi of Memnon. Rameses II used its design (as well as much of its stone) for his own funerary temple, the Ramesseum.

The Ramesseum contained two huge open courts entered through towering pylons and leading to a lofty hypostyle hall and a smaller hall with astronomical carvings on the ceiling. Vast statues stood before the second pylon, one of which, now toppled and ruined, has been estimated to weigh more than 1,000 tons.

The basic layout of a New Kingdom temple

PYLON

(FAR LEFT) HATSHEPSUT'S TEMPLE AT DEIR EL-BAHRI, WITH ITS BEAUTIFUL DESIGN, IS ONE OF THE GREAT LEGACIES OF HER REIGN. (LEFT) ABU SIMBEL WAS BEGUN EARLY IN THE REIGN OF RAMESES II AND TOOK AROUND 35 YEARS TO COMPLETE. IN THE 1960s IT WAS CUT INTO PIECES AND REASSEMBLED ON HIGHER GROUND TO SAVE IT FROM THE RISING FLOOD WATERS OF LAKE NASSER.

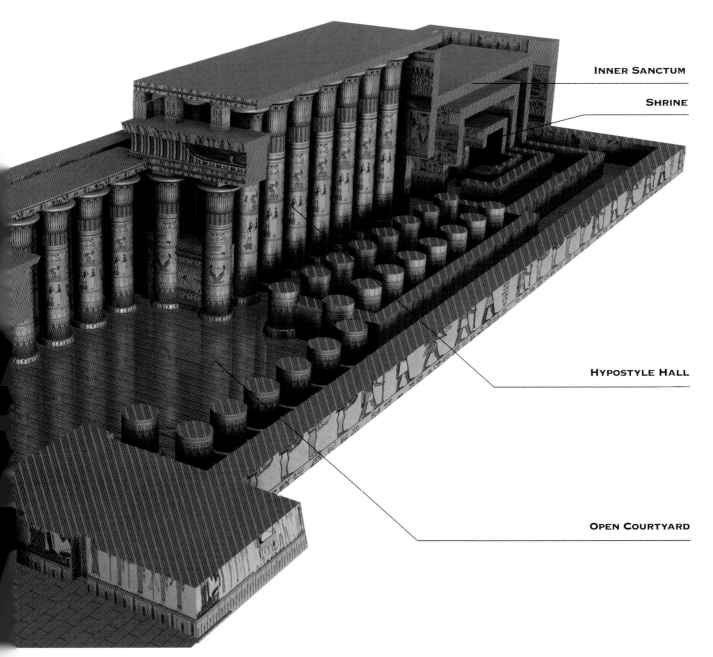

INNER SANCTUM

SHRINE

HYPOSTYLE HALL

OPEN COURTYARD

The Temple of Karnak

Cult temple dedicated to three gods. Dating from around 2055 BC to around 100 AD. The largest religious building ever constructed.

The Temple of Karnak was known as Ipet-isu—or "most select of places"—by the ancient Egyptians. It is a city of temples built over 2,000 years and dedicated to the Theban triad of Amun, Mut, and Khonsu. This derelict place is still capable of overshadowing many wonders of the modern world and in its day must have been awe-inspiring.

For the largely uneducated ancient Egyptian population, this could only have been the place of the gods. It is the largest religious building ever made, covering about 200 acres (1.5 km by 0.8 km), and was a place of pilgrimage for nearly 2,000 years. The area of the sacred enclosure of Amun alone is sixty one acres and could hold ten average European cathedrals. The great temple at the heart of Karnak is so big that St. Peter's, Milan, and Notre Dame Cathedrals would fit within its walls. The hypostyle hall, at 54,000 square feet (16,459 m) and featuring 134 columns, is still the largest room of any religious building in the world. In addition to the main sanctuary there are several smaller temples and a vast sacred lake—423 feet by 252 feet (129 by 77 m).

The sacred barges of the Theban Triad once floated on the lake during the annual Opet Festival. The lake was surrounded by storerooms and living quarters for the priests, along with an aviary for aquatic birds.

(LEFT TO RIGHT ACROSS THE BOTTOM) RECONSTRUCTION LOOKING ACROSS THE SACRED LAKE AND SHOWING THE VIEW OF THE SOUTH ENTRANCE PYLONS; THE CHAPEL BUILT BY RAMESES III: THE FORECOURT HAS A ROOFED GALLERY SUPPORTED BY EIGHT FIGURES OF THE KING IN THE IMAGE OF OSIRIS; THE AVENUE OF RAM-HEADED SPHINXES LEADS TO THE FIRST PYLON, BUILT BY THE ETHIOPIAN KINGS (656 BC). (FAR RIGHT, TOP TO BOTTOM) THE COURT OF THE BUBASTITES, BUILT BY THE LIBYAN PHARAOHS (935–730 BC). THE COLUMN WAS ONCE PART OF THE KIOSK OF TAHARKA, WHERE THE PROCESSIONAL BARQUE WAS KEPT; THE COLOSSAL STATUE (49 FT [15 M]) OF PINUDJEM (AROUND 978 BC), HIGH PRIEST OF AMUN AND PHARAOH OF THE TWENTY-FIRST DYNASTY.

TEMPLES OF MONTU

TEMPLE OF PTAH

CHAPEL OF OSIRIS-HEKADJET

THE FESTIVAL HALL BUILT BY THUTMOSE III

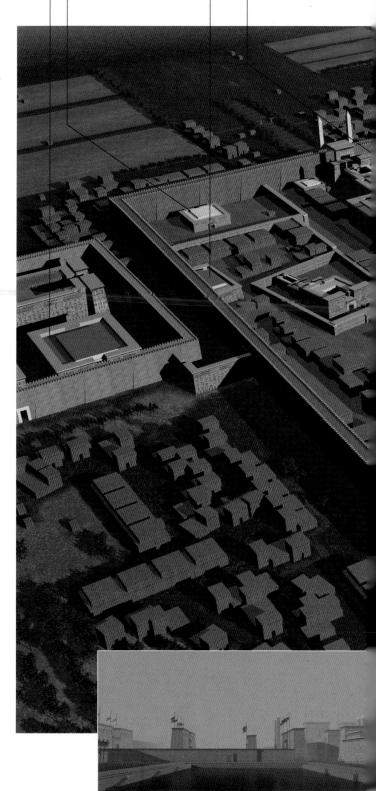

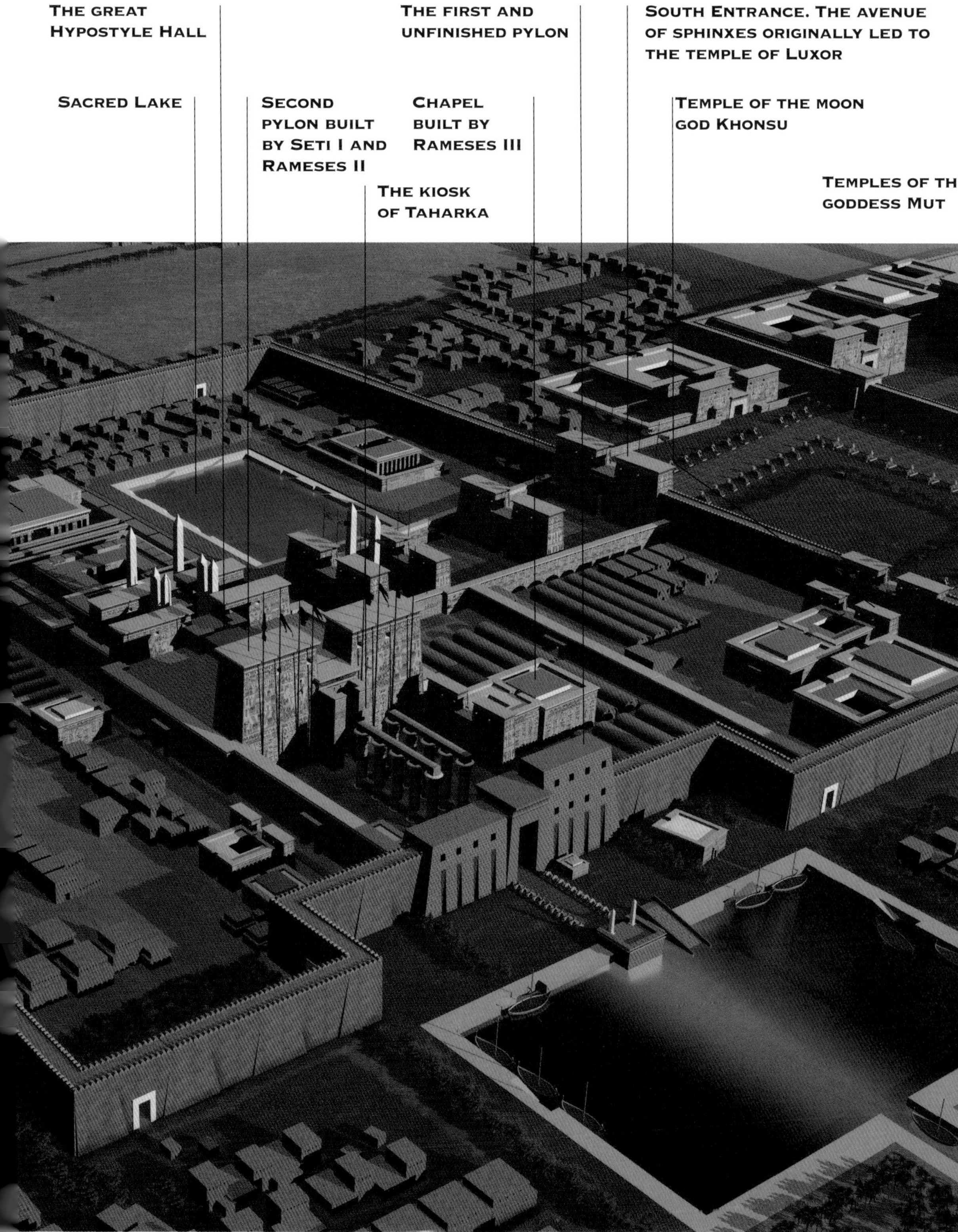

THE GREAT
HYPOSTYLE HALL

THE FIRST AND
UNFINISHED PYLON

SOUTH ENTRANCE. THE AVENUE
OF SPHINXES ORIGINALLY LED TO
THE TEMPLE OF LUXOR

SACRED LAKE

SECOND
PYLON BUILT
BY SETI I AND
RAMESES II

CHAPEL
BUILT BY
RAMESES III

TEMPLE OF THE MOON
GOD KHONSU

THE KIOSK
OF TAHARKA

TEMPLES OF THE
GODDESS MUT

In its day, the most important event held at Karnak was the annual Opet Festival, which lasted for twenty-seven days and was held during the Nile's inundation, when the people could not work in the fields.

The festival was a celebration of the link between pharaoh and the god Amun, who, in the New Kingdom, became the state god. The procession began at Karnak and ended at Luxor Temple, one and a half miles (2.4 km) to the south. The statue of the god Amun was bathed with holy water, dressed in fine linen, and adorned in gold and silver jewelry. The priests then placed the god in a shrine and onto a ceremonial barque (boat) supported by poles for carrying. Pharaoh emerged from the temple, his priests carrying the barque on their shoulders, and together they moved into the crowded streets. A troop of Nubian soldiers serving as guards beat their drums and musicians accompanied the priests in song as incense filled the air.

At Luxor, Pharaoh and his priests entered the temple and ceremonies were performed to transfer Amun's power to Pharaoh. This was thought to ensure the fertility of the earth and bring forth abundant harvests. When Pharaoh finally emerged from the temple sanctuary, the vast crowds cheered him.

During the festival the people received free bread and beer, and some were allowed into the temple to ask questions of the god. The priests spoke the answers through a concealed window high up in the wall or from inside hollow statues.

Hypostyle

means "under pillars." A hypostyle hall is an interior space with a roof supported by pillars or columns.

(OPPOSITE PAGE) THE
HYPOSTYLE HALL AS
IT MIGHT HAVE ONCE
APPEARED, WITH ITS
DEEP SHADOWS ILLUMI-
NATED BY SHAFTS OF
SUNLIGHT RECREATING
AN IDEALIZED MARSH-
LAND OF THE GODS.
(LEFT) THE MASSIVE
COLUMNS OF THE
HYPOSTYLE HALL
TOWER ABOVE PEOPLE.
(ABOVE) THE SEVENTH
PYLON OF THUTMOSE III
AND THE COLOSSAL
STATUES OF THE WAR-
RIOR KING; THE OBELISK
OF HATSHEPSUT IS
WELL PRESERVED
BECAUSE, TO HIDE HER
NAME FOR ALL ETERNI-
TY, THUTMOSE III BUILT
A WALL AROUND IT.

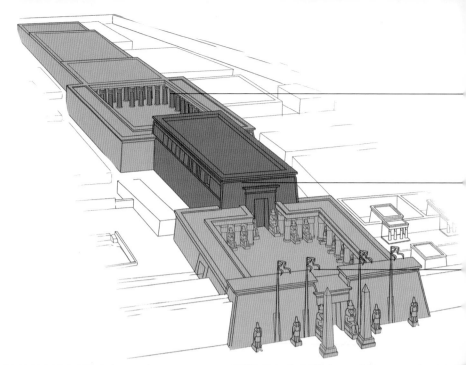

(BELOW) A RECONSTRUCTION OF THE PYLON SHOWING SCENES FROM THE BATTLE OF KADESH. MASSIVE STATUES OF RAMESES II GUARD THE GATEWAY AND ARE FLANKED BY TWO EIGHTY-FOOT (25 M) OBELISKS. (PHOTO INSET) TODAY ONLY ONE OBELISK REMAINS. THE OTHER STANDS IN PARIS.

THE SANCTUARY, HYPO-
STYLE HALL, AND FIRST
OPEN COURTYARD WERE
BUILT BY AMEN-HOTEP III
1390–1352 BC.

THE COLONNADE WAS
FINISHED BY TUTANKH-
AMUN
1336–1327 BC.

THE SECOND OPEN
COURTYARD AND NEW
ENTRANCE PYLON WERE
BUILT BY RAMESES II
1279–1213 BC.

Luxor Temple

Cult temple dedicated to three gods. Dating from around 1392 BC. Still a place of worship.

The modern town of Luxor is the site of the famous city of Thebes (Waset, in ancient Egyptian), the City of a Hundred Gates. It was the capital of Egypt from the twelfth dynasty on (1991 BC) and reached its zenith during the New Kingdom.

It was from here that Thutmose III planned his campaigns, Akhenaten first contemplated the nature of god, and Rameses II set out his ambitious building program. Only Memphis could compare in size and splendor but today there is nothing left of Memphis: It was pillaged for its masonry to build new cities, and little remains.

Although the mud-brick houses and palaces of Thebes have disappeared, its stone temples have survived. The most beautiful of these is the temple of Luxor.

Luxor Temple is close to the Nile and laid out parallel to the riverbank. It is dedicated to Amun-Ra, his consort Mut, and their son Khons.

Luxor was built by Amenhotep III (1390–52 BC) but completed by Tutankhamun (1336–27 BC) and Horemheb (1323–1295 BC) and then added to by Rameses II (1279–13 BC). Toward the rear is a granite shrine dedicated to Alexander the Great (332–305 BC).

The temple has been in almost continuous use as a place of worship right up to the present day. Then, for thousands of years, the temple was buried beneath the streets and houses of Luxor. Eventually the mosque of Sufi Shaykh Yusuf Abu al-Hajjaj was built over it. This mosque was carefully preserved when the temple was uncovered and forms an integral part of the site today.

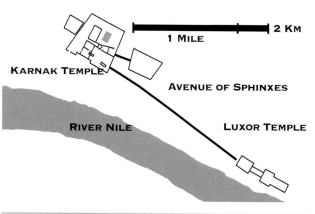

KARNAK TEMPLE

AVENUE OF SPHINXES

RIVER NILE

LUXOR TEMPLE

1 MILE   2 KM

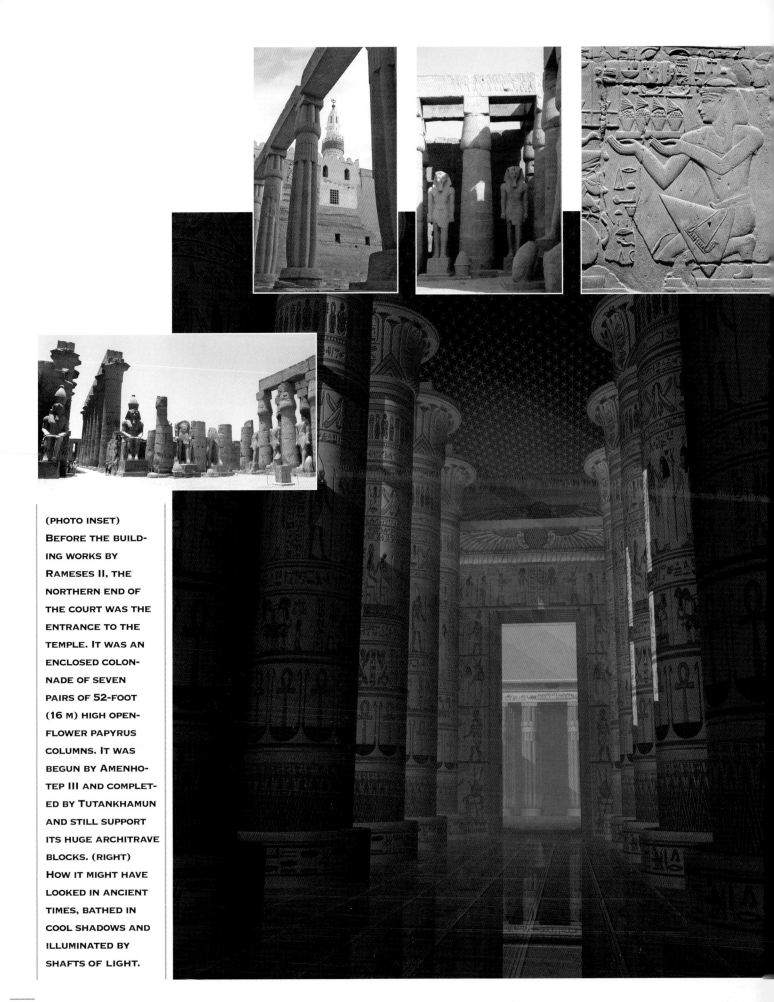

(PHOTO INSET)
BEFORE THE BUILDING WORKS BY RAMESES II, THE NORTHERN END OF THE COURT WAS THE ENTRANCE TO THE TEMPLE. IT WAS AN ENCLOSED COLONNADE OF SEVEN PAIRS OF 52-FOOT (16 M) HIGH OPEN-FLOWER PAPYRUS COLUMNS. IT WAS BEGUN BY AMENHOTEP III AND COMPLETED BY TUTANKHAMUN AND STILL SUPPORT ITS HUGE ARCHITRAVE BLOCKS. (RIGHT) HOW IT MIGHT HAVE LOOKED IN ANCIENT TIMES, BATHED IN COOL SHADOWS AND ILLUMINATED BY SHAFTS OF LIGHT.

During the Christian era, the temple's hypostyle hall was converted into a Christian church, and the remains of another Coptic church can be seen to the west.

Coptic Church

Most Egyptian Christians are Copts and claim descent from the native ancient Egyptians who, before the Arab conquest in 639 AD, were Christians. Before that time, the Coptic language, which descended directly from ancient Egyptian, was the language of daily life.

(TOP LEFT TO RIGHT) THE COURT OF AMENHOTEP III LEADS INTO A HYPOSTYLE HALL, WHICH HAS THIRTY-TWO COLUMNS. AT THE REAR OF THE HALL ARE FOUR SMALL ROOMS AND AN ANTECHAMBER LEADING TO THE BIRTH ROOM, THE CHAPEL OF ALEXANDER THE GREAT, AND THE SANCTUARY. AMENHOTEP III MAKES AN OFFERING. THE COURT MEASURES 148 FEET LONG (45 M) BY 184 FEET WIDE (56 M), WITH DOUBLE ROWS OF PAPYRUS-SHAPED COLUMNS ON THREE SIDES. (INSET AND BELOW) A RECONSTRUCTION SHOWING HOW IT MIGHT HAVE APPEARED IN ANCIENT TIMES.

Madinat Habu

Mortuary temple dating from 1550 to 332 BC. The temple of Rameses III.

In ancient times, Madinat Habu was known as Djanet and, according to ancient belief, was the place where Amun first appeared. Both Hatshepsut and Thutmose III built a temple dedicated to Amun here, and later Rameses III (1184–1153 BC) constructed his larger mortuary temple on the site.

Djanet then became the administrative center of western Thebes and the whole temple complex was surrounded by a massive, fortified enclosure wall with an unusual gateway at the eastern entrance known as the pavilion gate. This structure, a copy of a Syrian migdol fortress, is something you would not expect to see in Egypt. But Rameses III, a military man, would have seen the virtue in such a structure. A royal palace was attached at the south of the open forecourt, while priests' dwellings and administrative buildings lay on either side of the temple. Originally a canal connected the temple to the Nile, with a harbor outside the entrance, but this was obliterated by the desert long ago.

The exterior walls are still carved with religious scenes and portrayals of Rameses III's wars against the Libyans and

(BACKGROUND) RAMESES III'S SOLDIERS PARADE DEFEATED CAPTIVES. (OPPOSITE TOP) A GATEWAY BUILT DURING THE GREEK AND ROMAN PERIOD STILL SHOWS TRACES OF PAINT WORK. (OPPOSITE MIDDLE) THE MASSIVE FIRST PYLON IS COVERED IN CARVINGS SHOWING RAMESES III RITUALLY SLAYING EGYPT'S ENEMIES. (OPPOSITE BOTTOM LEFT) MUCH OF THE 3,000-YEAR-OLD WALLS STILL RETAIN THEIR PAINT. (OPPOSITE BOTTOM RIGHT) THE ENTRANCE TO THE TEMPLE SHOWS THE REMAINS OF A FORTIFIED TOWER. (BELOW LEFT) THE FIRST OPEN COURTYARD CONVEYS A SENSE OF THE TEMPLE'S HUGE SCALE. (BELOW RIGHT) A RECONSTRUCTION SHOWING THE RIGHT SIDE OF THE COURTYARD WITH THE IMAGE OF RAMESES III IN THE FORM OF OSIRID COLUMNS.

Wives of Amun chapel

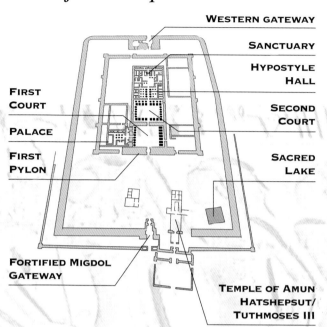

- WESTERN GATEWAY
- SANCTUARY
- HYPOSTYLE HALL
- SECOND COURT
- SACRED LAKE
- TEMPLE OF AMUN HATSHEPSUT/ TUTHMOSES III
- FIRST COURT
- PALACE
- FIRST PYLON
- FORTIFIED MIGDOL GATEWAY

the Sea Peoples. The first pylon depicts the king smiting his enemies and includes a list of conquered lands. The interior walls feature a wealth of well-preserved bas reliefs, some of which still retain their original paint work.

The pharaohs of the twenty-fifth and twenty-sixth dynasties (700 BC), used the strong fortifications of Madinat Habu as a place of refuge during the civil war between the High Priest of Amun at Karnak and the viceroy of Kush. The site was expanded during the Greek and Roman periods, and then, between the first and ninth centuries AD, a Coptic city was built around it and the temple was used as a Christian church.

Temple of Dendara

Cult temple dedicated to the goddess Hathor dating from 380 BC. One of the best-preserved temples in Egypt.

The Temple of Dendara was known as the "Castle of the Sistrum" or "Pr Hathor"—House of Hathor. Hathor was the goddess of love, joy, and beauty.

With the exception of its supporting pillars, which had capitals sculpted in the image of Hathor and were defaced by the Christians, the walls, rooms, and roof are complete and extraordinarily well preserved. The stone steps of the spiral staircase are time-worn but may still be used to ascend to the roof, where there is a small chapel decorated with Hathor-headed columns.

In ancient times, Dendara was associated with healing. Patients who traveled there for cures were housed in special buildings where they could rest, sleep, and commune with the gods in their dreams. There is something else special about this temple, as well: It bears the name of Cleopatra and her son, whose father was Julius Caesar. It is possible that these celebrated rulers climbed the same stairs and contemplated the same landscape stretching out for miles below.

Today, the place sings with the music of birds. Hundreds of them roost in small cracks and hollows in the walls, seemingly contemplating their own carved likenesses in the hieroglyphic reliefs.

THERE HAVE BEEN TEMPLES ON THIS SITE EVER SINCE THE OLD KINGDOM, BUT THE PRESENT TEMPLE WAS BEGUN IN THE REIGN OF PTOLEMY VIII. THE BUILDING WE SEE TODAY WAS CONSTRUCTED AND ADDED TO FROM ABOUT 116 BC TO 34 AD. (RIGHT) A RECONSTRUCTION SHOWING THE FAÇADE OF THE TEMPLE, WITH ITS SIX HATHOR-HEADED COLUMNS. (OPPOSITE PAGE, TOP TO BOTTOM) THE HYPOSTYLE HALL WAS BUILT BY THE ROMANS IN THE FIRST CENTURY AD. ITS FOREST OF COLUMNS STILL SUPPORTS THE ROOF, WHICH CAN BE ACCESSED BY A STONE SPIRAL STAIRCASE; THE HYPOSTYLE HALL LEADS INTO THE INNER SANCTUM; PHARAOH GIVES AN OFFERING TO THE GODDESS HATHOR; THE SMALL ROOF CHAPEL WITH ITS HATHOR-HEADED COLUMNS; THE REAR OF THE TEMPLE SHOWS CLEOPATRA AND HER SON CAESARION GIVING OFFERINGS TO THE GODS; THE SACRED LAKE IS NOW DRY AND HAS BECOME A GARDEN OF TREES. IT HAS FOUR FLIGHTS OF STEPS THAT ONCE LED DOWN TO THE WATER'S EDGE.

SMALL ROOF CHAPEL

ROOF

SACRED LAKE

HYPOSTYLE HALL

TEMPLE OF
HATHOR

CHRISTIAN BASILIKA

ROMAN MAMMISI

Temple of Philae

Cult temple dedicated to the goddess Isis. Dating from 380 BC–300 AD. A beautiful temple rescued from the flood waters.

"Philae" in Greek (or "Pilak" in ancient Egyptian) means "the end," and appropriately, it defined the southernmost limit of Egypt. Ptolemy II started the work which was completed by the Roman Emperors. The temple was dedicated to the goddess Isis, the wife of Osiris and mother of Horus. These three characters dominated ancient Egyptian culture and their story possesses all the drama of a Shakespearian tragedy.

Isis is an important figure in the ancient world. She is associated with funeral rites, but as the enchantress who resurrected Osiris and gave birth to Horus, she is also the giver of life, a healer and protector of kings. She was known as "Mother of God" and was represented with a throne on her head. During the Roman period, her cult spread throughout the empire. There was even a temple in London dedicated to her.

The temple at Philae was nearly lost under water when the high Aswan dam was built in the 1960s. Fortunately, the temple was rescued by a joint effort of the Egyptian government and UNESCO. In an engineering feat to rival those of the ancients, the whole island was surrounded with a dam and the inside pumped dry. Then every stone block of the temple complex was labeled and removed.

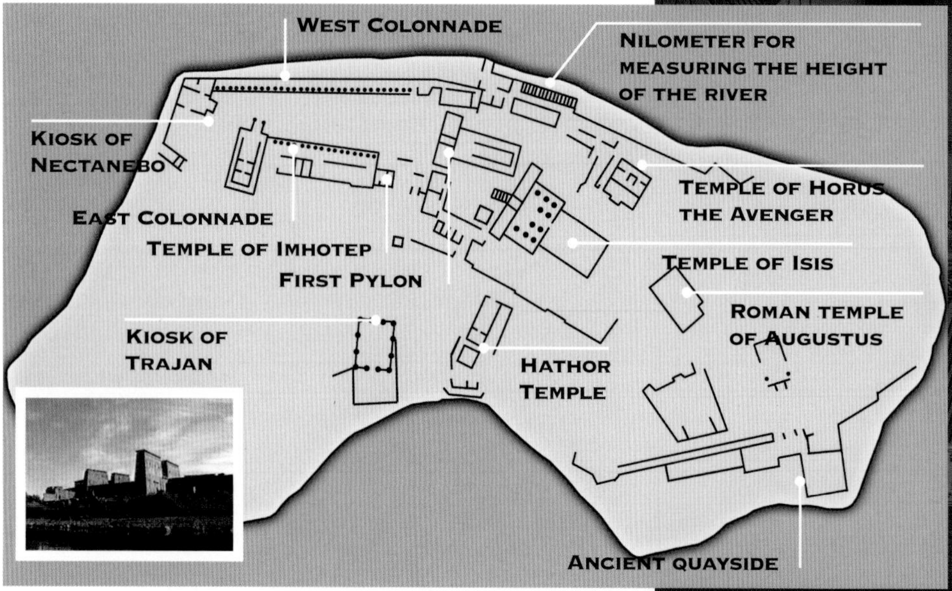

(BELOW) A RECONSTRUCTION OF THE HYPOSTYLE HALL INSIDE THE TEMPLE OF ISIS. ITS COLUMNS AND WALLS WERE ONCE BRIGHTLY PAINTED.

The Island of Philae

WEST COLONNADE

NILOMETER FOR MEASURING THE HEIGHT OF THE RIVER

KIOSK OF NECTANEBO

EAST COLONNADE

TEMPLE OF IMHOTEP

FIRST PYLON

TEMPLE OF HORUS THE AVENGER

TEMPLE OF ISIS

KIOSK OF TRAJAN

ROMAN TEMPLE OF AUGUSTUS

HATHOR TEMPLE

ANCIENT QUAYSIDE

UNESCO

United Nations Educational, Scientific, and Cultural Organization is an agency created in 1946 to promote international collaboration in education, science, and culture.

(FROM TOP LEFT) THE WESTERN SIDE CONSISTS OF THIRTY-TWO COLUMNS WITH FLORAL AND PALM-LEAF CAPITALS. THEY SUPPORT A ROOF DECO-RATED WITH STARS AND VULTURES AND ITS OUTER WALL HAS WINDOWS OVERLOOKING THE RIVER. YOU CAN STILL SEE THE ROUGH-CUT STONE CYLINDERS IN AN UNFINISHED COLUMN AT KARNAK. THE APPROACH IS LINED BY TWO COLONNADES. THE EASTERN SIDE HAS SEVENTEEN COLUMNS BUT ONLY SIX WERE COMPLETED. THE VIEW FROM THE TEMPLE OF NECTANEBO LOOKING TOWARD THE FIRST PYLON OF THE TEMPLE OF ISIS.

this material to construct the temples. The first and largest pylon at Karnak, which was never finished, still features the remains of a mud-brick rampart against the inside wall (left). It's safe to assume it was used to haul the stone blocks into position and would normally have been dismantled on completion of the pylon.

The erection of columns was more difficult because the stone blocks were heavier and the process required a lot of preparation. Again, mud-brick ramparts may have been used to create a level surface. The rough-cut stone cylinders that make up a column would have been hauled into place and, as the height of the columns grew, so did the mud-brick ramparts. When the columns, and the roofing blocks that they supported, were in place, these mud-brick ramparts were removed. During the mud-brick removal phase, the masons would finish and dressed the stone.

Herodotus, the Greek historian (450 BC), mentions that the pyramids were built with wooden machines—probably cranes and levers. It is possible that these same types of machines were also used to lift stone blocks. Finally the walls, ceilings, capitals, and columns were decorated by artists. Wooden scaffolding (right) may have been use for this purpose, as well as for alterations and maintenance after the temple was finished.

These were later reassembled, like a giant jigsaw puzzle, on the higher ground of Agilka Island. The whole project took ten years and saved one of Egypt's most beautiful temples from destruction.

The ancient Egyptians left us little documentary evidence showing how they constructed their buildings. There are some references to building techniques here and there, but we don't really understand the methods used to build the pyramids or how obelisks were erected. Ancient quarries still exist, bearing evidence of how stone was extracted. But how did they transport these massive blocks of stone to the construction sites? Luckily, there are illustrations that give us a clue: They did not use wheeled vehicles, and because of the necessity for careful control over the pulling movement, animals were not used either. (It would have been disastrous if a finely carved statue was damaged by panicking animals all pulling in different directions.) Ancient drawings show wooden sledges, sometimes pulled over rollers but more often pulled by teams of men using tow ropes made from papyrus over specially prepared tracks. Men poured water in front of the runners as a lubricant, while others delivered supplies. A foreman beat out a rhythm for the men doing the pulling.

The most common building material was mud brick and all the ancient houses and palaces were made from it. (Indeed, it is still used in Egypt today to construct houses.) Mud bricks are easy to manufacture on a large scale and there is some physical evidence showing how they used

Obelisks are an ancient Egyptian invention, and although we know how they were quarried and transported, we have no clue as to how they were erected. All Egyptian obelisks came from the same quarry in Aswan, where the granite was extremely strong and without faults. The

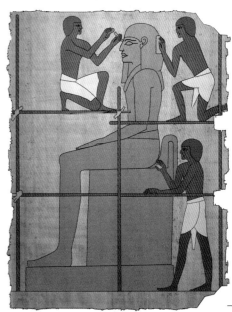

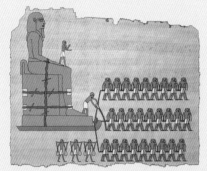
task involved in quarrying a single piece of hard granite almost 100 feet (30 m) in length and weighing 300 tons or more is one of the wonders of the ancient world, and just how they managed to set it upright on a three-meter-high plinth is still a mystery.

There is an unfinished obelisk in the granite quarry at Aswan (left) which, at 137 feet (42 m) and 1,150 tons, would have been the largest obelisk of all time had it been successfully erected. Fortunately for us, it cracked in several places and was never detached from the rock, providing us with an insight into the methods employed in making it. First, the architect selected a fault-free site and marked out the obelisk shape. It was then freed from the rock by large numbers of men hammering the granite with an even harder stone called dolerite. This was an arduous operation and must have taken many months of continuous work.

Once released from the surrounding rock, the obelisk was hauled to the river, probably on rollers. A canal was dug and the obelisk was supported on timber beams above the water. A barge filled with heavy stones was floated into position under it and when the stones were removed, the barge rose up, lifting the obelisk. The barge was then towed down river to the building site.

The most extraordinary thing about obelisks is that they were lifted into an upright position and balanced

How an obelisk might have been erected.

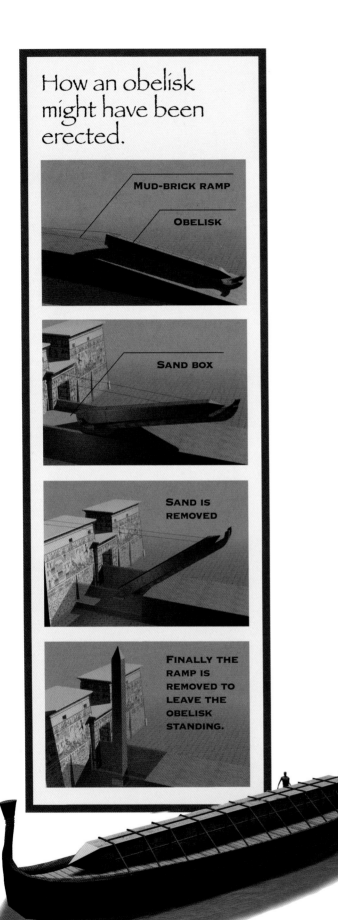

MUD-BRICK RAMP

OBELISK

SAND BOX

SAND IS REMOVED

FINALLY THE RAMP IS REMOVED TO LEAVE THE OBELISK STANDING.

on their plinths with nothing holding them up but their own weight. There are no records showing exactly how this amazing feat was achieved, so we can only speculate. One theory is that they built giant mud-brick ramps with a huge enclosed box at one end filled with sand. An obelisk might have been hauled up the ramp until half its length rested on the sand. Then the sand was removed, allowing the base of the obelisk to fall gradually onto a groove cut into the plinth. At this point it would not be horizontal but held up at an angle by the mud-brick rampart. Then, using ropes slung over the pylon wall and the groove as a pivot, teams of men could haul it into an upright position. That's one theory, anyway. But clearly, however it was done, it remains a marvel.

Ancient Egyptian temples were not just places of worship, they were also doorways from the everyday world of the profane into a world of the sacred. Their function was to maintain the stability of Egyptian civilization against the destructive supernatural powers of nature. As long as the temples carried out their sacred rituals, the sun would continue to rise each morning, the Nile would continue to flood each year, and the forces of nature (the gods) would continue to favor the Egyptian way of life. In some sense they were correct in this assumption, because their civilization ended with the closure of Philea in 391 AD, which was the last working temple in Egypt.

Egyptian temples do not possess the elegance of Greek or Roman buildings. Egyptian architecture is similar to a force of nature and photographs never really convey the buildings' solid power, their heavy weight, and their real sense of permanence.

More monuments survive in Egypt than from any other ancient civilization—and this is no accident. This is because the Egyptians believed they would live for eternity in the afterlife and their spirits would be able to return to the world of the living. Indeed they would even be able to magically inhabit a stone statue carved with their name and see out of its eyes. Therefore, they deliberately built their temples and tombs to last forever. That's why they called their temples "Houses of millions of years."

So far they have succeeded in building for eternity and it's a good bet that in another 3,000 years, when our modern buildings and skyscrapers are dust, perhaps not even a memory, that the pyramids and temples of Egypt will still stand—defying the ravages of time.

HIEROGLYPHS
"Hieroglyph" is a Greek word meaning "Sacred Carved Letter"

IN 391 AD THE BYZANTINE EMPEROR THEODOSIUS I CLOSED ALL PAGAN TEMPLES THROUGHOUT THE EMPIRE, DEALING A FINAL BLOW TO A 3,000-YEAR-OLD CULTURE AND BURYING FOR 1,500 YEARS THE MESSAGES OF HIEROGLYPHIC WRITING. IT WAS NOT UNTIL THE DISCOVERY OF THE ROSETTA STONE AND THE WORK OF JEAN-FRANÇOIS CHAMPOLLION (1790–1832 AD) TO DECIPHER IT THAT THE ANCIENT EGYPTIANS AWOKE FROM THEIR LONG SLUMBER.

Early in their history the Egyptians invented paper made from papyrus. Other civilizations used clay, leather, or wax to keep records—but paper proved itself a better medium, due to its lightness and portability. All governments need to keep records in order to function, and writing on paper was the tool that allowed Egypt's highly centralized form of government to run so successfully.

The millions of documents generated required filing systems and libraries to store them. In addition to accounts, legal documents, and government files, the Egyptians produced a huge body of literature, from books of poems and hymns to novels and articles on mathematics and medicine.

No other ancient culture set down such a meticulous record of its history, and because at least some of these documents survived, we now have access to a vast quantity of ancient Egyptian literature. For that reason we know more about their society than we do of most other ancient cultures. Unfortunately, paper is easily damaged and though we are lucky to have what we do, we can only wonder at what existed and has now been lost.

A highly educated, literate elite of scribes was required to sustain the complex machinery of state. These people held a privileged position within society. It was the scribe who organized the great building projects, assessed taxes, and generally ran the country.

Training to become a scribe began at an early age, in one of the many schools known as the "Houses of Life," and such training was compulsory for the ruling class. However, it was possible for commoners to rise to high office if they had been taught to read and write.

Craftsman
The sign for "craftsman" is an image of a tool that was used to grind out the inside of stone vases. The shaft was made of wood, with a fork at one end that held a piece of hard stone. A heavy stone was fastened to the top of the shaft to maintain pressure during the grinding process and above this was a handle used for turning. Note that above you can see the hieroglyph for craftsman is written twice in the Instruction of Ptahhotep.

Scribes
Those who could read and write, were essential to the operations of state. The hieroglyph for "scribe" appears to the right while an Old Kingdom illustration of scribes is shown at the left.

> "No limit may be set to art, neither is there any craftsman that is fully master of his craft."

The Instructions of Ptahhotep

(ABOVE) FROM THE INSTRUCTIONS OF PTAHHOTEP: PTAHHOTEP WAS THE FIRST MINISTER DURING THE REIGN OF DJEDKARA (2414–2375 BC). HIS WRITINGS ARE ONE OF THE EARLIEST EXAMPLES OF WISDOM LITERATURE: TEACHING THE VIRTUES OF MODERATION, SELF-CONTROL, KINDNESS, GENEROSITY, TRUTHFULNESS, AND JUSTICE. ONLY FOUR COPIES EXIST: THE MOST COMPLETE IS THE PAPYRUS PRISSE IN THE BIBLIOTHÈQUE NATIONALE OF FRANCE. (CENTER) A DETAIL FROM THE SECOND PYLON OF RAMESES III'S TEMPLE AT MEDINAT HABU.

Hieratic

The hieroglyphs we are all familiar with were not used in day-to-day business but reserved for formal and religious purposes, such as inscriptions on monuments. For the more mundane communications of daily life, a quick handwritten script called hieratic was developed.

Hieratic was the most common form of writing and was always written from right to left, whereas the orientation of hieroglyphs varied; and unlike hieroglyphs, hieratic continued to evolve over the centuries. By the twenty-sixth dynasty, business hieratic had changed into the simplified demotic script.

The Rosetta Stone

Beginning with the conquest of Alexander the Great in 332 BC, Greek was the language of the governing elite in Egypt. These Greek rulers could neither speak the language of the people nor read their hieroglyphs, and this fueled resentment amongst the population. By Ptolemy V's reign in 205 BC the country was in open revolt and the Rosetta stone was one of many that Ptolemy commissioned as a piece of political propaganda in 196 BC, to state publicly his claim to be the rightful pharaoh of Egypt.

HIEROGLYPHS

DEMOTIC

GREEK

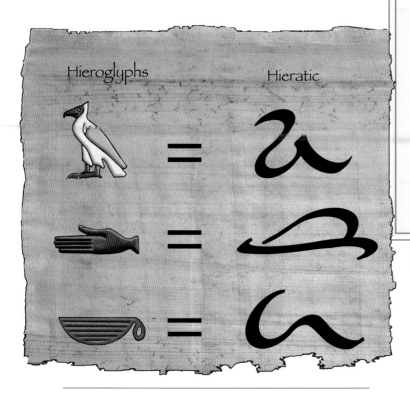

(ABOVE) THREE HIEROGLYPHS WITH THEIR HIERATIC EQUIVALENTS. (RIGHT) AN EXAMPLE OF DEMOTIC SCRIPT. (BELOW) AN EXAMPLE OF HIERATIC SCRIPT.

The Rosetta Stone is probably the most important archaeological artifact in the world.

Without the Rosetta Stone, we would know nothing of the ancient Egyptians, and the details of their three thousand years of history would remain a mystery.

The stone is a block of basalt 3' 9" (114 cm) high and 2' 4½" (72 cm) wide. It was discovered by a French captain named Pierre Bouchard in 1799 AD, during the Napoleonic wars. Captain Bouchard was supervising the restoration of an old fort near the town of Rosetta when he found the stone. He saw that it contained three different types of writing and realized its importance to the scholars who had accompanied the French army to Egypt. After the French surrender of Egypt in 1801, it passed into British hands and is now in the British Museum.

The content of the inscriptions is not what makes the stone significant—the text is simply a decree listing benefits bestowed on Egypt by King Ptolemy V. But—so that all could read and understand it at the time—it was written in two languages, Egyptian and Greek, and

Cartouche

The word "cartouche" was used by the soldiers of Napoleon's expedition in Egypt, who saw in the sign a similarity to the cartridges, or "cartouches" they used in their guns. A cartouche is an oval ring that represents a length of rope tied at one end to form a loop with no beginning or end.

The ancient Egyptian term for it was shenu, and was derived from the hieroglyph "sheni," which means "to encircle." It was a symbol of everything that the sun encircled and indicated the nature of pharaoh's universal rule.

KING OF UPPER AND LOWER EGYPT

RA

MEN

KHEPER

The Greek pharaohs (332–30 BC) wrote their foreign names using alphabet symbols. Here, you can see a cartouche containing the throne name of Tuthmosis III, who lived over 1,200 years before Ptolemy. To achieve a pleasing design the signs were not always placed in the order they were spoken.

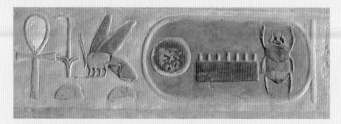

MENKHEPERRA, MEANING "ESTABLISHED IS THE MANIFESTATION OF RA"

THE OTHER SYMBOLS IN THE CARTOUCHE OF PTOLEMY REPRESENT HIS TITLE, "EVERLIVING, BELOVED OF PTAH."

in three writing systems, hieroglyphic, demotic, and the Greek alphabet. This is what makes the Rosetta Stone such an important discovery. Since we have never lost our understanding of ancient Greek, the Greek inscriptions provided a key to decoding their Egyptian equivalents. The last sentence of the Greek text says, "Written in sacred and native and Greek characters." Scholars were quick to figure out that this meant that the same text was set down in three scripts, and that the "sacred" referred to the hieroglyphic system, while the "native" referred to the demotic script of the ordinary Egyptians.

Deciphering the stone was largely the work of two people, Thomas Young of England and Jean-François Champollion of France. Young was a physician, physicist, and all-around genius. He was the first to give the word "energy" its scientific meaning and is remembered mainly for his study of light. Egyptology was one of his hobbies and he began studying the texts of the Rosetta stone in 1814. Young correctly identified the cartouche, the oval loop containing hieroglyphs, as the name of King Ptolemy by finding the corresponding name written in Greek. From this he determined which hieroglyphs spelled the name of Ptolemy. This, in turn, gave him the key to the hieroglyphs for p, t, m, y, and s; and, by examining the orientation of the Egyptians' bird and animal characters, he also figured out the direction in which the hieroglyphs should be read.

Hieroglyphs are written in rows or columns and can be read from left to right or from right to left. You can distinguish the direction in which the text is to be read because the human or animal figures always face toward the beginning of the line.

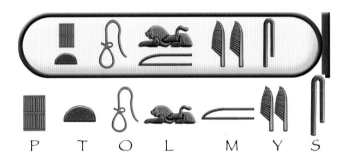

P T O L M Y S

Young's work was invaluable—but he had many other projects on his energetic mind, and it became clear that the job of cracking the hieroglyphic code called for someone who could focus entirely on the task. That person was Jean-François Champollion, the founder of scientific Egyptology. An historian and brilliant linguist, by the age of sixteen Champollion had mastered not only Latin and Greek but six ancient Oriental languages including Coptic, the late form of ancient Egyptian that was written phonetically in Greek.

In 1821 AD, Champollion started where Young left off, and eventually established an entire list of Egyptian symbols with their Greek equivalents. He was the first Egyptologist to realize that the symbols were not only alphabetic but syllabic, and in some cases determinative, meaning that they depicted the meaning of the word itself. He also established that the hieroglyphic text of the Rosetta Stone was a translation from the Greek, not, as had been thought, a translation from Egyptian into Greek. But more important, because he understood

Coptic he was able to translate the meaning of the ancient Egyptian words.

The work of these two men, especially Champollion, established the basis for the translation of all Egyptian hieroglyphic texts.

The Hieroglyphic Script

The hieroglyphic script was developed about thirty-five hundred years before Christ, along with a decimal system of numeration up to a million. Unlike other cultures the Egyptians never discarded their early picture forms, probably because they are so very lovely to look at. The Egyptians called the hieroglyphs "the words of God" and they were used mainly by the priests. These painstakingly drawn symbols were great for decorating the walls of temples—but hieratic was used for day-to-day business.

Hieroglyphs are written in rows or columns and can be read from left to right or from right to left. You can distinguish the direction in which the text is to be read because the human or animal figures always face toward the beginning of the line. Also the upper symbols are read before lower symbols.

Hieroglyphic signs are divided into four categories: alphabet signs, syllabic signs, determinative signs, and word signs.

THE TWENTY-FOUR HIEROGLYPHS OF THE ANCIENT EGYPTIAN ALPHABET.

Alphabet Symbols

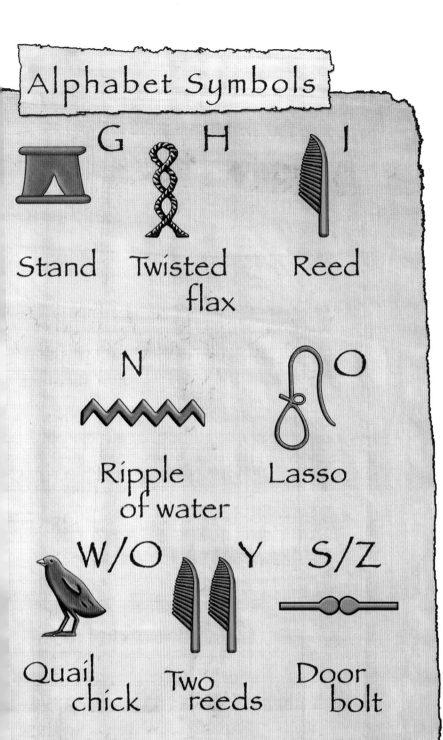

G Stand

H Twisted flax

I Reed

N Ripple of water

O Lasso

W/O Quail chick

Y Two reeds

S/Z Door bolt

How would your name have looked in ancient Egypt?

There are twenty-four alphabet symbols, each one representing a single sound. The Egyptians did not include vowels in their writing and there are no signs for e, u, v, or x although these sounds were present in the spoken language. For example, Sbk is the name of the god we call Sobek, but the Egyptians might have pronounced his name Sebek—there is no way to tell from the written word.

NEFER

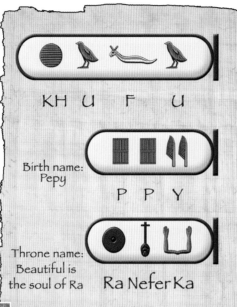

KH U F U

Birth name:
Pepy

P P Y

Throne name:
Beautiful is
the soul of Ra   Ra Nefer Ka

The Beloved   Son of Ra   Give Life

BELOVED OF

GIVEN LIFE

It is possible to write a whole word using only symbols from the ancient Egyptian alphabet. The fourth dynasty pharaoh, Khufu (2589–2566 BC), who built the great pyramid at Giza, wrote his name in this way (left). By the time of the sixth dynasty the names and titles of the pharaohs had become more elaborate. In addition to their birth name there would also be a "throne name" which invariably incorporated the name of the sun god Ra. You can see (left) that Pepi II's birth name is composed of alphabet symbols but his throne name, NeferKaRa, is made using symbols that do not appear in the alphabet. These signs represent a combination of two or three

---

(LEFT) "NEFER," THE WORD FOR BEAUTIFUL, IS WRITTEN USING IMAGES OF A HEART AND A WINDPIPE TOGETHER WITH TWO ALPHABET SYMBOLS. (PHOTO INSET LEFT) A DETAIL FROM THE WALLS OF HATSHEPSUT TEMPLE AT DEIR EL-BAHARI.

Syllabic Symbols

SHA — pool with flowers	DR — Bundle of flax — Say der	WR — swallow — Say wer	IR — eye
MS — three fox skins — Say mes	BIT — bee — Say bity	DW — Valley between hills — Say dja	NTR — pennant — Say netjer
MN — game board — Say men	NB — basket — Say neb	PR — plan of house — Say pair	TM — sledge — Say tem
MR or — hoe or canal — Say mer	THA — Duckling	RA — disk of the sun	MA — sickle
HPR — dung beetle — Say kheper	SW — duck — Say soo	NFR — heart and windpipe — Say nefer	KM — burning charcoal with flames — Say kem
NK — sandal strap — Say ankh	KA — raised arms	BA — jabiru stork	MT — Vulture — Say moot

letters and are called syllabic symbols. They represent word sounds such as "buy" and "pie" in English or "Sha" and "Ka" in ancient Egyptian.

A word can be made up of a combination of alphabet and syllabic symbols (left). For example, two reeds and a hoe stand for *mery* "the beloved." Images of a duck and a disk are frequently placed before a king's cartouche, representing "SaRa" or "Son of Ra." Sometimes other symbols that aren't part of the name appear inside a cartouche, such as an offering loaf, meaning "to give," along with an "ankh"—the cross with a loop at the top—the symbol for life. This suggested that the king was "ever living."

A determinative sign is a picture of an object that helps the reader understand the meaning of a word. Written words did not represent all of the sounds of spoken words. So, for example, the word for boat was expressed in hieroglyphs as "dpt" (it might have been pronounced "depet"), but Depet might also have been a person's name. To prevent the reader from mistaking it for another word, the writer included a picture of a boat to clarify the word's meaning.

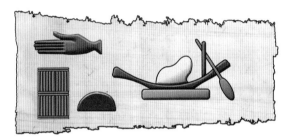

If a word expressed an abstract idea, such as "happy," a picture of a sealed papyrus scroll was included to show that the meaning of the word could be expressed in writing but not pictorially.

Word signs are pictures of objects used as the words for those objects. Each word sign is followed by an upright stroke to indicate that the word is complete in one sign. For example, if there wasn't enough space to write "boat" in hieroglyphs, the ancient writer just used the picture of a boat followed by an upright stroke to indicate that the sign should be read as "boat."

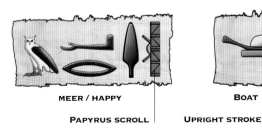

MEER / HAPPY

PAPYRUS SCROLL

BOAT

UPRIGHT STROKE

Determinative Symbols

King

Man

Woman

Old man/ old/ lean on

Child

Eat/ drink/ speak/ think/

Enemy/ foreigner

Walk/ travel

Offer

Eye/see

Water

Come

Desert

Life

Town/ village/place

Sun

Love

Truth

God

Several/plural

There are more than 700 hieroglyphs, many of which are both syllabic and determinative. You can find a full list of them online, on the Egypt Alive resources page at: www.discoveringegypt.com.

Hieroglyphic writing does not use articles and conjunctions such as "the," "a," or "and." When reading hieroglyphs you insert these words according to the context of the sentence. For example (below) "Brother Sister" would be read as "brother and sister."

The name of a god, for example, might appear first—for fear of insulting the god's dignity. The extract from Hatshepsut's obelisk at Karnak (below) literally reads "Amun Ra lord of gods beloved give life Ra forever" but it should be read as "The beloved Amun Ra lord of the gods gives life as Ra forever."

THE SUN IS IN THE SKY.

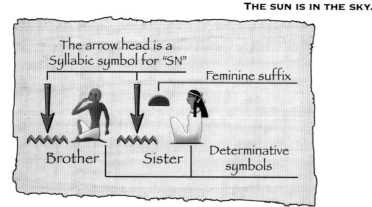

The alphabet symbol for *t* is also a female determinative symbol used as a suffix to indicate a feminine noun. Masculine nouns do not have suffixes but may end with a male determinative symbol. Plurals are indicated by adding three strokes at the end of a word, as in these examples right showing "god and gods," "house and houses."

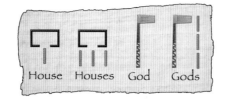

Figuring out the meaning of hieroglyphs is like solving a puzzle. There are no linking words and sometimes the word order within a sentence is deliberately changed.

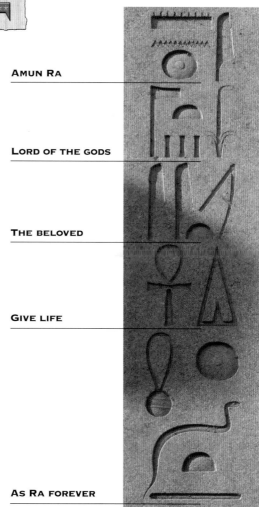

AMUN RA

LORD OF THE GODS

THE BELOVED

GIVE LIFE

AS RA FOREVER

Egyptian language

The Egyptian language can be divided into Old, Middle, and Late Egyptian (there is also Demotic and Coptic from the very late periods). These divisions describe the common speech of the people from different eras in the same way that Old English differs from the English spoken today. Old Egyptian was the spoken language of the Old Kingdom, while Middle and Late Egyptian belong to the Middle and New Kingdoms, respectively. Demotic dates from the third Intermediate Period, and Coptic, which uses the Greek alphabet, was the final form of the language.

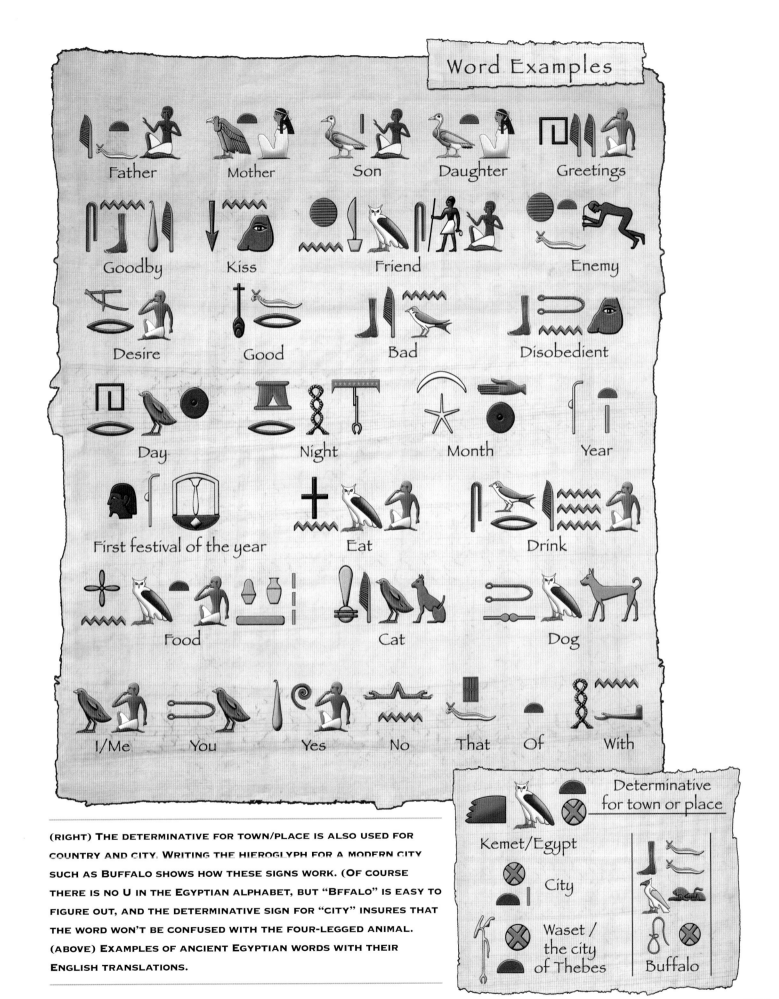

Word Examples

Father

Mother

Son

Daughter

Greetings

Goodby

Kiss

Friend

Enemy

Desire

Good

Bad

Disobedient

Day

Night

Month

Year

First festival of the year

Eat

Drink

Food

Cat

Dog

I/Me

You

Yes

No

That

Of

With

(RIGHT) THE DETERMINATIVE FOR TOWN/PLACE IS ALSO USED FOR COUNTRY AND CITY. WRITING THE HIEROGLYPH FOR A MODERN CITY SUCH AS BUFFALO SHOWS HOW THESE SIGNS WORK. (OF COURSE THERE IS NO U IN THE EGYPTIAN ALPHABET, BUT "BFFALO" IS EASY TO FIGURE OUT, AND THE DETERMINATIVE SIGN FOR "CITY" INSURES THAT THE WORD WON'T BE CONFUSED WITH THE FOUR-LEGGED ANIMAL. (ABOVE) EXAMPLES OF ANCIENT EGYPTIAN WORDS WITH THEIR ENGLISH TRANSLATIONS.

Determinative for town or place

Kemet/Egypt

City

Waset / the city of Thebes

Buffalo

How to Read the Names of the Pharaohs

Kings of Egypt had five names and many titles, but the two most important ones for our purposes, for recognizing inscriptions on ancient artifacts, are their Birth Names and Throne Names.

Normally, the king's name begins with a word combining the emblem for Lower Egypt, the bee, and the emblem for Upper Egypt, the sedge plant. This combination means "Lord (or King) of Upper and Lower Egypt."

Next comes a cartouche containing the king's Throne Name, and this is often followed by "Son of Ra," composed of the duck and the sun. The second cartouche contains the king's Birth Name, probably the name by which we know him today. These cartouches can also contain other titles and they are usually followed by extra titles such as "Beloved of Ra" and "given life for ever." The example at the right shows the cartouche of Thutmose III's Throne Name, MenKheperRa, but it also contains two extra symbols: the Crook and the Feather. The shepherd's crook was a symbol of authority and translates as "ruler." The feather represents Maat, the goddess of truth. "Maat" also stands for harmony, so we can assume that Thutmose III wants us to believe that he was a legitimate king whose reign was harmonious.

To reinforce this idea, the inscription goes on to say that he was loved by the god Amun Ra, who gave him life forever. This second part is frequently attached to pharaohs' names, although it sometimes features other gods.

The names of pharaohs also included a message affirming their authority. For example, Hatshepsut, a woman, legitimized her right to become pharaoh by proclaiming that her father was the god Amun. Her name, which translates as "Amun is joined with the First Noble Lady," reinforces this claim.

Incorporating a god into the name of a pharaoh also made a statement about the political policies of a new administration. Akhenaten's Birth Name was Amenhotep (Amun is Satisfied) but a few years into his reign he changed it to Akhenaten (Servant of the Aten). Likewise, Tutankhamun's birth name was Tutankhaten (Living Image of the Aten), but was changed to the "Living Image of Amun" in order to emphasize a shift in the religion and politics of his era.

KING OF UPPER AND LOWER EGYPT

RA

MEN

KHEPER

THE CROOK SAYS "RULER" AND THE FEATHER "TRUTH" OR "HARMONY"

THE GOD AMUN RA

BELOVED OF

GIVEN LIFE

FOR EVER

Pharaohs' Names

The god Amun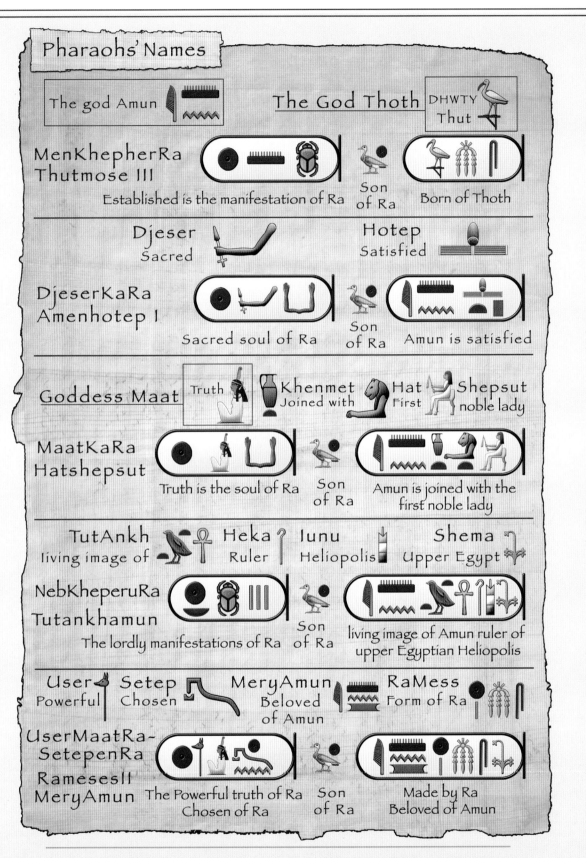

The God Thoth — DHWTY Thut

MenKhepherRa Thutmose III
Established is the manifestation of Ra — Son of Ra — Born of Thoth

Djeser Sacred

Hotep Satisfied

DjeserKaRa Amenhotep I
Sacred soul of Ra — Son of Ra — Amun is satisfied

Goddess Maat — Truth — Khenmet Joined with — Hat First — Shepsut noble lady

MaatKaRa Hatshepsut
Truth is the soul of Ra — Son of Ra — Amun is joined with the first noble lady

TutAnkh living image of — **Heka** Ruler — **Iunu** Heliopolis — **Shema** Upper Egypt

NebKheperuRa Tutankhamun
The lordly manifestations of Ra — Son of Ra — living image of Amun ruler of upper Egyptian Heliopolis

User Powerful — **Setep** Chosen — **MeryAmun** Beloved of Amun — **RaMess** Form of Ra

UserMaatRa-SetepenRa RamesesII MeryAmun
The Powerful truth of Ra Chosen of Ra — Son of Ra — Made by Ra Beloved of Amun

FIVE NEW KINGDOM PHARAOHS AND HOW THEIR NAMES WERE CONSTRUCTED.

105

Numbers and Mathematics

The Egyptians used a decimal system for counting.

The ancient Egyptians were possibly the first civilization to explore science. Indeed, "chemistry" is derived from "alchemy," which itself comes from the word *kemy*, an ancient term for "Egypt."

Where the Egyptians really excelled was in applied mathematics, but there are few surviving records of how they reached their conclusions. They must have had an advanced understanding of the subject, because without it their innovations in engineering, astronomy, and administration would not have been possible.

The ancient Egyptians used mathematics for measuring the level of the Nile flood, calculating areas of land, and working out taxes. With their expertise they even got very close to calculating the "true year"—and of course mathematical skills were essential for the computations needed to build temples, tombs, and pyramids.

Hieroglyphic numbers were not used in the day-to-day running of the state. Like hieroglyphic words, they were used to decorate the tombs and great temples. But there was a hieratic numbering system that made it easier to write numbers, although it had more symbols to remember. The hieratic system included the numbers 1 to 9, then 10, 20, 30...90, 100, 200, 300, and so on.

Unlike the Greeks, the Egyptians did not think of numbers as abstract quantities; their awkward numbering

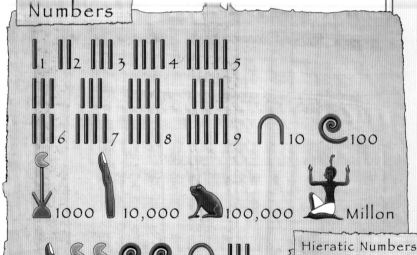

Numbers

12,427

Hieratic Numbers

Hieroglyphic Numbers

The conventions for reading and writing numbers are quite simple. The higher number is always written in front of the lower number, and where there is more than one row of numbers, the reader must start at the top.

1 is shown as a single stroke.
10 is a drawing of a hobble for cattle.
100 is represented by a coil of rope.
1,000 is a drawing of a lotus plant.
10,000 is represented by a finger.
100,000 is a tadpole or frog.
1,000,000 is the figure of a god with his arms raised above his head.

(BACKGROUND) A COPY OF PART OF THE RHIND PAPYRUS. (LEFT) HIERATIC SYMBOLS EVOLVED OVER SIX DISTINCT PERIODS. THE HIERATIC NUMERALS SHOWN HERE DATE FROM AROUND 1800 BC.

system was probably responsible for this failing. However, surviving mathematical papyri, written in hieratic, show they invented clever ways around the problem.

The Rhind papyrus contains the oldest examples of arithmetic trigonometry and algebra. It is about 18 feet (6 m) long and 13 inches (33 cm) wide, and was written around 1650 BC by the scribe Ahmes, who acknowledged that he was making a copy of a 200-year-old document. It contains the sort of problems a typical Egyptian school student had to solve in his mathematics class, such as "From a certain amount of grain, how many loaves can be baked?" or "Given a ramp of length x and height y, how many bricks are needed?"

The geometry we attribute to Pythagoras, Eudoxus, and Euclid was actually being practiced more than a thousand years earlier by Egyptian mathematicians. They knew that the area of a rectangle was equal to its length multiplied by its width. They understood that if a triangle was drawn inside a rectangle with the same length as its sides and the same height as its width, then its area would be half that of the rectangle. They were even able to calculate a value for pi of 3.16.

Having a standard value for weights and measures was essential to trade and the running of the state, although

Ancient Egyptian Arithmetic

The Egyptians had some clever methods for making calculations. For example a multiplication problem such as 24 X 53 would have been answered by successively doubling 24 while at the same time successively dividing 53 in half and rounding down to a whole number.

The illustration below shows how this was done. To find the answer only numbers in the first column neighboring the odd numbers in the second column are added together. This method works with any two numbers.

24	53	Odd
48	26	
96	13	Odd
192	6	
384	3	Odd
768	1	Odd

24+96+384+768
Answer 1272

these values altered during different periods. During the New Kingdom the royal cubit was approximately the length of a man's forearm—around 20½ inches (52.4 cm). Measuring rods were used as rulers and knotted ropes as tape measures.

Weights were made in units known as *deben*, which were about 3.3 ounces (93.3 grams). A deben was a quantity of copper, silver, or gold and was used to calculate the value of other goods such as grain, thus allowing a standard pricing system before the invention of money.

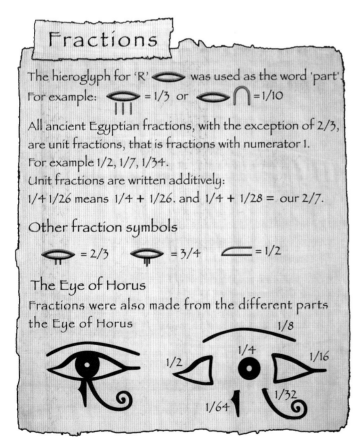

Fractions

The hieroglyph for 'R' ⬯ was used as the word 'part'. For example: ⬯ = 1/3 or ⬯∩ = 1/10

All ancient Egyptian fractions, with the exception of 2/3, are unit fractions, that is fractions with numerator 1.
For example 1/2, 1/7, 1/34.
Unit fractions are written additively:
1/4 1/26 means 1/4 + 1/26. and 1/4 + 1/28 = our 2/7.

Other fraction symbols

⬯ = 2/3   ⬯ = 3/4   ⬳ = 1/2

The Eye of Horus
Fractions were also made from the different parts the Eye of Horus

1/2 1/4 1/8 1/16 1/32 1/64

Papyrus, the Wonder Plant

The Egyptians started making paper from the papyrus plant over five thousand years ago, and our word "paper" comes from their word "papyrus," meaning "that which belongs to the house" (referring to the government bureaucracy of ancient Egypt).

This ancient invention was exported all around the Mediterranean and was used by the Roman Empire—in fact, it became the most important writing material in the ancient world and revolutionized how records were kept. (Many things were written down that might never have been, if not for the ease of using papyrus.) Papyrus was used throughout the Byzantine Empire and continued to be used after the Arab conquest of Egypt, until the seventh century AD, when an embargo on exporting it forced the Europeans to use parchment—and then paper made from cotton, a Chinese invention. Although cotton paper was less durable then papyrus, it was easier to make, and gradually, the production of papyrus died out. The papyrus plant itself soon disappeared from Egypt.

Ironically, the ancient Egyptians left no written records of how they made papyrus, but the method was rediscovered in 1965 by the Egyptian scientist Dr. Hassan Ragab. Through careful study of ancient papyri, he worked out how it was made and reintroduced the papyrus plant into Egypt. Today, papyrus paper is easily obtained and is widely used for painting reproductions of ancient Egyptian art.

In the dry climate of Egypt, papyri have lasted in excellent condition for well over 4,000 years and today, there are many papyrus collections around the world. These include personal and business letters, legal and historical scripts, "magical" papyri, as well as mathematical and scientific works. The existing works of fiction, theology, poetry, and books of proverbs provide us with invaluable insight into the minds of ancient people.

Through philosophical treatises written in the form of dialogues, the ancients attempted to deal with the great problems of existence. Such works as the Instructions of Ptah-hotep were ancient at the time of the New Kingdom—and yet their message is timeless. Many fictional works bear an uncanny resemblance to stories written thousands of years later. Parts of *The Thousand and One Nights* and the story of Cinderella originated in ancient Egypt. Amenemhat I wrote a book of instruction on the principles of good government for his son that is still worth reading today.

Most surviving papyri date from the Greco-Roman Period until the middle of the seventh century AD. More than sixty of the famous Dead Sea Scrolls are made of papyrus, and most of the early Christian texts were written on papyrus as well.

Recovered Literature

RECENTLY, SCIENTISTS HAVE BEEN ABLE TO RECOVER PARTS OF LOST TEXTS BY FAMOUS ANCIENT WRITERS SUCH AS THE ATHENIAN PLAYWRIGHT SOPHOCLES, AND AN EPIC POEM BY ARCHILOCHOS DESCRIBING THE EVENTS LEADING UP TO THE TROJAN WAR. THE TECHNIQUE THEY ARE USING IS CALLED MULTISPECTRAL IMAGING, WHICH WAS DEVELOPED AT NASA. THIS PROCESS WAS FIRST USED IN THE MID 1990S TO READ CARBONIZED SCROLLS FROM AN ANCIENT LIBRARY AT HERCULANEUM THAT HAD BEEN BURIED IN VOLCANIC ASH WHEN MOUNT VESUVIUS ERUPTED IN 79 AD. THAT EVENT DESTROYED THE TOWNS OF HERCULANEUM AND POMPEII—BUT THANKS TO THE DURABILITY OF PAPYRUS AND THE INGENUITY OF MODERN SCIENCE, WE HAVE ACCESS TO THESE ENLIGHTENING RECORDS.

MULTISPECTRAL IMAGING IS NOW BEING USED AT OXFORD UNIVERSITY IN ENGLAND TO READ THE OXYRHYNCHUS PAPYRI, WHICH WERE SALVAGED FROM AN ANCIENT RUBBISH DUMP IN EGYPT. FOR THE FIRST TIME IN 2,000 YEARS, CLASSICAL GREEK AND ROMAN LITERATURE IS BEING RECOVERED, PROVIDING US WITH FASCINATING INSIGHTS INTO THE ANCIENT WORLD.

How the Egyptians Make Papyrus Paper

1. **THE STEMS OF THE PAPYRUS PLANT ARE CUT AND THE SKINS REMOVED, REVEALING THE WHITE INTERIOR PITH.**
2. **THIS IS THEN SLICED INTO THIN STRIPS.**
3. **THE STRIPS ARE BEATEN WITH A WOODEN HAMMER TO BREAK DOWN AND FLATTEN THE FIBERS AND TO STRENGTHEN THE FINISHED PAPER.**
4. **THE STRIPS ARE SOAKED IN WATER FOR A FEW DAYS. THE PITH ABSORBS THE WATER AND SOFTENS THE STRIPS.**
5. **A ROLLING PIN IS USED TO SQUEEZE OUT THE EXCESS WATER.**
6. **THE STRIPS ARE LAID OUT AT RIGHT ANGLES AND OVERLAPPING ONE ANOTHER TO FORM A SHEET.**
7. **THESE SHEETS ARE THEN SANDWICHED BETWEEN LINEN AND PRESSED UNTIL DRY.**
8. **THE ANCIENT PAPERMAKERS USED HEAVY STONES TO PRESS THE SHEETS, BUT NOWADAYS THE SAME RESULT IS ACHIEVED WITH A SCREW PRESS. THE FINISHED PAPER IS EXTREMELY STRONG AND DOES NOT TEAR EASILY; THE SURFACE IS SMOOTH, MAKING IT A PERFECT MEDIUM FOR WRITING AND PAINTING.**

Papyrus

The ancient Egyptians used the versatile papyrus plant in many other ways as well. It was used for food and for medicinal purposes, and the reeds were bundled together to make boats. It was also used to make sandals and woven into mats and baskets. The strength and flexibility of the plant made it perfect for making the rope that was used to haul the massive stone blocks needed for building temples and pyramids. Indeed many temple columns are based on the form of the papyrus plant.

Fun with Hieroglyphs

The word 'Name'

Everyone wants to see how his or her name appears in hieroglyphs. But is it possible to write your name like an ancient Egyptian? The answer, unless your name is Moses, is no. In ancient Egypt a person's name was considered to be a living part of that person and it had to be given immediately at birth or, it was thought, the individual would not properly come into existence.

The names of pharaohs offered clues to their personality, the period in which they lived, and the gods they worshipped. But it was not only the kings who placed great store in names. All Egyptians' names were carefully chosen for commoners and royalty alike.

Ordinary words often formed part of the name, such as "ankh" (life), "mery" (beloved), "hotep" (satisfied or peace) and "nefer" (beautiful). For example Neferet, means "beautiful woman," Nefertiti "the beautiful one has come" and Rahotep means "Ra is satisfied."

So how do you write your name in hieroglyphs? The chief problem is the missing vowels especially "E", "U" and "V" and the answer is to follow the principles the ancient Egyptians used to write the names of their foreigners Greek rulers during the Ptolemaic period.

In this chapter we have seen how Ptolemy was written now lets look at the names Cleopatra and Alexander.

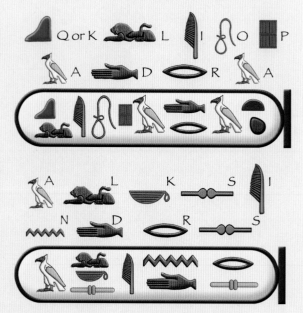

A name like "Sarah," for example, is easily written in hieroglyphs but "Peter" is more difficult.

"Cleopatra" replaced the "E" in her name with an "I". So the "E" in Peter could be left out altogether or the symbol for "I" can be used. The "R" symbol alone represents the "ER" sound.

"Cameron" is both a girl and boy's name so the determinative symbol is used at the end of the word.

By using the information in this chapter you will be able to write your name in hieroglyphs. It is even possible to write an English word using alphabet, syllabic, and determinative symbols.

Imagining Egypt Resources

All the hieroglyphs in this chapter are available for you to download and use in your own Word documents. Go to: WWW.DISCOVERINGEGYPT.COM

You will also find all sorts of free downloads and fun activities such as Egyptian math, the hieroglyphic translator, the game of Senet, and glyph eCards you can send to a friend.

Click the Imagining Egypt Resources button and you will be asked to translate these three hieroglyphs.

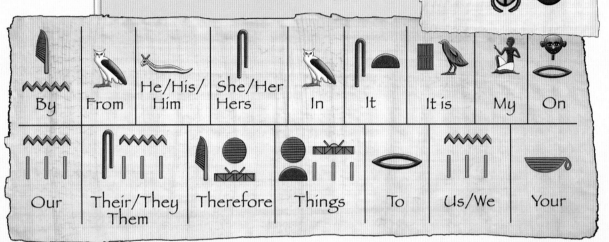

By	From	He/His/Him	She/Her/Hers	In	It	It is	My	On
Our	Their/They/Them	Therefore	Things	To	Us/We	Your		

Year · 2007 · Month · Six · Day · 20

(ABOVE) SOME USEFUL ANCIENT EGYPTIAN WORDS. (LEFT) A FORMULA FOR WRITING DATES. (BELOW) A SENTENCE WRITTEN USING HIEROGLYPHS FROM THIS CHAPTER. SEE IF YOU CAN DECODE IT.

THE GODS AND GODD

The Book of the Dead lists more than 500 deities

MANY OF THE ANCIENT EGYPTIAN RELIGIOUS STORIES AND RITUALS HAVE BEEN LOST, MAKING IT DIFFICULT TO FULLY UNDERSTAND THE CONFUSING MULTITUDE OF DEITIES. REPRESENTATIONS OF EGYPTIAN GODS HAVE OFTEN BEEN MISUNDERSTOOD AND DESCRIBED AS "VISIONS OF HELL." IMAGES OF HUMAN DEITIES WITH ANIMAL HEADS WERE DEEPLY SHOCKING TO THE PROPHETS OF ISRAEL AND THE EARLY CHRISTIANS—AND YET THERE ARE SIMILARITIES IN THE SYMBOLISM AND PHILOSOPHIES OF THE ANCIENT EGYPTIANS AND THE CHRISTIANS, SUCH AS THE WORSHIP OF THE HOLY MOTHER EMBODIED IN BOTH THE GODDESS ISIS AND THE CULT OF THE VIRGIN MARY.

Egypt was the first country to adopt Christianity, and many Egyptian temples were converted into churches, so it is not really surprising that elements of the old religion were incorporated into the new. Indeed the Bible was first translated into Greek in Alexandria, and it is possible to detect themes from Egyptian myths in the Old Testament Bible, which appeared much later.

The peoples of the ancient Near East and Mediterranean world held Egyptian civilization in awe. The Greeks and Romans were especially fascinated by Egypt, which was as old to them as their civilization is to us.

On the whole, ancient peoples were more tolerant of other religions than their modern counterparts are, and they had no difficulty in recognizing the characteristics of foreign gods in their own deities.

Believers in today's prevailing religions tend to be contemptuous of the ancient Egyptians, who worshipped

a multitude of gods. But for thousands of years, the Egyptian religion brought comfort to millions of people and held their society together.

The Creation

In the beginning there was nothing but the watery chaos of Nun. There was no light and no darkness and nothing solid or still. Within this turmoil was the essence of all the things of creation, but they were inert and helpless.

Then something stirred inside the Nun. It was the god Atum, also called Ra—the rising sun—in the form of Khepre.

When Khepre rose out of the ocean of Nun, he found himself in a vast, empty space. There was no place for him to stand, so he made a solid bank by thinking in his heart of the thing he wished to make. By uttering the words that described it, it came into being.

When he pondered all the things he had to do, he determined to create two other gods to help him. They were Shu, the god of the air, and Tefnut, the goddess of moisture and rain. In this way the atmosphere came into being. Shu and Tefnut then united and produced Geb, god of the earth, and Nut, the sky goddess. Shu supported Nut above Geb and Khepre, who was now transformed into Ra the sun god, who shone down upon the world and produced the day.

Geb and Nut had five children: the gods Osiris, Horus the Elder, Seth, Isis, and Nephythys. Men and women sprang from the tears that fell from the eyes of Khepre.

This is only one of a number of Egyptian creation myths. Another credits the god Ptah as the original creator. In this story, Ptah forms the gods, the world, and everything in it with his thoughts and words.

The Egyptians had no problem reconciling contradictory stories to explain the creation of the world. Their religion was polytheistic—meaning that they worshipped many gods. For 3,000 years, new gods appeared and others ceased to be worshipped but for most of that time, the Egyptian religion did not change much. (The only exception was that for a short period during the eighteenth dynasty, Akhenaten established a revolutionary monotheistic cult of the one god Aten.)

For the ancients, the world was filled with mystery. Much of what they experienced in the world around them was unknown and frightening. The gods represented the many aspects of the Egyptians' natural and "supernatural" surroundings and helped them understand its many

aspects, and Egyptian gods took on a much wider range of roles than the deities of monotheistic religions, even including what might be termed "demons." Demons had more power than human beings, were usually immortal, could be in more than one place at a time, and could affect the world as well as the people in it in extraordinary ways. But there were certain limits to their powers and they were neither all-powerful nor all knowing.

Most Egyptian gods represented one principle

aspect of the world: Ra was the sun god, for example, and Nut was goddess of the sky. The characters of the gods were not clearly defined. Most were generally benevolent but their favor could not be counted on. Some gods were spiteful and had to be placated. Some, such as Neith, Sekhmet, and Mut, had changeable characters. The god Seth, who murdered his brother, embodied the malevolent and disordered aspects of the world.

(LEFT) KHEPRE, THE CREATOR GOD, IN THE FORM OF THE SCARAB OR "DUNG" BEETLE. IT WAS BELIEVED THAT KHEPRE PUSHED THE SUN ACROSS THE SKY LIKE A BALL OF DUNG. (BELOW) THE SKY GODDESS NUT IS HELD ABOVE THE EARTH GOD GEB BY THEIR FATHER SHU, THE GOD OF THE AIR.

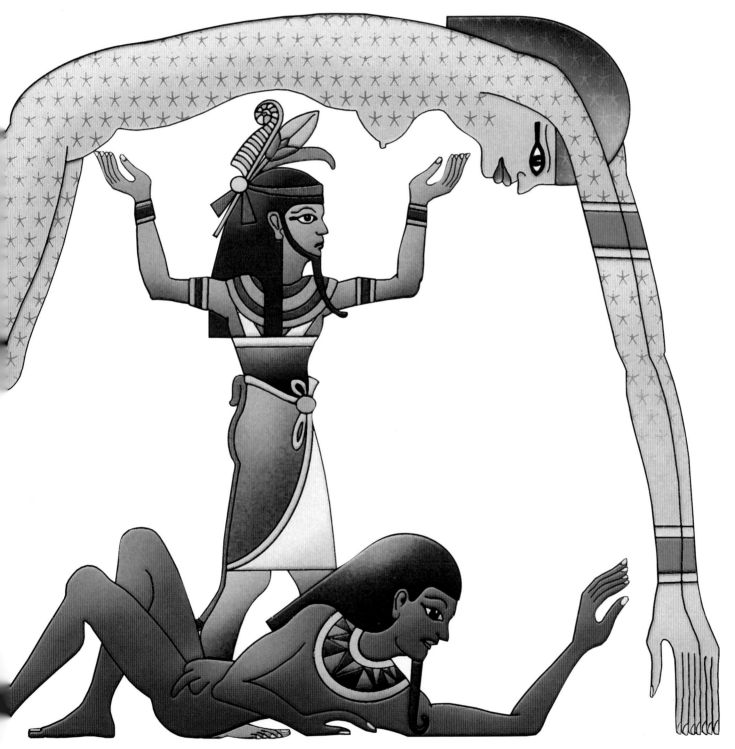

(CLOCKWISE FROM TOP) THE CROCODILE GOD SOBEK FROM A COLUMN AT KOM OMBO TEMPLE; A RAM-HEADED SPHINX FROM KARNAK TEMPLE; A HUMAN-HEADED SPHINX FROM THE AVENUE OF SPHINXES AT LUXOR TEMPLE; THE GOD OSIRIS SITS ON HIS THRONE AT THE GATES OF PARADISE WHILE HIS SON HORUS PRESENTS A DEAD MAN WHO HAS PASSED INTO THE AFTERLIFE; ANUBIS, THE JACKAL-HEADED GOD WHO WAS THOUGHT TO PROTECT THE DEAD; THE IMAGE OF AMUN RA IN THE FORM OF THE RAM FROM KARNAK TEMPLE; THE GOD BES FROM DENDARA TEMPLE, A GUARDIAN OF CHILDREN ALSO ASSOCIATED WITH GOOD TIMES AND ENTERTAINMENT; HORUS IN THE FORM OF THE FALCON, FROM HIS TEMPLE AT EDFU.

The physical form taken on by the various Egyptian gods was usually a combination of human and animal, and many were associated with one or more animal species. And an animal could express a deity's mood. When a god was angry, she might be portrayed as a ferocious lioness; when gentle, a cat. The convention was to depict the animal gods with a human body and an animal head. The opposite convention was sometimes used for representations of a king, who might be portrayed with a human head and a lion's body, as in the case of the sphinx.

Sphinxes might also appear with other heads, particularly those of rams or falcons.

Many deities were represented only in human form. Among these were such very ancient figures as the cosmic gods—Shu of the air, Geb of the earth, the fertility god Min, and the craftsman Ptah. There were a number of minor gods that took on grotesque forms, including Bes, a dwarf with a mask-like face, and Taurt, a goddess whose physical form combined the features of a hippopotamus and a crocodile. Among demons the most important figure was Apepi (sometimes called Apophis). He was the enemy of the sun god in his daily cycle through the cosmos and is depicted as a colossal snake.

Deities were often grouped together in what were known as Enneads. These were groups of nine deities.

These nine gods formed the basic model of the universe for the ancient Egyptians, providing a sense of order for people faced with the chaotic and mysterious forces of their environment. Belief in these gods also helped establish a common language for understanding and communicating the meaning of their existence. Belief in the gods even helped form the laws that held their society together.

Belief in the gods helped form the laws that held Egyptian society together.

Gods and Men

The ancient Egyptians believed that at the dawn of history, all of the gods and goddesses lived upon the earth and ruled Egypt in much the same way as the pharaohs did in their own time. The divine ones went about among men and took an interest in their affairs, ruling with justice and caring for their people.

The gods had distinctive personalities and physical forms similar to those of mortals, and, like men, they experienced emotions and passions and were prone to the same accidents that befell human beings. They even grew old and died. The greatest of all the gods was Ra, who ruled Egypt for 992 years. His reign was marked by justice and righteousness and throughout ancient Egypt's history he was regarded as the very model of what a king should be.

The nine gods of the Great Ennead

The Egyptian myth of creation revolves around the Great Ennead

THE SUN GOD, RA

THE DEITY OF AIR, SHU

THE DEITY OF MOISTURE, TEFNUT

THE SKY GODDESS, NUT

THE EARTH GOD, GEB

THE GODS WHO ESTABLISHED CIVILIZATION AND KINGSHIP OSIRIS, ISIS, NEPHYTHYS, AND SETH

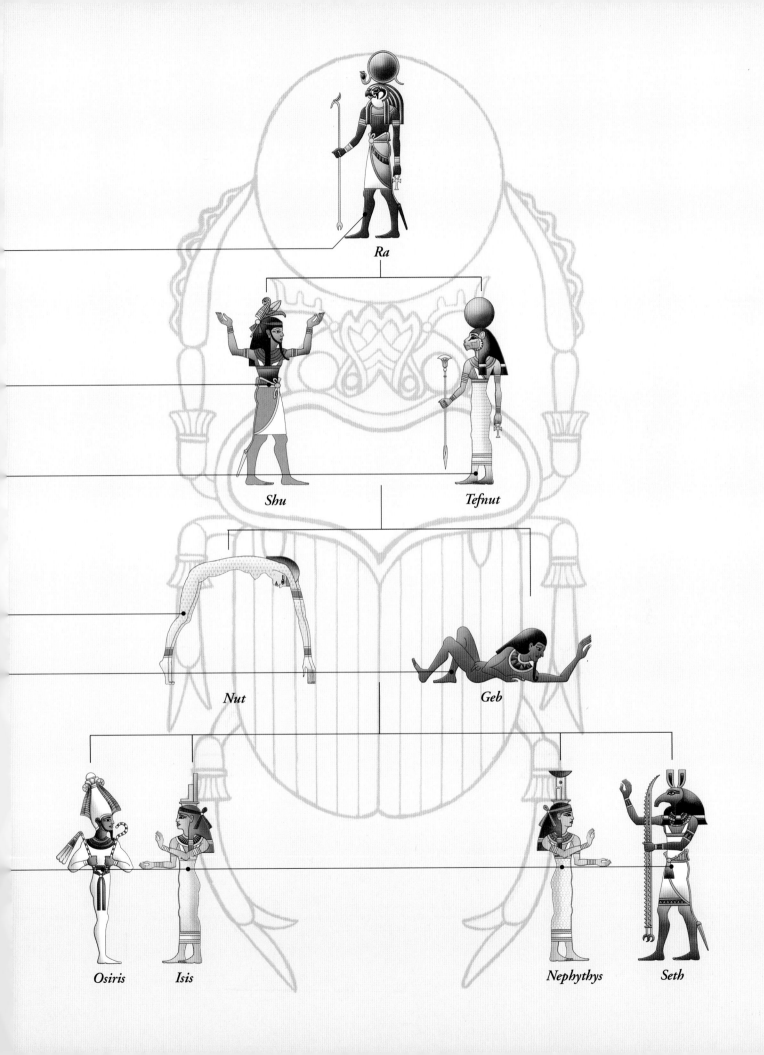

Ra

Shu

Tefnut

Nut

Geb

Osiris

Isis

Nephythys

Seth

The Gods

 Ammut

Devourer of the Dead

Ammut, a female, was an extravagantly imagined creature, depicted as part crocodile, part lioness, and part hippopotamus. She was often shown near the scales on which the hearts of the dead were weighed against the Feather of Truth. She devoured the hearts of those whose wicked deeds in life made them unfit to enter the afterlife.

A DETAIL FROM THE EGYPTIAN BOOK OF THE DEAD SHOWING AMMUT BESIDE THE SCALES WHERE THE HEART OF THE DECEASED IS WEIGHED AGAINST THE FEATHER OF TRUTH.

 Amun

Also Known as Amen, Amun, Ammon

Amun was the chief Theban deity whose power grew as the city of Thebes grew from an unimportant village, in the Old Kingdom, to a powerful metropolis in the Middle and New Kingdoms. He rose to become the patron of the Theban pharaohs and was eventually combined with sun god, Ra—who had been the dominant deity of the Old Kingdom—to become Amun-Ra, King of the Gods and ruler of the Great Ennead.

Amun's name means "Hidden One, Mysterious of Form," and although he is most often represented as a human wearing a double-plumed crown, he is sometimes depicted as a ram or a goose. The implication is that his true identity can never be revealed.

Karnak was Amun's chief temple, but his fame extended well beyond the boundaries of Egypt. His cult spread to Ethiopia, Nubia, Libya, and through much of Palestine. The Greeks thought he was an Egyptian manifestation of their god Zeus. Even Alexander the Great thought it worthwhile consulting the oracle of Amun.

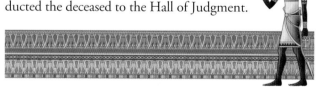 Anubis

Protector of the Dead

Anubis is shown as a jackal-headed man, or as a jackal. His father was Seth and his mother Nephythys. His cult center was Cynopolis, now known as El Kes. He was closely associated with mummification and as protector of the dead. It was Anubis who conducted the deceased to the Hall of Judgment.

 Aten

A God Without a Male or Female Aspect

Aten was the God of the pharaoh Akhenaten, who considered Aten to be the father and mother of all creation. Aten is depicted as the sun disk with radiating beams ending in hands that sometimes hold the Ankh, a symbol of life itself. Akhenaten declared all other gods to be false and decreed that only Aten could be worshipped. Many temples were closed down and all references to other gods destroyed. But the doctrine that there is but one God was unpopular. The people took great comfort in their belief in many gods, and believed that Anubis and Osiris were essential to their entry into the afterlife. The worship of Aten was abandoned after Akhenaten's death.

Apepi

A Demon Also Known as Apophis

Apepi was a huge snake symbolizing darkness, storm, night, the underworld, and death. He was the evil ally of Seth and the enemy of the sun. He did nightly battle with the sun god Ra, but fortunately was always defeated, thus permitting the sun to shine upon the earth each morning. Sometimes he was partially successful in his eternal battle, causing an eclipse of the sun; it was believed that during eclipses he swallowed the boat of the sun god, but he always regurgitated it and light was restored.

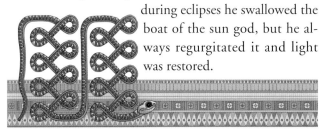

Apis

A Living Bull God

Apis was the sacred animal of Ptah and is depicted as a bull god who wears the solar disc and royal *uraeus* (coiled cobra). An actual bull was kept at Memphis and was regarded as the physical manifestation of the god Ptah. When the Apis bull died, there was national mourning and its body

was mummified and buried in a vast subterranean complex at Saqqara. Its successor was recognized by certain marks on its body.

Atum

Atum was one of the creator gods who lay dormant in the primeval waters of Nun long before creation. He was said to have created the other gods and was thought to be the ancestor of the human race. He was depicted as a man wearing the double crown of Egypt but also appeared as the scarab, a lion, a bull, or a lizard. Atum was regarded as a protector god and was particularly associated with the rituals of kingship. It was thought that Atum carried the dead king from his pyramid into the sky and transformed him into a star god.

Atum's cult center was at Heliopolis, where over time, he was united with the sun god Ra.

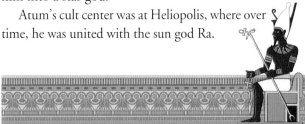

Bastet

Bastet is depicted as a woman with a cat's head or simply as a cat. Originally an avenging lioness deity, she evolved into a goddess of pleasure.

Her cult center was in the town of Bubastis in the Western delta. Many cats lived at her temple and were mummified when they died. An immense cemetery of mummified cats has been discovered in the area.

Bes

Unlike the other gods, Bes is represented full face rather than in profile, as a grotesque, bandy-legged dwarf with his tongue sticking out. He was associated with good times and entertainment but was also considered a guardian god of childbirth. Bes chased away demons of the night and guarded people from dangerous animals.

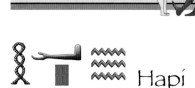

Geb

Geb was the father of Osiris, Isis, Seth, and Nephythys, and was a god without a cult. As an earth god he was associated with fertility and it was believed that earthquakes were the laughter of Geb. He is mentioned in the Pyramid Texts as imprisoning the buried dead within his body.

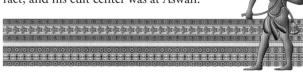

Hapi

Hapi was not the god of the river Nile but of its inundation. He is represented as a pot-bellied man with breasts and a headdress made of aquatic plants. He was thought to live in the caves of the first cataract, and his cult center was at Aswan.

Hathor

Hathor was the daughter of Ra and the patron goddess of women, love, beauty, pleasure, and music. She is depicted in three forms: as a cow, as a woman with the ears of a cow, and as a woman wearing the headdress of a cow's horns. In this last manifestation, she holds the solar disc between her horns. She was the consort of Horus, and her name actually means "House of Horus." She had many temples the most famous of which is at Dendara.

There was a dark side to Hathor. It was believed that Ra sent her to punish the human race for its wickedness, but Hathor wreaked such bloody havoc on Earth that Ra was horrified and determined to bring her back. He tricked her by preparing vast quantities of beer mixed with mandrake and the blood of the slain. Murdering mankind was thirsty work, and when Hathor drank the beer she became so intoxicated that she could not continue her slaughter.

THE GREAT PYLON ENTRANCE INTO THE TEMPLE OF HORUS AT EDFU REMAINS ONE OF THE BEST PRESERVED TEMPLES IN EGYPT.

Horus

Horus was the son of Osiris and Isis and the enemy of the wicked god Seth. He is depicted as a hawk or as a man with the head of a hawk. Sometimes he is shown as a youth with a side lock, seated on his mother's lap. He was the god of the sky and the divine protector of kings.

Horus was worshipped throughout Egypt and was particularly associated with Edfu, the site of the ancient city of Mesen, where his temple can still be seen.

There are many stories of his wars against his uncle Seth, who murdered his father and usurped the throne. Eventually Horus defeated Seth and became the king of Egypt.

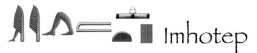

Imhotep

Imhotep is notable among the gods, as he was a common man who lived in the Old Kingdom. He was the architect of King Djoser, builder of the first pyramid, and is credited as the inventor of the building technique that used dressed stone. Because of his genius, he rose to the highest level below pharaoh and after his death was revered as a god of wisdom, writing, and medicine. Imhotep's cult center was at Memphis. He is usually shown seated with an open manuscript roll on his knees, sporting the shaved head of a priest.

Isis

A very important figure in the ancient world, Isis was the wife of Osiris and mother of Horus. She was associated with funeral rites and said to have made the first mummy from the dismembered parts of Osiris. As the enchantress who resurrected Osiris and gave birth to Horus, she was also the giver of life, a healer and protector of kings.

THE FIRST PYLON OF THE TEMPLE OF ISIS AT PHILAE.

Isis is represented with a throne on her head and is sometimes shown breast-feeding the infant Horus. In this manifestation she was known as "Mother of God." To the Egyptians she represented the ideal wife and mother: loving, devoted, and caring.

Her most famous temple is at Philae, though her cult spread throughout the Mediterranean world and, during the Roman period, extended as far as northern Europe. There was even a temple dedicated to her in London.

Khepre

Also known as, Khepri, Khepra, Khepera, Khepre was a creator god depicted as a Scarab beetle or as a man with a scarab for a head. The Egyptians observed young scarab beetles emerging spontaneously from balls of dung and associated them with the process of creation. Khepre was one of the first gods, self-created, and his name means "he who has come into being." Atum took his form as he rose out of the chaotic waters of the Nun in a creation myth. It was thought that Khepre rolled the sun across the sky in the same way a dung beetle rolls balls of dung across the ground.

Khepre's name was often incorporated into the king's throne name. For example, Thutmose III's throne name, "Men-kheper-Ra," means "Lasting is the Mani-festation of Ra."

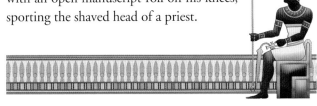

Khnum

Khnum, was depicted as a ram-headed man. He was a god of the cataracts, a potter, and a creator god who guarded the source of the Nile. His sanctuary was on Elephantine Island but his best-preserved temple is at Esna. The Famine Stele, a carved stone tablet, contains appeals to Khnum during a famine caused by a low inundation of the Nile.

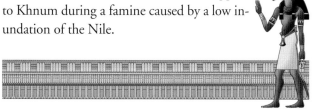

Khonsu

Also known as Khons Khensu, Khuns

Khonsu was the son of Amun and Mut, with whom he formed the Theban Triad. He was a moon god depicted as a man with a falcon head wearing a crescent moon headdress surmounted by the full lunar disc. Like Thoth, who was also a lunar deity, he is sometimes represented as a baboon. Khonsu was be-

THE OPEN COURTYARD IN THE TEMPLE OF KHONSU AT KARNAK.

lieved to have the ability to drive out evil spirits. Rameses II sent a statue of Khonsu to a friendly Syrian king in order to cure his daughter of an illness.

His temple was within the precincts of Karnak.

Maat

Maat was the goddess of truth and justice, embodying the essential harmony of the universe. She was depicted as a seated woman wearing an ostrich feather, or sometimes just as the feather itself. Her power regulated the seasons and the movement of the stars. Maat was the patron of justice and the symbol of ancient Egyptian ethics, so the vizier who was in charge of the law courts went by the title Priest of Maat.

Maat was the ultimate judge in the afterlife, and the heart of the newly deceased was weighed against her feather in the Hall of Two Truths. Ammut, devourer of the dead, ate those who failed her test.

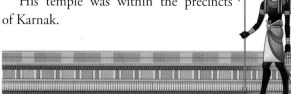

Montu

Montu was a warrior god who rose to become the state god during the eleventh dynasty. He was associated with King Montuhotep I ("Montu is satisfied") who reunited Upper and Lower Egypt after the chaos of the First Intermediate Period.

During the twelfth dynasty Montu was displaced by the rise of Amun, but he took on the true attributes of a war god when warrior kings such as Thutmose III and Rameses II identified themselves with him.

Mut

Mut formed part of the Theban Triad. She was one of the daughters of Ra, the wife of Amun, and mother of Khonsu. She was the vulture goddess and is often depicted as a woman with a long, brightly colored dress and a vulture headdress surmounted by the Double Crown. In her more aggressive aspect she is shown as a lion-headed goddess.

Like Isis and Hathor, Mut played the role of divine mother to the king. Her amulets, which depict her as a seated woman suckling a child, are sometime confused with those of Isis.

Nephythys

Daughter of Geb and Nut, sister of Isis, wife of Seth and mother of Anubis, Nephythys is depicted as a woman with the hieroglyphs for a palace and *neb* (a basket) on her head. She is thus known as "Lady of the Mansions" or "Palace." Nephythys was disgusted by Seth's murder of Osiris and helped her sister, Isis, against her husband, Seth. Together with Isis she was a protector of the dead, and they are often shown together on coffin cases, with winged arms. She seems to have had no temple or cult center of her own.

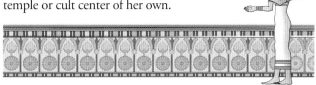

Nut

Mother of Osiris, Isis, Seth, and Nephythys, Nut is usually shown in human form, her elongated body symbolizing the sky. Each limb represents a cardinal point as her body stretches over the earth. Nut swallowed the setting sun (Ra) each evening and gave birth to him each morning. She is often depicted on the ceilings of tombs, on the inside lid of coffins, and on the ceilings of temples.

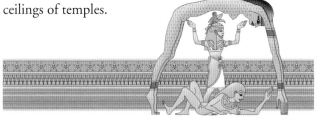

Osiris

Osiris was originally a vegetation god linked with the growth of crops. He was the mythological first king of Egypt and one of the most important of the gods. It was thought that he brought civilization to the race of mankind. He was murdered by his brother Seth, brought back to life by his wife Isis, and went on to become the ruler of the underworld and judge of the dead.

He is usually depicted as a mummy holding the crook and flail of kingship. On his head he wears the white crown of Upper Egypt flanked by two plumes of feathers. Sometimes he is shown with the horns of a ram. His skin is depicted as blue, the color of the dead; black, the color of the fertile earth; or green, representing resurrection.

Osiris's head was thought to have been buried at Abydos, his main cult center. Each year, during his festival, there was a procession and a reenactment of his story in the form of a mystery play.

Ptah

Ptah was a creator god, said to have made the world from the thoughts in his heart and his words. He was depicted as a mummy with his hands protruding from the wrappings and holding a staff. His head was shaven and he wore a scull cap. Ptah was associated with craftsmen, and the high priest of his temple at Memphis held the title Great Leader of Craftsmen.

Why a Year Has 365 Days

Nut was the sky Goddess and wife of all-powerful Ra. She dared to take Geb, the god of the Earth, as her secret lover. When Ra discovered his wife's infidelity he was furious and pronounced a curse on her, and it is this curse that explains why we have 365 days in a year, rather than 360.

Ra declared that Nut's children should not be born in any month or in any year, meaning that she would be pregnant for eternity. Distressed, Nut called upon Thoth for help. Thoth was clever. He immediately challenged the moon goddess to a game of tables. The moon staked a part of her illumination and lost the game, and this is why the moon waxes and wanes, and is no longer a rival to the sun.

With the moonlight Thoth had won, he was able to fashion five extra days, which he added to the calendar. But these days belonged to no month or year, and Nut was able to give birth during this time without contradicting the will of Ra.

 Ra

Also known as Re

The supreme sun god was represented as a man with the head of a hawk, crowned with a solar disk and the sacred serpent. However, in the underworld through which he passes each night, he is depicted as ram-headed.

Each day Ra traveled across the sky in the form of the sun, riding in his solar boat, and each night he journeyed through the underworld where he defeated the allies of chaos. He was reborn each morning in the form of the sunrise. His influence on the other gods was so strong that he subsumed many of their identities. Thus Amun became Amun-Ra, Montu became Montu-Ra, and Horus became Ra-Horakhty. Pharoah Akenaten's god, the Aten, was another form of Ra, the solar disk.

The Egyptian kings claimed to be descended from Ra and called themselves "The Son of Ra." His cult was very powerful during the period of the Old Kingdom, when

Sun Temples were built in his honor. His cult center was at Heliopolis, which today is covered by the northern suburbs of Cairo.

The Eternal Battle of Apepi and Ra

Apepi was the evil arch enemy of Ra, the sun god, and was associated with savage animals, monsters, serpents, and venomous reptiles. Every day he would take the form of a huge serpent and lie in wait near the entrance of the dawn, attempting to swallow up Ra as he was about to rise in the eastern sky.

Apepi was accompanied by legions of devils and the powers of storm, hurricane, thunder, and lightning. He was the deadly foe of all physical and moral order and of all the good of heaven and earth.

At night priests at the Temple of Karnak would perform hymns and magical ceremonies intended to strengthen the arms of Amun-Ra and give him the power to overcome Apepi. They would also recite spells to paralyze the demon just as he was about to attack, thus allowing the sun god enough of an advantage to shrivel up Apepi with the burning heat of his rays. At this, all the devils of darkness would flee shrieking in terror and the sun could once again rise into the sky, inspiring the spirits of the morning and all the gods of heaven to sing for joy!

 Sobek

Sobek was a crocodile god, depicted as a crocodile on an altar or as a man with a crocodile head wearing a headdress in the form of the sun disk with upright feathers and horns. Sobek's main cult centers were at Medinet el Fayum and at the temple of Kom Ombo, which he shared with Horus and which still exists today. There was a pool at Kom Ombo containing sacred crocodiles and it is still possible to see original mummified crocodiles at the temple.

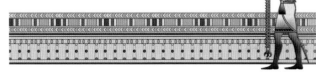 Seth

Also known as Set, Setekh, Suty, and Sutekh

Seth was the son of Geb and Nut, and the evil brother of Osiris. He was the god of darkness, chaos, and confusion, and is represented as a man with an unknown animal head, often described as a Typhonian by the Greeks who associated him with the god Typhon. He is sometimes depicted as a hippopotamus, a pig, or a donkey. Seth murdered his brother and usurped the throne of Egypt and most of the other gods despised him.

Horus eventually defeated Seth, but it was thought that their battle was an eternal struggle between good and evil. Although Seth failed to keep the throne of Egypt he continued to be a companion of Ra. He sometimes accompanied Ra across the sky in his solar boat, causing storms and bad weather.

Shu

Shu was the husband of Tefnut and the father of Nut and Geb. He and his wife were the first gods created by Atum. Shu was the god of the air and sunlight—or, more precisely, dry air—and his wife represented moisture. He was normally depicted as a man wearing a headdress in the form of a plume, which is also the hieroglyph for his name.

Shu's function was to hold up the body of the goddess Nut and separate the sky from the earth. He was not a solar deity but his role in providing sunlight connected him to Ra. Indeed, he was one of the few gods who escaped persecution under the heretic king Akhenaten.

 Tefnut

Tefnut was the wife of Shu and mother of Nut and Geb. She and her husband were the first gods created by Atum. She was the goddess of moisture or damp, corrosive air, and was depicted either as a lioness or as a woman with a lioness's head.

 Thoth

Thoth was the god of writing and knowledge, and was depicted as a man with the head of an ibis holding a scribe's pen and palette, or as a baboon. The Greeks associated him with Hermes and ascribed to him the invention of all the sciences as well as the invention of writing. He is often portrayed writing or making calculations.

Thoth stands apart from most of the other gods. He was as old as the oldest gods and often acted as an intermediately between gods. He was associated with

the moon and is sometimes shown wearing a moon disk and crescent headdress. One of his most important roles was to record the deeds of the dead at the day of their judgment and is often seen doing this in the *Book of the Dead*. His main temple was at Hermopolis in Middle Egypt.

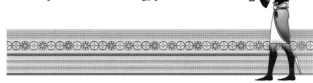

The ancient Egyptians were deeply religious people whose sense of national unity was strengthened by their religious values, enabling their rise to become the first regional superpower in the ancient world. They viewed their victories in war, the abundance of their sacred land, and their personal prosperity as favors from the gods.

When they looked at other people living in comparatively impoverished lands, they believed themselves favored above all others and for this they honored their gods by creating monuments that have stood the test of time. In fact, all of the great monuments along the Nile valley that still exist today were inspired by their belief in their gods and the afterlife. The ancient Egyptians still hold the record for the largest religious building: the Great Pyramid at Giza is still the largest stone building in the world and although their religion in now dead, it lasted for well over 3,000 years, making it one of the most durable religions in human history.

The Egyptians believed themselves favored above all others and for this they honored their gods.

DAILY LIFE IN ANCIENT

MOST EGYPTIANS WERE PEASANT FARMERS WHO WORKED SMALL LOTS OF LAND

NCIENT EGYPT WAS A LAND WITH FEW EXTERNAL ENEMIES. IT WAS THE MOST POWERFUL COUNTRY OF ITS TIME, A SUPER POWER OF THE ANCIENT WORLD. THE PEOPLE WERE PROSPEROUS AND CONFIDENT, AND COUNTED THEMSELVES FORTUNATE TO HAVE BEEN BORN EGYPTIAN. THE NILE BROUGHT RICHES BUT ALSO DANGERS IN THE FORM OF CROCODILES, HIPPOPOTAMUSES, AND PARASITIC WORMS THAT CAUSED BLINDNESS. MOST EGYPTIANS WERE PEASANT FARMERS, BUT MUCH OF THE LAND BELONGED TO THE STATE, SO MANY OF THEM WERE TENANT FARMERS OR AGRICULTURAL LABORERS WORKING FOR THE KING, THE TEMPLES, OR THE NOBILITY.

The lives of the people revolved around the annual flooding of the Nile, which deposited rich black silt on its banks and made the land around it verdant and fertile. By August of each year, the farmland was flooded and only the cities and towns remained above water. During this time, the farmers could not work the land, so many of them were recruited to work on state building projects such as the construction of pyramids. In October, when the waters receded, the property boundaries were once again marked out, irrigation channels were dug, and the planting of crops could begin. As the crops ripened, tax assessors traveled the land noting the yield and fixing the fees to be paid.

The forces of nature were not always kind, and they were not understood in the way that we take for granted today. Many of the uncertainties and mysteries of the world were explained as vagaries of the gods, who could

EGYPT

be spiteful, playful, selfish, or generous. The Egyptians believed fervently that their actions could either anger or placate the gods, and that it was crucial to avoid offending them and to make frequent offerings to them. Perhaps this sounds primitive nowadays but, for its time, Egypt was probably the most civilized place in the world to live.

Men and Women

Monogamous marriage was the general rule in ancient Egyptian society. Only kings and people of great power had harems. In many cases a king's chief wife was a sister or half sister, or another member of the royal family. This practice of intermarriage was confined to the royal household.

Egypt was a male-dominated society and the status of women was lower than that of men at all levels. The father was the head of the family. Upon his death, his oldest son became the head of the family. Boys received an education and followed in their father's trade. A carpenter's son would be a carpenter and a scribe's son would be a scribe.

Marriage was conducted without ceremony, and an agreement between the couple was considered an adequate bond—but marriage was taken quite seriously. In general, a woman's place was in the home, taking care of children and cooking. The goddess Isis was a model of the ideal wife and mother, whereas the goddess Hathor represented aspects of feminine sexuality and fertility. Unlike women in other ancient cultures, such as Rome, Egyptian women did have legal status similar to that of men. They were able to engage in business, inherit

Menna *was the Fields Scribe of Thutmose IV and Amenhotep III. He supervised temple farmlands and state granaries, recorded crop yields, measured land for taxation, and inspected the work of field laborers. He had a wife named Henuttawi, two sons, and four daughters, all of whom are pictured in his tomb.*

The tomb features superb paintings of everyday life in ancient Egypt, depicting Menna working in the fields and hunting in the marshes with his wife and sons.

There are some lovely details, including an image of a little girl taking a thorn out of a friend's foot and one of a mother cradling her baby. One of Menna's daughters is shown picking lotus flowers. There is evidence that Menna's wife may have been literate: several scenes depict a scribal palette under her chair.

The most famous scene in Menna's tomb shows the abundant wildlife of the marshes, including butterflies and flocks of birds in flight.

property, and own land, and a wife could even obtain a divorce if she was mistreated by her husband. Cruelty to women was not tolerated within Egyptian society and could be punished by flogging.

From the numerous wall paintings that survive, we can assume that the moral principles of a close and loving family were valued in Egyptian society. The wife is always shown next to her husband and all of their children. Couples are often shown engaging in

A MAN CARVED THIS LETTER ON THE BACK OF A MEMORIAL STONE TO HIS DEAD WIFE. IT WAS WRITTEN OVER 4,000 YEARS AGO.

How are you?
Are you happy in the afterlife?
Look! I am your beloved on earth, so fight for me, speak for me.
I have made sure you were buried properly so drive off the illness in my limbs.

activities together, hunting in the marshes, playing games, or attending a banquet. The tender, loving relationship between the gods Osiris and Isis was seen as the role model for marriage.

Children

Egyptians never indulged in the practice of abandoning unwanted babies to the elements, as was common in poorer societies of the ancient world. They were fond of children and liked to spend time with them.

Rameses III built a beautiful tomb in the Valley of the Queens for his son Amunhirknopshef, who died while still a boy. There are touching scenes painted on the walls of the father guiding his son through the underworld and introducing him to the gods.

(ABOVE) AMUNHIRKNOPSHEF—SON OF RAMESES III. (BELOW LEFT) AN AGRICULTURAL SCENE FROM THE TOMB OF MENNA.

Children usually went naked and had their heads shaved except for a side lock, a tress of hair hanging over the ear. This was worn until around the age of ten. They spent a lot of time playing games and sports. A number of toys have survived, such as dolls, tops, stuffed leather balls, and board games. Children also kept pets,

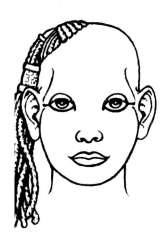

including cats, dogs, monkeys, baboons, and birds.

Most working-class boys received an informal education confined to the practical trades and crafts passed from one generation to the next. There is little evidence to suggest that girls received any education at all. Upper- and middle-class boys learned to read and write, and the sons of the elite were schooled in the "House of Life," where they learned mathematics, ethics and literature. The teaching method consisted of repetitive copying of exercises, and discipline was harsh. A surviving papyrus text includes the words "A boy's ear is on his back—he listens when he is beaten."

Children learned an unquestioning respect for their elders and a duty to their parents. After their parents' death they were expected to bring food to their tombs regularly.

Slaves

The concept of slavery in the ancient world is often confused in translation. We live in a world where the institution of slavery is abhorrent by definition. The use of slaves in ancient Egyptian society, however, was not the same at all.

Most of the Egyptian population was tied to the land of their fathers or inherited their professions from the previous generation. These people were often included as possessions of kings, high-ranking officials, or temple estates. "Serfs" might be a better term to describe them, although it is important to understand that these Egyptian farmers were allowed to own property. They weren't legally tied to the land, but tied to it by tradition.

The popular notion that the pyramids were built by multitudes of slaves is entirely wrong. The work on royal funerary monuments was mostly conducted though conscription during the annual flood of the Nile and indeed, gave the population the security of paid work during this time. True slavery, in the modern sense of the word, seems to have been rare. What slaves existed were either convicts or, more commonly prisoners of war. It was not until the Middle and New Kingdoms that prisoners of war were numerous enough to play any part in Egyptian society. Foreign prisoners of war sometimes carried out the unpleasant tasks of quarrying and mining.

On the whole, however, slaves were well treated. Both male and female owners of slaves had the right to free them, and it was possible for slaves to own land.

Egyptian costume changed very little over 3,000 years.

Although few ancient Egyptian garments have survived, there are many wall paintings and sculptures showing how the ancient Egyptians dressed. These illustrations are colorful and, because of the diagrammatic nature of Egyptian art, the details of the material are clearly shown. Egyptian costume changed very little over three thousand years. Basic garments were loosely draped and needed little sewing. The material was simply held in place around the body by knotted belts, sashes, and collars. Fashion staples were loincloths, skirts or kilts, shirts, capes, and robes.

Most clothing was fashioned of linen made from the flax plant. The dyeing of fabric was not common in Egypt, so most garments remained the color of the original fibers. A decorative collar featuring brightly colored bands was worn by both sexes. It was made of embroidered and beaded materials, and often included semiprecious stones. The collar was worn over a garment or over bare shoulders as protection from the sun.

A GOLD COLLAR WITH SEMI-PRECIOUS STONES, FROM THE TOMB OF PRINCESS NEFERERUP-TAH, 1831-1786 BC.

The skins of various animals were used to make leather belts and straps, as well as sandals and other footwear. Men and women occasionally wore woolen cloaks for warmth.

The production of garments was considered a household chore, so women were most often in charge of the manufacturing of textiles and the making of clothes. Women also worked in spinning and weaving shops, making clothing for the aristocracy.

During the Old Kingdom, men wore a short skirt tied at the waist or held there by a belt. Important people wore a decorative, colored pendant hanging from their waist belt, as well as a shoulder cape or corselet partly covering their bare torsos. A gown that covered the body from just below the breasts to the ankles, held up by decorative shoulder straps, was typical female attire.

During the Middle Kingdom, the man's skirt grew to ankle length, and eventually a double skirt was introduced. At some point during the New Kingdom, more elaborate pleats and ways of draping the material for both sexes evolved—but all of these garments were variations on the same theme.

Embroidered and carved ornamental items were worn, including the lotus flower, the papyrus bundle, birds in flight, and geometric forms. Priests and royalty wore sacred emblems, such as the scarab beetle and the asp. Children and servants usually wore nothing, though household servants and field laborers might wear loincloths. Many

The Police

During the Old and Middle Kingdoms order was kept by local officials with their own private police forces. During the New Kingdom a more centralized police force developed, made up primarily of Egypt's Nubian allies, the Medjay. They were armed with staffs and used dogs. Neither rich nor poor citizens were above the law and punishments ranged from confiscation of property, beating and mutilation (including the cutting off of ears and noses) to death without a proper burial. The Egyptians believed that a proper burial was essential for entering the afterlife, so the threat of this last punishment was a real deterrent, and most crime was of a petty nature.

"They went to the granary, stole three great loaves and eight sabu-cakes of Rohusu berries. They drew a bottle of beer which was cooling in water, while I was staying in my father's room. My Lord, let whatsoever has been stolen be given back to me." (Eighteenth Dynasty)

people went barefoot, but those of rank are depicted in sandals made from palm leaves, papyrus, or leather.

The Egyptians took great care of their hair and were eager to conceal graying and baldness. Hair was usually washed and scented, and the wealthy employed hairdressers. Both men and women often wore wigs of genuine human hair (or plaits of nonhuman hair) on public occasions and at banquets. Wigs were styled and arranged into extremely complex braids and coiffures. Women often wore long, heavy wigs with lotus flowers and cones of perfumed beeswax attached for decoration. Men generally wore shorter wigs.

On their chins Egyptian men grew hair that they sometimes dyed and braided with threads of gold. Kings sometimes wore false beards held in place by ribbons tied over their heads. Children's heads were shaved, leaving a side lock. This side lock of youth regularly appears in the images of young deities such as the infant Horus.

Cosmetics were used by both sexes. They applied

rouge to their cheeks, red ointment to their lips, and henna to their nails and hair. A black liner called kohl was applied around the eyes, along with a green eye shadow made from powdered malachite.

THE LATIN TERM FOR FLAX (LINUM USITATISSIMUM) MEANS "MOST USEFUL PLANT."

THE ANCIENT EGYPTIANS USED THE FLAX PLANT TO MAKE LINEN CLOTH. PICTURES ON TOMB AND TEMPLE WALLS OFFER EVIDENCE THAT THE BLUE FLOWERING FLAX PLANTS WERE USED FROM THE EARLIEST TIMES.

FLAX IS MADE FROM THE SKIN OF THE PLANT'S STEM, AND THE RAW FIBER IS SOFT, FLEXIBLE, AND STRONGER THAN COTTON.

FLAX IS STILL USED TODAY. THE BEST GRADES ARE USED TO MAKE LINEN FABRICS AND THE COARSER GRADES ARE USED TO MAKE ROPE. THE SEEDS ARE USED IN COOKING AND IN THE PRODUCTION OF LINSEED OIL. THE FIBERS ARE USED IN THE PRODUCTION OF HIGH-QUALITY PAPER SUCH AS THAT USED FOR BANK NOTES.

Egypt was a land of plenty, with enough food for everyone.

Food

Wheat and barley were the principal crops of Egypt—the former used to make bread and the latter to make beer. Another important crop was flax, the raw material used in the production of linen clothing. Of course vegetables were grown as well, including onions, cucumbers, lettuce, peas, lentils, radishes, pumpkins, watermelons, leeks, garlic, and turnips. Rock salt from the western desert and spices were used to flavor food. Figs, dates, mulberries, and pomegranates were also plentiful, and grapes were grown in vineyards on the great estates.

The poorer people ate fish. According to Herodotus, fish-eaters were considered unclean and the priests shunned fish. On the whole, meat was abundant and such domestic animals as sheep, goats, oxen, and geese were reared and fattened. There was also a multitude of such game animals as gazelle, antelope, duck, pigeons, and several other kinds of wild bird found in the marshes all over Egypt.

Little is known about Ancient Egyptians cooking – food was baked, boiled, fried, grilled, and roasted. Few actual recipes have survived but they flavored their dishes with herbs and spices such as cumin, dill, coriander, mustard, cinnamon, and rosemary.

Bread

The ancient Egyptians grew emmer wheat, which had strong husks and required a lot of threshing and grinding. The flour was made by grinding the emmer in simple stone mills and, as a result, fine grains of sand and little flakes of stone found their way into the bread. The resulting abrasion of the teeth caused the population to suffer poor dental health.

IN THIS SCENE FROM THE TOMB OF NAKHT, FARM LABORERS USE WOODEN SCOOPS TO THROW THE THRESHED GRAIN IN THE AIR TO WINNOW IT.

Drink

Unlike contemporary Egyptians, their ancestors liked a drink. In myth, Osiris taught humans to brew beer; in fact beer was invented in ancient Egypt and all classes drank it—as a mealtime beverage and in religious ceremonies. There were different types of beer, including a sweet beer made from honey. Egyptologists have studied beer residue from Egyptian vessels and have made brews using a recipe derived from their analysis. They found it to be fruity, sweet, and without the bitterness of modern beer.

The other common drinks were milk and wine. The production of wine began early in Egyptian history. Kings of the first dynasty had extensive cellars where they fermented and stored the wine in earthenware jars sealed with tar. They kept accurate records, carefully labeling each jar with its vintage and quality. The Egyptian grape was famous in antiquity, and both red and white wine were made. The Egyptians also made a date wine by pouring water over ripe dates and letting it stand for a week or two. This is still made today.

(ABOVE) A SCENE FROM THE TOMB OF NAKHT SHOWS MEN MAKING WINE BY PRESSING THE JUICE FROM GRAPES. (RIGHT) AN OFFERING TABLE OF FOOD FROM HATSHEPSUT'S TEMPLE AT DEIR EL-BAHRI.

Date palms *are believed to have originated around the Persian Gulf and were cultivated in Egypt from the earliest times for their sweet fruit, which was fermented to make date wine. The palm's leaves were used for making baskets.*

Herodotus

Herodotus was a Greek historian who lived in the 5th century BC. He traveled extensively and visited Egypt. His many history books earned him the title "The Father of History"

On Egyptian food and cooking he says "they use habitually a wine made out of barley." This is a reference to beer. He continues: "Of their fish some they dry in the sun and then eat them without cooking, others they eat cured in brine. Of birds they eat quails and ducks and small birds without cooking, after first curing them." He goes on the say birds and fishes are also roasted or boiled.

He also states that sacred animals were not eaten and "he pig is accounted by the Egyptians an abominable animal." The Egyptians regarded pork as unclean and did not eat it.

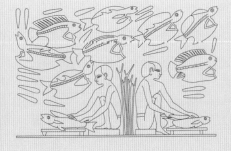

AN ILLUSTRATION FROM THE OLD KINGDOM TOMB OF TI, DEPICTING MEN FILLETING FISH.

All houses were made from mud brick.

The House

All houses were made from mud brick. Stone was used only in the construction of temples and other state buildings. Most homes were small, had flat roofs, and were built close together. They had small windows placed high in the walls to help keep out the sun. The floor was of beaten earth, and wet mats were laid out on the floors to help cool the air. On hot nights, people often slept on the roof where it was cooler. Cooking was done in domed clay ovens in kitchen yards. Each house also included a shrine for the patron god of the family.

The rich Egyptians often had town houses and country estates, some with as many as seventy rooms, featuring tile floors and walls painted with pastoral scenes. These estates might also have large gardens with orchards, swimming pools, and many servants.

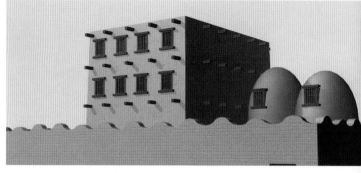

(ABOVE) RECONSTRUCTIONS OF A FARM HOUSE WITH GRAIN SILOS; A GROUP OF TOWN HOUSES. (TOP RIGHT) EXAMPLES OF INFORMAL ORNAMENTAL PATTERNS. (BOTTOM RIGHT) A RECONSTRUCTION OF AN OLD KINGDOM PALACE BASED ON A SARCOPHAGUS IN THE FORM OF A PALACE.

The Palace

The Egyptian royal family used many different types of buildings: There were ritualistic or symbolic palaces attached to New Kingdom mortuary temples, such as the Ramesseum and Medinet Habu; and there were huge buildings used to receive foreign visitors and for ceremonial occasions. The "king's house" a set of domestic apartments, was, like all other residences, made of mud brick—which is why no pharaoh's palace has survived the ravages of time.

Many palaces included a "window of appearances," a ceremonial window at which the king appeared when receiving visitors, conducting ceremonies, or dispensing rewards to his loyal courtiers. The architectural style and decoration of the palaces varied to some extent, although they tended to combine a large-scale domestic room, reception halls, courtyards, pools, and ceremonial areas suitable for religious rituals. A number of surviving fragments of painted plaster and glazed tile suggest that the walls and floors were decorated in a less formal style than the temples.

Made of mud brick, no pharaoh's palace has survived the ravages of time.

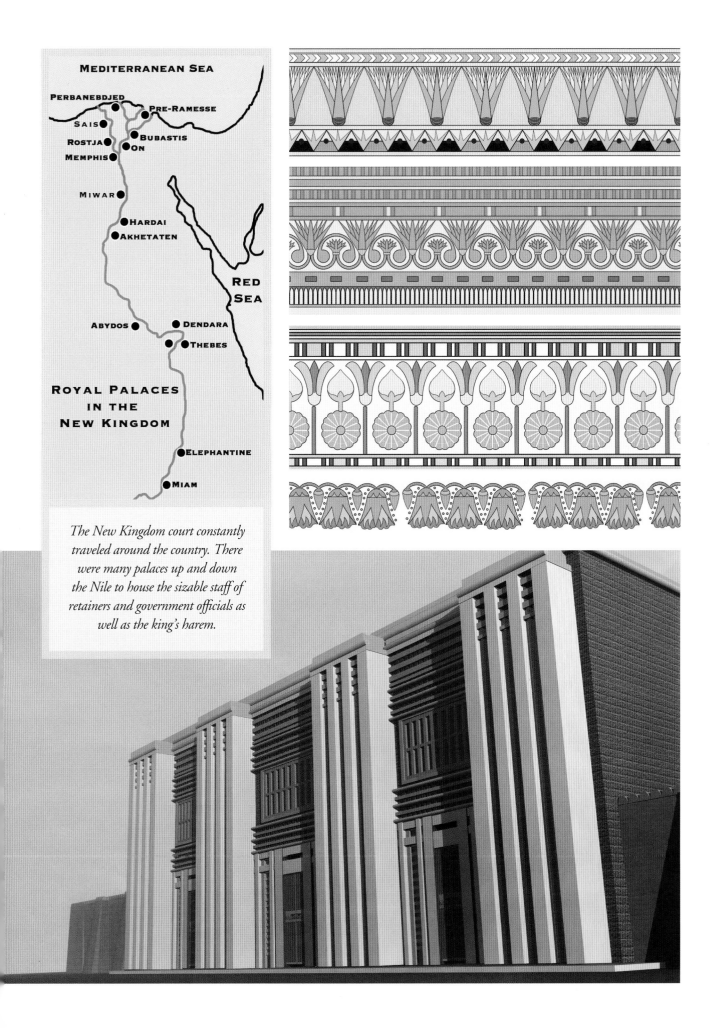

MEDITERRANEAN SEA

PERBANEBDJED
PRE-RAMESSE
SAIS
BUBASTIS
ROSTJA
ON
MEMPHIS

MIWAR

HARDAI
AKHETATEN

RED
SEA

ABYDOS
DENDARA
THEBES

ROYAL PALACES
IN THE
NEW KINGDOM

ELEPHANTINE

MIAM

The New Kingdom court constantly traveled around the country. There were many palaces up and down the Nile to house the sizable staff of retainers and government officials as well as the king's harem.

Games and Sport

Board games were a favorite pastime in Egypt, and Senet was the most popular of these. It was played by two people, either on elaborately carved and inlaid boards, like the one found in Tutankhamen's tomb, or on a "board" simply scratched into the earth. The oldest known representation of Senet is in a painting from the tomb of Hesy, from 2686 BC.

Many actual boards, with their counters and throw sticks (or "knucklebones"), have survived intact. There have been a number of attempts to reconstruct the game but the rules are not fully understood.

The game board consisted of thirty squares laid out in three rows of ten. Some of the squares had symbols on them and the path of the counters probably followed a reverse "S" across the board. The symbols represented either good or bad fortune, and affected play accordingly. The movement of the counters was decided by throwing four two-sided sticks or, in some cases, knucklebones. The word Senet meant "passing" and had a religious significance: the aim of each player was to move his pieces around the board while avoiding hazards. Good luck was considered a blessing from the gods and the first to "pass" into the afterlife by getting all of his pieces off the board was the winner.

THE HIEROGLYPH FOR THE SYLLABIC SOUND FOR "MEN" IS A PICTURE OF A SENET BOARD.

The Ancient Game

Start → ... → Finish

You're safe if you land on Ankh.

Landing on Water Removes piece from board.

# of Senet

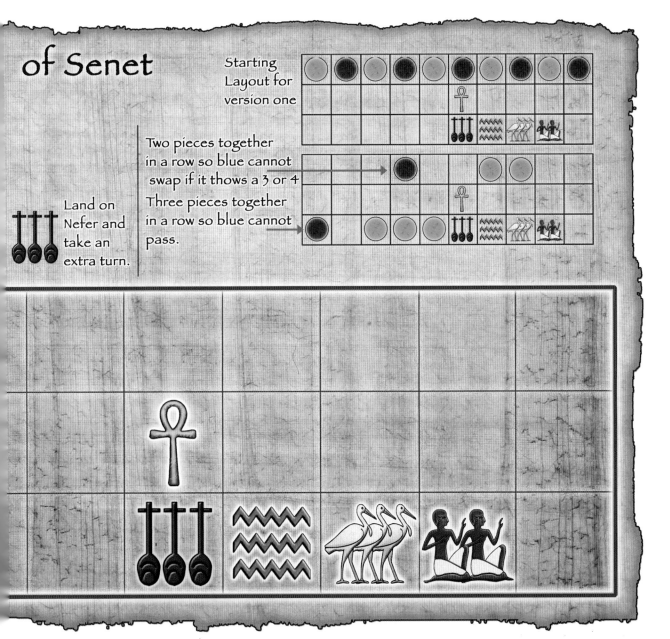

Starting Layout for version one

Two pieces together in a row so blue cannot swap if it thows a 3 or 4

Three pieces together in a row so blue cannot pass.

Land on Nefer and take an extra turn.

How to play Senet

VERSION ONE: Each player has five counters—you could use coins for counters and dice instead of sticks. See diagram (above) for the starting layout.

If you throw a four, or six, you get an extra turn. You can't land on one of your own counters. If you land on the other player's counter, you switch places with them. You can't switch with them if they have two or more counters together in a row. If the other player has three or more counters in a row, you can't pass them. Your counter is safe on the "Ankh" square. Landing on the "Nefer" square gives you another throw of the dice. Landing on the "Water" square knocks your counter off the board and requires a four or six to get it back into play. The functions of the squares with the birds and two men are unknown, so you can make your own rules for

YOU CAN DOWNLOAD AND PRINT THE ABOVE SENET BOARD FROM THE IMAGINING EGYPT RESOURCES WEB SITE AT WWW.DISCOVERINGEGYPT.COM.

them. The first player to get all of their counters off the board wins the game.

VERSION TWO: Each player has seven counters, which are not on the board at the start. You need a four or six to get a counter on the board. You get an extra turn if you throw a six. If you land on your opponent's counter it is knocked off the board. The function of the picture squares is the same as in version one. The first player to get all of their counters off the board wins the game. You can play this version online by going to the Imagining Egypt resources page at **WWW.DISCOVERINGEGYPT.COM**

The Egyptians loved to watch people perform various feats and contests. Some of the most popular contests were wrestling, acrobatics, and gymnastics,

Nakht

Nakht lived some time in the eighteenth dynasty, possibly during the reign of Thutmose IV. He was a scribe at Karnak with the title "Astronomer of Amun," and his job was to schedule festivals and religious rituals for the temple. He did this by studying the night sky and recording the locations of the stars and moon. In this way Nakht could accurately calculate the correct time and date.

He was a wealthy man, and his tomb includes beautiful paintings of country life on his estates. Many of the images depict activities such as canal building for irrigation, plowing, sowing, and harvesting. There are also images of men threshing grain and making wine.

Like many Egyptians, Nakht enjoyed hunting and had a large painting made of himself with his wife and sons hunting birds in the marshes. There are even paintings of cooks plucking and cleaning the catch.

Besides wine and hunting, Nakht liked music. A painting of three musicians playing the harp, lute, and flute has made his tomb famous. (See Music and Dance)

(RIGHT) A NEW KINGDOM HUNTING SCENE FROM THE TOMB OF NAKHT.

Music and Dance

Music and dance were important aspects of daily and religious life in ancient Egypt. Many artifacts have illustrations of musicians and singers—the blind singer is a common motif, as is a banquet scene that includes musicians and dancers.

In ancient cultures, there was no system of music notation, so we cannot know the tunes and melodies that people enjoyed. Fortunately, a large number of musical instruments have survived, so we can get an idea of the sounds that were produced. These include percussion instruments such as bells, clappers, tambourines, drums, and

An Ancient Egyptian Love Song

New wine it is, to hear your voice;
I live for hearing it.
To see you with each look,
Is better than eating and drinking.

the sacred sistrum, which is often associated with religious ceremonies. Wind instruments include flutes, clarinets, double oboes, and trumpets or bugles. And we have found stringed instruments, such as harps, lutes, and lyres.

Music and song accompanied many activities, including religious festivals, parties, and funerals. Rowers used percussion instruments to beat the time. From depictions of athletic dancers, it is quite likely that there was a great deal of lively rhythmic music as well as hymns and songs written in verse.

The ancient Egyptians played double flutes with two parallel pipes. Double oboes, with one pipe longer than the other in order to play deeper notes, were also popular. Harps were usually made of wood and had up to twelve strings made of animal gut. They could be played in a sitting, standing, or kneeling position. Lutes had a rectangular wooden sound box perforated with holes and a long neck like the fretboard on a modern guitar. They had up to four strings and could be played by plucking the strings or strumming them with the fingers or a plectrum.

These instruments were played in various combinations or with drums, tambourines, hand-clapping, and the sistrum. The sistrum (left) was a sort of rattle with a handle and a curved head that contained clappers made of wood, bone, or ivory. It kept the beat for the other musicians and was associated closely with Hathor, the goddess of music.

Music was not reserved for parties, festivals, and religious ceremonies but was very much a part of everyday life. The countryside must have echoed with the chanting and songs of farm laborers—but what did it sound like? This we will never know, but by looking at the position of the holes in flutes discovered in tombs, it seems likely that ancient Egyptian music was based on a minor pentatonic scale. This is a scale formed out of only five notes and would have sounded something like playing only the black keys on a piano.

The first doctors in ancient Egypt were priests

In the ancient world, Egypt was famous for its physicians. It was not uncommon for subject kings to ask pharaoh to send a doctor if one of their relatives became ill. Herodotus, the Greek historian, says of the medical practices of the Egyptians,

> *"The art of medicine is thus divided: each physician applies himself to one disease only and not more. Some for the eyes, others for the head, others for the teeth, others for the intestines, and other for internal disorders."*

Pharaoh might have a whole army of doctors, each looking after a different part of his body. From an inscription in the tomb of Doctor Iry, who lived around 2500 BC, we learn that he was known as the *"Keeper of the King's Rectum,"* but there was also a *"Keeper of the King's Left Eye"* and a *"Keeper of the King's Right Eye,"* among others.

Diodorus Siculus, another Greek historian, records that,

> *"The sick are all treated free of charge because doctors are paid by the state."*

This is probably the first recorded instance of state-sponsored universal health care.

Ancient Egyptian medicine was not based on science; rather, it was practiced by people who were believed to hold a "secret knowledge" and was mainly concerned with ridding patients of demons. The goddess Isis was associated with healing because of the powerful magic she was thought to have used to resurrect her husband Osiris. Thoth was not only the god of writing but also of medicine—it was Thoth who restored the Eye of Horus—and many ancient Egyptian physicians came from the temple of Thoth. In fact, the temples functioned as clinics of a sort. Holy water from a temple was greatly valued as a cure-all because it had been poured over a statue of a god and was thought to have healing properties.

There are many surviving papyrus scrolls which list remedies for wounds and ailments. Egyptian doctors used a combination of spells, rituals, and practical treatments; although dissection of the human body was a common practice in the mummification process, the Egyptians were ignorant of how the body's organs functioned. They did not realize, for example, that the brain had anything to do with thought, but believed that all thought emanated from the heart.

Although most remedies for illness were based on the use of magic, the treatment of trauma injuries, such as broken bones, was based on observation. The ancient doctors were skilled in treating these injuries. The Edwin Smith Surgical Papyrus, dating from 1700 BC, describes forty-eight cases, beginning with injuries to the head and continuing on through the body like a modern anatomy textbook. It includes the first accounts of surgical stitching and of various types of dressings, as well as the first descriptions of the external surface of the brain. There are discussions of injuries to the head, throat, neck, collarbone, arm, breastbone, ribs, shoulder, and spine. For example:

> "If thou examine a man having a gaping wound in his head penetrating to the bone, thou should lay thy hand upon it and palpate the wound. If his skull is uninjured, not having a perforation in it, thou should bind it with fresh meat on the first day. There after apply two strips of linen, and treat with grease, honey, and lint every day until he recovers."

The Ebers Papyrus has more than seven hundred magical formulas for illness and includes many magical incantations, but it also describes experimental practice and observation. There are remedies for intestinal parasites, eye and skin problems, dentistry, abscesses and tumors, bone-setting, and burns. A number of the remedies call for the use of toxic substances such as

Amulets were charms that protected the wearer from harm or imbued him with certain qualities.

THE EYE OF HORUS (left), or Udjat eye, represents the eye of the god Horus, which was torn from his head by the storm god Seth. It resembles a composite of the human eye and that of a falcon, and was used as an amulet against injury.

TYET (right) is sometimes called the knot or girdle of Isis. It was usually red and sometime made from red jasper, symbolizing the menstrual blood of Isis.

ANKH (left) – The hieroglyphic symbol of a sandal strap stands for "life." There are many surviving representations of the ankh, for example, Osiris rising from the coffin holds an Ankh in each hand. In fact, most of the gods are shown holding this symbol. Many of the great temple wall reliefs show gods bestowing eternal life on a king in the form of an Ankh.

THE SCARAB (right) – The Egyptians called the scarab beetle "Khepre" after the god of regeneration, new life, virility, and resurrection. He was sometimes shown with outstretched wings, but the most common forms were the little amulets worn as ornaments or buried with the dead. The reverse side of the scarab is often inscribed with names of kings. Scarabs were made and worn as late as 1,000 years after the death of the kings whose names they bear.

hemlock, aconite, lead, copper, and antimony, as well as the opiate found in the poppy.

The most common remedy for illness was a combination of medicines, amulets, and magic spells. Prescribing the appropriate spells along with medicine was considered essential for the recovery of the patient. In the margin of a 3,500-year-old papyrus, a doctor wrote, "This spell is excellent, successful many times."

An examination of preserved mummies has given us insight into some of the diseases suffered at the time, including arthritis,

(LEFT) THOTH, THE GOD OF WRITING AND MEDICINE. (RIGHT) A DRAWING FROM THE TOMB OF ANKHMAHOR (SIXTH DYNASTY) SHOWS BOYS BEING CIRCUMCISED.

LAND OF THE DEAD

TO DIE IN A FOREIGN LAND WAS A TERRIBLE FATE FOR AN EGYPTIAN.

THE EGYPTIANS RESPECTED THEIR ELDERS, WORSHIPPED THEIR AN-CESTORS, AND FELT A STRONG SENSE OF DUTY TOWARD THOSE WHO HAD PASSED FROM THIS LIFE. THEY REG-ULARLY VISITED THE TOMBS OF THEIR DEAD WITH FOOD AND OTHER OFFERINGS.

The Egyptians believed that death was a temporary interruption, rather than the end of life. They believed that the afterlife was an idealized version of life on earth, where they would enjoy all of life's good things without having to endure any of its suffering. To gain admittance to this paradise, they believed that they must live a good and honorable life by obeying their superiors, assisting and protecting the poor, and showing proper respect for the gods. The other essential factor for entry into the afterlife was that body be preserved through mummification, so that the aspect of the spirit called the "Ka" could return to it and be sustained.

The Egyptian's concept of soul or spirit was complex. They believed that, in addition to the physical body, a human being consisted of five crucial elements:

THE KA *(left) was represented by the hieroglyph of uplifted arms.*

This is the creative life force, a vital and defining element of life. It is translated as either "double" or "sustenance." The Ka comes into existence at birth and is thought to be the protecting, divine spirit. When someone dies, the Ka survives and might reside in a picture or statue of the person. Offerings of food are given to the dead person's Ka in the form of real or pictorial representations of food and drink. The Egyptians did not suppose that food was really eaten by the Ka, but rather that the life force within the food was absorbed. There was a special "offering formula" that activated the power within the images.

THE BA *(left) was represented by the bird form.*

The Ba expresses the mobility of the soul after death, the personality or nonphysical elements that make a person unique. The Ba has to journey from the tomb to rejoin with the Ka, enabling the trans-formation into the Akh.

THE AKH *(left) was represented as a mummy or crested Ibis.*

This is the form in which the dead inhabit the underworld, the successful reunion of the Ka and Ba. Once the Akh has been created, it is immortal. The Akh can assume any form it desires and revisit the earth as a ghost to the living.

THE SHWT OR SWT *meaning "shadow" or "shade" – represented as a feather, palm fan (left) or a human silhouette.*

The Shadow protects the person from harm. It is portrayed in funeral texts as an entity of great power, capable of moving at great speed. Although it was a seperate entity it always was thought to stay near the Ba.

THE NAME *(left) was regarded as a living part of the person.*

The Name must be given at birth. Without a name an individual cannot come into existence in any meaningful way. In one version of the creation myth, the god Ptah creates everything in the universe by speaking its name.

The Mummification Process

The word "mummy" comes from the Arabic *mummiya*, meaning bitumen or coal.

Egyptian embalmers were highly skilled, so skilled that people who died 4,000 years ago and mummified are still in good enough condition to recognize such physical features as skin, hair, and even scars and tattoos. Every Egyptian, except the most abject criminal, was entitled to be embalmed and receive a decent burial. For the kings and nobles who could afford the full treatment, it was an elaborate process that took seventy days to complete.

When someone died, the body was taken to the embalmers by the relatives, who then chose the method and quality of mummification. The best and most expensive methods were used on the wealthy, but there were cheaper alternatives for the poor. In the most expensive method, the body was washed and the brain removed by inserting a hook through the nostrils, scooping it out bit by bit. An incision was made in the body's left side, and the liver, lungs, stomach, and intestines were removed. These organs were preserved in a naturally occurring salt called "natron" and placed in canopic jars. Then the body cavity was cleaned with palm wine.

Next, the body was covered with natron and left for forty days. This absorbed all the fluids, leaving the flesh dry. The body was then washed and rubbed with oil and fragrant spices. The inside was stuffed with resin

(LEFT) AN ANTHRO-
POID COFFIN. THE
TERM COMES FROM
THE GREEK FOR
"HUMAN LIKE-
NESS."

Canopic Jars

Except the heart, which was needed by the deceased in the Hall of Judgment, the ancient Egyptian embalmers removed all of the internal organs from the body. These were placed into four vases called Canopic Jars. The lids formed the shape of the Four Sons of Horus.

The liver was associated with Imset, who was depicted with a human head.

The lungs were associated with Hapi, who was shown with a baboon's head.

The stomach was associated with Duamutef, who appeared with the head of a jackal.

The intestines and viscera of the lower body were associated with the falcon-headed Kebechsenef.

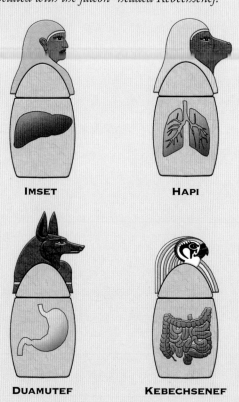

IMSET

HAPI

DUAMUTEF

KEBECHSENEF

THE HEART

and natron before being wrapped in linen. The face was painted to make it look lifelike and the hair neatly arranged.

The chief embalmer, dressed as Anubis (god of embalming), would bless the mummy. The priests then said prayers to help the dead person on his way through to the next world. Finally, the body was wrapped in linen bandages previously soaked in resin. First the fingers and toes were wrapped, followed by the legs and arms. Magical amulets were placed within the mummy's bandages as symbols of power, protection, and rebirth. The body was then returned to the relatives who placed it in a wooden coffin.

Natron *is a naturally occurring white, crystalline mineral salt that absorbs water from its surroundings. In ancient Egypt, natron was mined from dry lake beds and used in the mummification process to extract water from the body.*

It was also added to castor oil to produce a smokeless fuel for the lamps used by artisans painting artworks inside tombs.

THE HEAD AND LIMBS WERE WRAPPED FIRST.

AMULETS WERE PLACED IN THE LAYERS OF LINEN WRAPPED AROUND THE BODY.

THE ARMS AND LEGS WERE TIED TOGETHER AND, FOR THOSE WHO COULD AFFORD IT, A FUNERARY PAPYRUS SUCH AS *THE BOOK OF THE DEAD* **WAS INCLUDED.**

THEN THE WHOLE BODY WAS WRAPPED IN LINEN AND COVERED IN A SHROUD DECORATED WITH AN INK DRAWING OF OSIRIS, THE GOD OF THE DEAD.

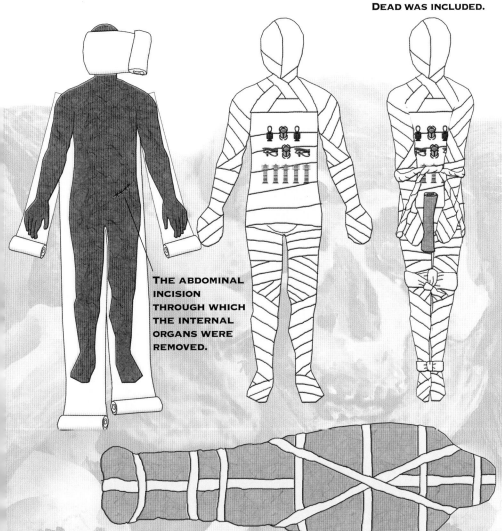

THE ABDOMINAL INCISION THROUGH WHICH THE INTERNAL ORGANS WERE REMOVED.

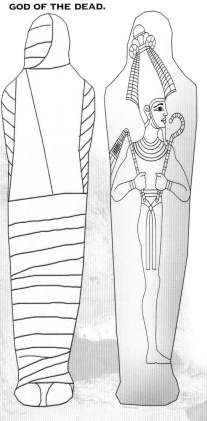

FINALLY, THE MUMMY WAS FINISHED WITH AN OUTER WRAPPING OF DYED LINEN AND RETURNED TO THE FAMILY OF THE DECEASED.

The preparation of the tomb would have been carried out long before the person's death, as he would need many things in the afterlife, including furniture and everyday objects. Pictures of daily life were painted on the walls of the tomb. Lists, models of food, and other useful items were placed in the tomb. It was believed that, through a magical process, these would become real when needed in the afterlife.

People were buried on the western side of the river, where the sun sets. On the day of the funeral the relatives crossed the river. The coffin was drawn along on a sledge, the mourners and guests led by a priest. Servants followed, carrying the objects and food to be used in the next world. Before the deceased was placed in the tomb, the priest performed the ceremony of "opening the mouth" to bring the dead person's senses to life again. This consisted of touching various parts of the mummy with a ceremonial instrument. When the instrument touched the mouth, the dead person would be able to speak and eat, and so on.

Finally, the coffin was placed in the tomb along with all of the accoutrements, and the door was sealed. Then the guests held a feast in honor the dead person.

The Funeral

A LONG PROCESSION OF FAMILY MEMBERS AND SERVANTS ACCOMPANIED THE COFFIN TO THE TOMB. INCENSE WAS BURNED TO PURIFY THE AIR AND MAGICAL SPELLS AND PRAYERS WERE RECITED BY A PRIEST. ANOTHER PRIEST, WEARING A JACKAL'S MASK, HELD THE MUMMY UPRIGHT AND RELATIVES EXPRESSED THEIR GRIEF. SOMETIMES PROFESSIONAL MOURNERS WERE EMPLOYED TO WAIL LAMENTATIONS.

THE MOST IMPORTANT PART OF THE FUNERAL WAS THE "OPENING OF THE MOUTH CEREMONY," IN WHICH THE PRIEST RAISED THE ADZE AND OTHER IMPLEMENTS TO THE MUMMY'S LIPS AND SYMBOLICALLY REANIMATED THE BODY SO HE OR SHE COULD BREATHE, SEE, HEAR, AND EAT THE FOOD OFFERINGS MEANT TO SUSTAIN THE KA. (THE FOOD AND DRINK OFFERINGS WERE ONLY A SYMBOL OF THE LIFE-GIVING ENERGY OF FOOD. THEY WERE LATER CONSUMED BY THE PRIESTS AND THE FAMILY OF THE DECEASED.)

A FUNERARY STELA WAS ERECTED OUTSIDE THE TOMB CHAPEL. THIS SLAB OF STONE WAS INSCRIBED WITH TEXT AND IMAGES RECORDING THE NAME OF THE DECEASED AND LISTING THE SUPPLIES NECESSARY FOR ETERNAL LIFE.

Coffins and Sarcophagi

The coffin was the rectangular or anthropoid (human-shaped) container that held the mummified body. The sarcophagus was the stone outer container that held the coffin or coffins.

Coffins were often decorated in a variety of styles on both the inside and outside. Some have been found with images of food offerings on the inside to sustain the deceased. The interior of many Middle Kingdom coffins were decorated with extracts of the Pyramid Texts known as the Coffin Texts.

The exteriors of many coffins were painted with eyes on the east-facing side (see below). It was believed that the dead person could look out at the world through these eyes and see the rising sun.

Anthropoid coffins (left) first appeared during the twelfth dynasty (1985-1795 BC) and were associated with Osiris. They were often decorated with images of Osiris, rebirth, and the judgment of the dead.

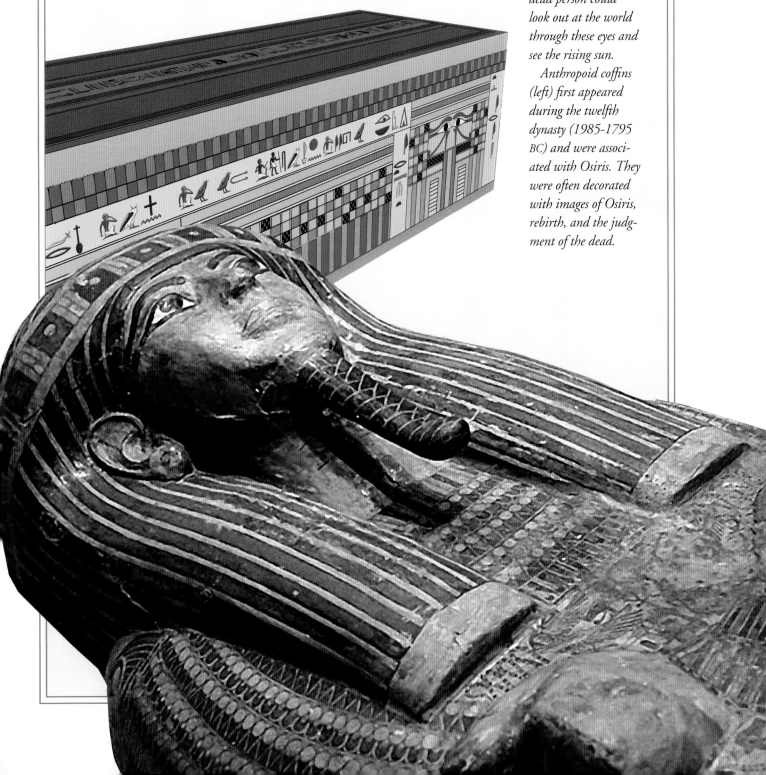

Each day they would take offerings of food and drink to the tomb so that the dead person's Ka might survive.

Deir el Medina is the site of an ancient village on the west side of the river at Luxor. It was the permanent settlement of the craftsman and their families who made the tombs in the Valley of the Kings. The inhabitants of Deir el-Medina also built their own tombs fifty-three of which still survive.

The tombs followed a standardized design with an entrance through a small pylon into an open courtyard and a chapel topped by a small pyramid. The chapel was for the worship of the deceased relative. The actual burial chambers were cut into the rock below the ground and contained the remains of several family members.

(ABOVE) SMALL PYRAMID CHAPEL AT DEIR EL-MEDINA. (BELOW) A RECONSTRUCTION OF A ROCK-CUT TOMB AT DEIR EL MEDINA FROM AROUND 1250 BC.

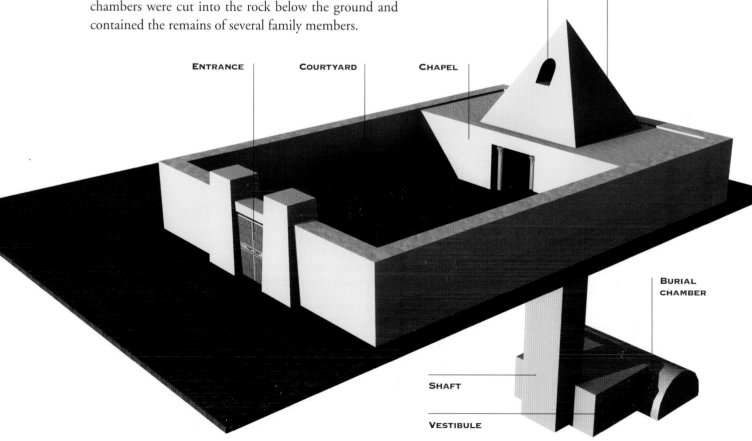

STELE NICHE

MUDBRICK PYRAMID

ENTRANCE   COURTYARD   CHAPEL

BURIAL CHAMBER

SHAFT

VESTIBULE

False Door

A false door or "Ka Door" was believed to be a magical link between the land of the living and the land of the dead through which the deceased could pass in order to partake of the food offerings left by relatives.

The earliest examples of Ka Doors were discovered in Old Kingdom tombs (2686-2181 BC). They were usually carved from one monolithic piece of limestone but were sometimes made of wood or simply painted on a wall.

They were not copies of real doors, but they did feature door elements such as door jambs and a rounded part called a drum that might represent a rolled-up woven curtain. The surface was often inscribed with the name and titles of the deceased, together with his or her image, prayers, and offering formulas.

(LEFT) A FALSE DOOR FROM THE TOMB OF NI-KAURE (OLD KINGDOM, FIFTH DYNASTY). THIS DOOR BELONGS TO NIKAURE'S WIFE, IHAT, A PRIESTESS OF HATHOR. NIKAURE AND IHAT ARE SHOWN SITTING AT AN OFFERING TABLE AND ON EACH SIDE ARE IMAGES OF THEIR SON AND DAUGHTER WITH OFFERINGS OF BIRDS.

Shabtis *were small human figurines that magically became animate in the afterlife. It was believed that a shabti would carry out any unpleasant task associated with hard physical work in the Fields of Yalu, so most shabtis were fashioned as laborers, wrapped like mummies and depicted with a pick, a hoe, and a basket. Over four hundred shabtis might be placed in a single tomb—one for each day of the year plus an overseer for every ten workers.*

They were made by the thousands, often hastily and poorly out of wood, clay, wax, or stone. But there are some fine faience shabtis from the Twenty-Sixth to Thirtieth Dynasties.

The ancient Egyptian's beliefs and duties towards their dead relatives were very different from our own. The connection with a dead relative was never broken because their spirit—the joined Ka and Ba in the form of the Akh—could watch over their family and influence their lives. This continued interaction was a part of the daily routine for the living because each day they would take offerings of foods and drink to the tomb so that the dead person's Ka might survive. But pictorial representations of food and drink, which could be magically activated, were also painted on the walls of a tomb as a form of insurance against neglect.

The tomb walls were also painted with representations of an idealized afterlife where there was no pain or illness and the land was abundant with plants and animals. This place was known as the "Elysian Fields" or "Fields of Yalu." We would call it "Paradise," but to get there the dead person had to pass through the "Duat" (Underworld) and be judged worthy by the gods.

Now we leave the land of the living and travel with the dead to the end of their journey. This is the moment of judgment when the heart is weighed against a feather.

Knowledge of the next world—the rules of behavior, magic formulas, and prayers—were very important. Meticulous preparations were made in life for the great journey. Special guide-

(BELOW) JUDGMENT OF THE DEAD. A COPY FROM *HUNEFER'S BOOK OF THE DEAD*, NINETEENTH DYNASTY, AROUND 1275 BC. THE TOP ROW OF HIEROGLYPHIC TEXT LISTS THE NAMES OF THE GODS. THE SECOND ROW INCLUDES A PRAYER BY HUNEFER THAT DESCRIBES HIS HEART BEING WEIGHED, AND AN ANNOUNCEMENT OF HIS INNOCENCE BY THOTH AND HORUS, WHO TELL OSIRIS THAT THE BALANCE REMAINED UNMOVED.

THE DECEASED HUNEFER KNEELS IN PRAYER BEFORE THE GODS.

THE SCALES, WITH THE HEAD OF MAAT, THE GODDESS OF TRUTH. HUNEFER'S HEART IS BALANCED AGAINST THE FEATHER OF TRUTH.

ANUBIS LEADS HUNEFER INTO THE JUDGMENT HALL OF OSIRIS.

ANUBIS CHECKS THE TONGUE OF THE BALANCE.

AMMUT, DEVOURER OF THE WICKED SOULS WHO FAIL THE TEST OF TRUTH.

books and maps of the after-world were designed to help the traveler overcome the trials awaiting him. The earliest of these are known as the "Pyramid Texts," and they were carved on the walls of the burial chamber in the pyramid of King Unas. Later texts included the "Coffin Texts," the "Book of the Dead," and the "Book of Amduat."

The Journey of the Dead

The heart is weighed against a feather and the wicked souls are eaten by a demon.

The Egyptians placed copies of the Book of the Dead with their dead relatives to help them successfully travel through the Underworld which was filled will all sort of terrifying dangers. The ordinary Egyptian could buy a standardized copy with blank spaces where they could insert their name. But the rich would commission a custom-made copy with their favorite chapters beautifully illustrated.

After death, it was believed that the Ka becomes separated from the body and the Ba is liberated. The kind and merciful goddess Isis receives the Ba and in turn

OSIRIS IS SEATED IN HIS SHRINE BY THE STREAM OF THE OTHER WORLD. A LILY GROWS FROM ITS SACRED WATERS, SUPPORTING THE FOUR CHILDREN OF HORUS. ABOVE OSIRIS IS THE EYE OF HORUS AND BEHIND HIM STAND THE GODDESSES ISIS AND NEPHTHYS.

THOTH, THE SCRIBE OF THE GODS, RECORDS THE RESULT OF THE WEIGHING.

HUNEFER IS INTRODUCED TO OSIRIS BY HORUS.

entrusts it to the wise god Anubis, who then comforts and guides it until the moment of judgment.

Anubis and the spirits of the dead make their way west from the city of Abydos toward one of the mountains that supports the sky. On the other side of the mountain they board Khephre's barge and sail down into the "Gallery of the Night," where the river of the Underworld flows. Anubis guides the boat through the dark caverns and churning waters until the barge enters the heart of the Underworld. Here, the waters swarm with the evil enemies of Osiris. This is a frightening place filled with the dreadful cries and screams of wandering lost souls. Monstrous creatures attempt to grasp the travelers and drag them down into the cold waters, but Anubis comforts and protects the Ba and together they continue their journey.

The Book of the Dead

THE EGYPTIANS KNEW IT AS THE THE BOOK OF COMING FORTH BY DAY. IT CONTAINED ALMOST TWO HUNDRED MAGIC SPELLS USED TO PROTECT THE DECEASED FROM THE MONSTERS OF THE UNDERWORLD. ONE OF THE MOST IMPORTANT SPELLS WAS THE ONE THAT PROTECTED THE DECEASED FROM HIS OWN HEART.

"My heart, which I had from my mother, do not stand up as a witness against me, do not oppose me in the tribunal, do not be hostile to me in the presence of the Keeper of the Balance, do not make my name stink to the Entourage who make men, and do not tell lies about me in the presence of the god."

Magic Spells from the Book of the Dead

The Galley of the Night

THE GALLEY OF THE NIGHT WAS A DANGEROUS PLACE FILLED WITH FIRE-SPITTING REPTILES, RAVENOUS SERPENTS, HEADLESS HUMANS, AND LOST SOULS. ALL OF THESE GROTESQUES WOULD TRY TO ENSNARE THE TRAVELER, BUT TERRIFIED TRAVELERS WHO OWNED A COPY OF THE BOOK OF THE DEAD COULD PROTECT THEMSELVES WITH ITS MAGIC SPELLS. THE BOOK ALSO CONTAINED THE NAMES OF THESE MALEVOLENT CREATURES—AND KNOWING THEIR NAMES GAVE THE USER THE POWER TO DEFEAT THEM.

BEFORE THE TRAVELER COULD EXIT THE GALLERY OF THE NIGHT, THE GREAT SERPENT, AND ENEMY OF OSIRIS, APEPI (APOPHIS), HAD TO BE DEFEATED.

Spell for passing the Evil Serpent Apepi

"You waxen one who takes by robbery and lives on the lifeless.

I will not be lifeless for you;

I will not be weak for you. Your poison shall not enter into my members, for my members are the members of Atum. If I'm not weak your suffering shall not enter my members.

I am Atum at the head of the Abyss, my protection is from the gods, the lords of eternity. My name is secret and more holy than the gods of Chaos."

Spell for Driving Off a Snake

O Rerek snake, take yourself off for Geb protects me.

Get up for you have eaten a mouse which Ra detests and you have chewed the bones of a putrid cat.

Spell for Driving Off a Crocodile

Get back, retreat, get back you dangerous one.

Do not come against me, do not live by my magic;

May I not have to tell this name of yours to the Great God who sent you;

"Messenger" is the name of one and "Bedty" is the name of the other.

The Realm of Duat

In due course, they arrive in the realm of Duat, where they must go through seven gates and then ten pylons to enter the great Hall of Osiris. Three divinities, the magician god, the guardian god, and the questioner god, guard each gate. The dead person must know the correct magical words as well as the secret name of each guardian in order to pass. Once through the seven gates, they pass through the ten pylons where each guardian reveals his secret name.

THE HIEROGLYPH FOR DUAT IS A STAR WITHIN A CIRCLE.

The Book of Amduat

THAT WHICH IS IN THE UNDERWORLD, IS ALSO CALLED THE BOOK OF THE SECRET CHAMBERS." IT DESCRIBES THE SUN GOD RA'S NIGHTLY JOURNEY FROM WEST TO EAST, THROUGH THE TWELVE REGIONS OF THE UNDERWORLD. EACH REGION CORRESPONDS TO ONE OF THE TWELVE HOURS OF THE NIGHT. THE EGYPTIANS BELIEVED IT WAS A REAL PLACE OF DARK WATERWAYS AND CAVERNS OF TORMENTED SOULS, DIVIDED BY GATES GUARDED BY GATEKEEPERS. EACH NIGHT RA DEFEATED THE EVIL AGENTS OF CHAOS AND FOR A BRIEF HOUR REVIVED THE LOST SOULS WHO HAD FAILED TO PASS THROUGH THE GALLERY OF THE NIGHT AND THE OTHER TESTS BEFORE THE HALL OF TRUTH.

IN ONE MYTHOLOGICAL STORY, THE SKY GODDESS NUT SWALLOWS THE SETTING SUN, WHICH PASSES THROUGH HER BODY DURING THE NIGHT TO BE REBORN EACH DAY AS THE RISING SUN. THIS CYCLE OF DEATH AND RESURRECTION WAS CENTRAL TO THE EGYPTIANS' BELIEFS.

The Seven Gates

IF THE TRAVELERS SURVIVED THE GALLERY OF THE NIGHT
THEY ENTERED THE WORLD OF THE DUAT AND HAD TO PASS
THROUGH THE SEVEN GATES. EACH GATE HAD ITS OWN MAGIC
WORDS FOR GAINING ENTRY. THE BOOK OF THE DEAD CON-
TAINS THE CORRECT FORMULAS.

HERE IS AN EXTRACT FOR THE FIRST GATE.

*If these words be recited by the spirit when he comes to the
Seven Gates he shall neither be turned back nor repulsed
before Osiris,*

The First Gate.

The name of the Doorkeeper is Sekhet-her-asht-aru.

The name of the Watcher is Smetti.

The name of the Herald is Hakheru.

*The deceased, whose word is truth, shall say when he cometh
unto the First Gate: "I am the mighty one who creates his
own light. I have come to you, O Osiris, and am purified
from that which would defile you, I adore you. Lead on."*

The Ten Pylons

AFTER THE SEVEN GATES, THE TRAVELERS WERE CONFRONT-
ED WITH YET ANOTHER OBSTACLE, THIS TIME TEN PYLONS,
AND ONCE AGAIN THE BOOK OF THE DEAD SUPPLIED THE
CORRECT FORMULAS TO GAIN ENTRY.

HERE IS AN EXTRACT:

*The following shall be said when one comes to the First
Pylon. "Lady of tremblings, high-walled, the sovereign
lady, the lady of destruction, who says the words which
drive back the destroyers, who delivers him that comes
from destruction. The name of her Doorkeeper is Neruit."*

The Elysian Fields

After the last pylon, the soul enters the "Grand Hall of Justice." All around sit the gods of the universe and at the center are the four high judges: Shu, god of the air, Tefnut, goddess of moisture, Geb, god of the earth, and Nut, goddess of the sky. The god of writing and knowledge, Thoth, is also there, bearing the scales for weighing the heart. Meanwhile, the monster Ammut, who is part crocodile, part lion, and part hippopotamus, waits to devour the souls that fail judgment. In the center of this gathering, on his throne, sits the god king Osiris.

Now comes the moment of truth. Anubis places the dead person's heart on one plate of the scales. On the counterweight is the feather of Ma'at, goddess of truth. The god Thoth takes notes. If the individual has committed evil acts against others during his life, the weight of his guilty conscience makes his heart heavier than the feather, and Ammut eats his soul, dragging it down into the gloom of Sokaris. However, if the person was good during his life, his conscience is light and his heart balances exactly with the feather. His entrance to the Elysian Fields is granted.

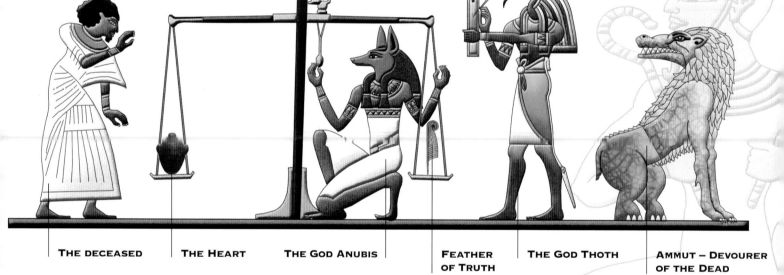

THE DECEASED | **THE HEART** | **THE GOD ANUBIS** | **FEATHER OF TRUTH** | **THE GOD THOTH** | **AMMUT – DEVOURER OF THE DEAD**

THERE ARE MANY ANCIENT TEXTS THAT GIVE ADVICE ON LIVING A GOOD AND HONORABLE LIFE.

"If you are great after having been small, if you are rich after having been poor, do not be miserly with your wealth. Because it has fallen on you as a gift from God.

"If then you cultivate your fields and they give you fruit, not only fill your own mouth, but remember your neighbor. Because abundance is given to you by God.

"Do not cause terror among men because God will give you battle in equal measure, whosoever pretends to conquer life by violence, God will take the bread out of his mouth, he will take away his riches, and he will reduce him to impotence. Therefore, do not cause terror among men; give them a life of peace and with peace you will have what you would obtain with war, for this is the will of God."

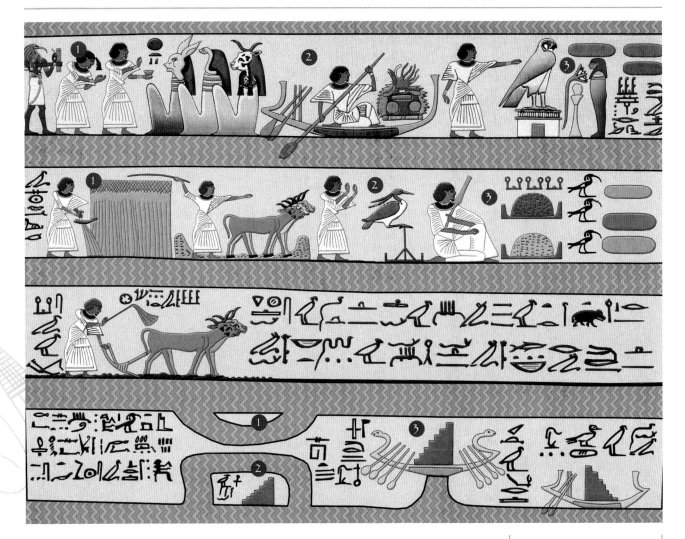

TOP ROW *1. The god Thoth. Ani makes an offering to "the company of the gods," a hare-headed god, a snake-headed god, and a bull-headed god. 2. He paddles his boat across the Lake of Offerings and then speaks to the Western Falcon, shown on a pedestal. 3. A table of offerings and a god in the form of a mummy. The text says, "Being at peace in the Field, and having air for the nostrils."*

SECOND ROW *1. Ani is shown reaping wheat, with the words "Osiris reaps." Then he is depicted driving the oxen as they tread the wheat. 2. Ani worships a Bennu bird (the Heron of Plenty), which represents the soul of the Sun-God Ra. 3. Ani seated, holding the kherp scepter in front of a heap of barley and wheat. The hieroglyphics mean "food of the spirits."*

THIRD ROW *The deceased had to toil in the Field of Rushes although he might have Shabtis do this for him. In this scene, Ani is using oxen to plough a field called Sekhet-aanre. The two lines of hieroglyphics say "Chapter of the River-horse. The river is one thousand cubits long, its width cannot be told. It contains neither fish nor serpents nor worms of any kind whatsoever."*

FOURTH ROW *1. A stream flows around a small island called the birthplace of the "god of the city." 2. An island with a flight of steps is called the "place of the spirits." The text to the left says "The seat of the shining ones. (the abode of the sacred dead), their length is seven cubits. 3. "The sacred dead reap the wheat which is three cubits."*

The eight-oared boat of Wennefer (another name for the god Osiris) is moored in a canal. It is shown with the heads of snakes. The second boat is called Tohefau.

The Valley of the Kings
The "Great and Majestic Necropolis of the Million Years of Pharaoh"

This is how the ancient Egyptians referred to the Valley of the Kings, located behind the hills, on the West Bank of the Nile at Luxor. They also called it the "Great Field." It remains the most famous cemetery in the world, and although many of its treasures were plundered in ancient times, it remains an extraordinary monument.

In all, sixty-three tombs have been discovered in the valley. They are so old that, even before Christ was born, forty of them were regarded as interesting historical monuments by early Greek and Roman tourists.

After the tomb robberies of the Old and Middle Kingdoms, the New Kingdom pharaohs devised a different strategy for protecting their final resting place. They selected a remote valley in the hills of western Thebes and forbade

---

(BELOW) THE VALLEY OF THE KINGS WAS THE BURIAL PLACE FOR MOST OF EGYPT'S NEW KINGDOM RULERS. IT IS SURROUNDED BY SHEER CLIFFS AND WOULD HAVE BEEN EASY TO GUARD. IT IS THOUGHT THAT THE SITE WAS CHOSEN BECAUSE THE MOUNTAIN THAT OVER-LOOKS IT RESEMBLES A PYRAMID.

Sixty-three tombs have been discovered in the valley. They are so old that forty of them were regarded as interesting historical monuments by early Greek and Roman tourists.

KV 63

In February 2006, a new tomb was discovered in the Valley of the Kings. An American team of Egyptologists from the University of Memphis found it near the tomb of Tutankhamun. The tomb appears to be from the late eighteenth dynasty and so far the excavation has uncovered a single chamber with five or six coffins and about twenty large funerary jars.

The coffins appear to have been coated in black resin, which is quite unusual, and Egyptologists are not sure if this was an attempt to preserve them or hide their inscriptions.

To find out about the latest developments on this discovery go to the Imagining Egypt Resources Web page at **WWW.DISCOVERINGEGYPT.COM**.

KV 34 The Tomb of Thutmose III

Thutmose III's tomb didn't escape the robbers despite its inaccessibility. But when it was discovered in 1898, there were still some items of funerary furniture left. The entrance is through a steep corridor ending in a shaft that goes nowhere. Nowadays, a bridge over the shaft leads into a two-pillared vestibule.

The walls in this early Valley of the Kings tomb were not carved but simply painted in a lively, no-nonsense cartoon style. The brushstrokes show the confidence of a master draftsman. The scene in this first room depicts the 741 divinities that generate the sun each day.

A few steps lead from the vestibule into the oval burial chamber, which has two pillars and four annexes. The only object it contains is a large sarcophagus made from red quartzite, carved with the image of the goddess Nut. The chamber itself is in the shape of a cartouche, the hieroglyphic symbol that contains the name of a king, and the walls are painted with the complete text of "The Book of Amduat" (This which there is in the Underworld). The pillars feature passages from "The Litanies of Ra."

Thutmose III's mummy does survive, having been found in a hiding place at Deir el Bahri in 1871.

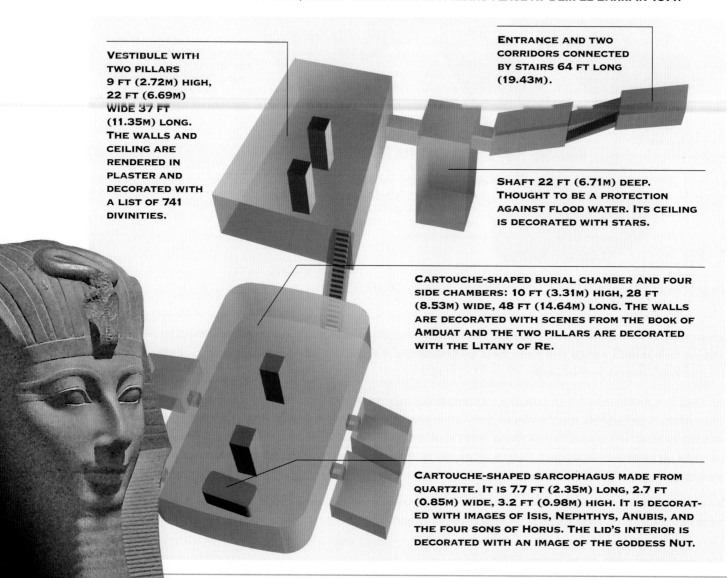

Vestibule with two pillars 9 ft (2.72m) high, 22 ft (6.69m) wide 37 ft (11.35m) long. The walls and ceiling are rendered in plaster and decorated with a list of 741 divinities.

Entrance and two corridors connected by stairs 64 ft long (19.43m).

Shaft 22 ft (6.71m) deep. Thought to be a protection against flood water. Its ceiling is decorated with stars.

Cartouche-shaped burial chamber and four side chambers: 10 ft (3.31m) high, 28 ft (8.53m) wide, 48 ft (14.64m) long. The walls are decorated with scenes from the Book of Amduat and the two pillars are decorated with the Litany of Re.

Cartouche-shaped sarcophagus made from quartzite. It is 7.7 ft (2.35m) long, 2.7 ft (0.85m) wide, 3.2 ft (0.98m) high. It is decorated with images of Isis, Nephthys, Anubis, and the four sons of Horus. The lid's interior is decorated with an image of the goddess Nut.

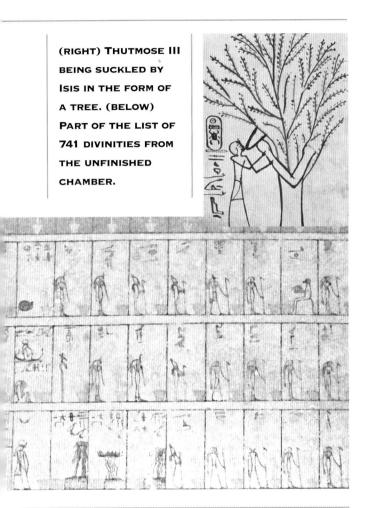

(ABOVE) PART OF THE SEVENTH HOUR OF THE THE BOOK AMDUAT. THE BARQUE OF THE SUN GOD RA APPROACHES THE SERPENT APEPI (APOPHIS).

had time to make fine tombs with many improvements to the original plans.

Before serious work could begin on any building project, the ritual of laying the foundation deposit was performed. This rite consisted of digging a hole into the foundation and filling it with objects such as tools, cups, jewelry, and food. After that, the stonecutters got to work quarrying a tunnel deep into the rock using copper and bronze chisels, wooden mallets, stone pounders, and baskets for removing rubble. The limestone was soft and easily removed, but it harbored large and extremely hard flint nodules that sometimes caused delays. In Merenptah's tomb is a boulder of hard rock left protruding from the wall of the first pillared hall.

As the work proceeded, far from the light of day, oil lamps were needed to illuminate the work area. The walls and ceilings had to be smoothed and plastered so that the scribes and artists could cover them with paintings and bas-reliefs depicting the dead king in the presence of the gods. These remarkable paintings were not intended as works of art. Rather, the surfaces of the tomb walls were covered with what were considered magical diagrams, precise instructions and maps of the underworld for the benefit of the dead king. The conventions of Egyptian visual representation that arose from these tomb paintings were founded on simplicity and ease of recognition.

The illustrations are accompanied by magical texts, usually extracts from various funerary texts such as *The Book of the Dead*, *The Book of Gates*, or *The Book of Amduat*.

Litany of Ra

"The Litany of Ra" (below) is in two parts. It acclaims the sun god in his seventy-five forms and praises the king's union with the sun. The work originated during Eighteenth Dynasty and first appeared on the pillars of the burial chamber of Thutmose III.

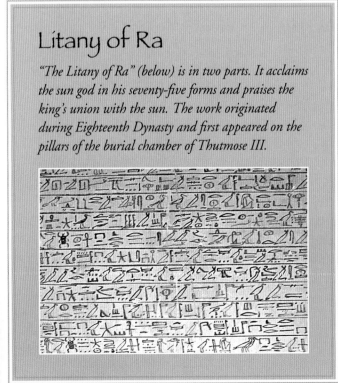

KV 9 The Tomb of Rameses VI

RAMESES VI'S TOMB IS FROM A LATER PERIOD AND EXEMPLIFIES A DIFFERENT ARTISTIC STYLE. IT WAS KNOWN AND VISITED IN THE TIME OF THE GREEKS AND ROMANS, WHO LEFT GRAFFITI ON ITS WALLS.

THE TOMB WAS ORIGINALLY MADE FOR RAMESES V, THE BROTHER OF RAMSES VI, WHO RULED FOR ONLY FOUR YEARS. THE HIGH-QUALITY PAINTED BAS-RELIEF WALLS DEMONSTRATE A SOPHISTICATED STYLE. THE SCENES ARE AN INTRICATE DEPICTION OF THE SUN ON ITS DAILY JOURNEY THROUGH THE UNDERWORLD.

THE FIRST THREE CORRIDORS ARE DECORATED WITH TEXTS FROM *THE BOOK OF GATES* AND *THE BOOK OF CAVERNS*, WHICH DESCRIBE THE GEOGRAPHY OF THE UNDERWORLD. THE FOURTH AND FIFTH CORRIDORS ARE DECORATED WITH EXTRACTS FROM *THE BOOK OF AMDUAT*. THE VESTIBULE BEFORE THE BURIAL CHAMBER HAS EPISODES FROM *THE BOOK OF THE DEAD.*

THE BURIAL CHAMBER ITSELF CONTAINS A BROKEN SARCOPHAGUS. THE WALLS ARE DECORATED WITH SCENES FROM *THE BOOK OF THE EARTH*, WHILE THE CEILING ILLUSTRATES *THE BOOK OF THE DAY* AND *THE BOOK OF THE NIGHT* WITH STARS, ASTRONOMICAL FIGURES, AND A DOUBLE IMAGE OF THE SKY GODDESS, NUT, SHOWN STRETCHING ACROSS THE FIRMAMENT, SWALLOWING THE SUN IN THE EVENING, AND GIVING BIRTH TO IT IN THEN MORNING.

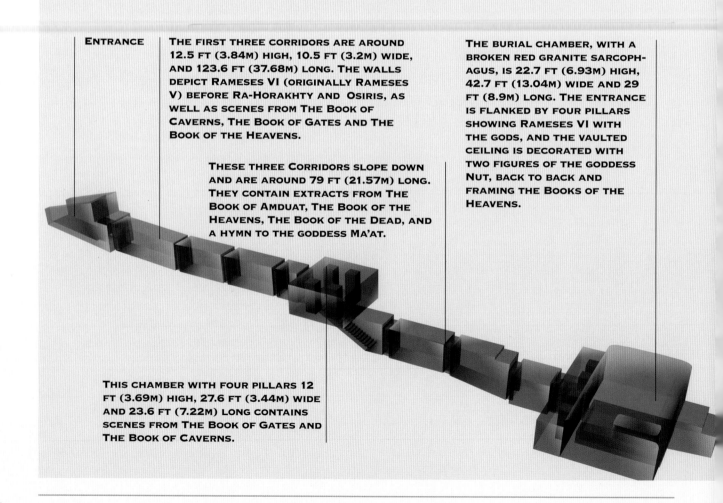

ENTRANCE

THE FIRST THREE CORRIDORS ARE AROUND 12.5 FT (3.84M) HIGH, 10.5 FT (3.2M) WIDE, AND 123.6 FT (37.68M) LONG. THE WALLS DEPICT RAMESES VI (ORIGINALLY RAMESES V) BEFORE RA-HORAKHTY AND OSIRIS, AS WELL AS SCENES FROM THE BOOK OF CAVERNS, THE BOOK OF GATES AND THE BOOK OF THE HEAVENS.

THESE THREE CORRIDORS SLOPE DOWN AND ARE AROUND 79 FT (21.57M) LONG. THEY CONTAIN EXTRACTS FROM THE BOOK OF AMDUAT, THE BOOK OF THE HEAVENS, THE BOOK OF THE DEAD, AND A HYMN TO THE GODDESS MA'AT.

THE BURIAL CHAMBER, WITH A BROKEN RED GRANITE SARCOPHAGUS, IS 22.7 FT (6.93M) HIGH, 42.7 FT (13.04M) WIDE AND 29 FT (8.9M) LONG. THE ENTRANCE IS FLANKED BY FOUR PILLARS SHOWING RAMESES VI WITH THE GODS, AND THE VAULTED CEILING IS DECORATED WITH TWO FIGURES OF THE GODDESS NUT, BACK TO BACK AND FRAMING THE BOOKS OF THE HEAVENS.

THIS CHAMBER WITH FOUR PILLARS 12 FT (3.69M) HIGH, 27.6 FT (3.44M) WIDE AND 23.6 FT (7.22M) LONG CONTAINS SCENES FROM THE BOOK OF GATES AND THE BOOK OF CAVERNS.

The quality of the work is astonishing even today; the tombs hold some of the greatest and best preserved examples of art by great but anonymous artists of the time. Among the finest is the tomb of Seti I. Unfortunately for today's tourists, Seti's tomb is often closed to the public because of the damage caused by the breath of thousands of visitors, which raises the moisture level and damages the delicate 3,500-year-old plaster and paintwork.

The ancient Egyptians believed that they could take their material wealth with them into the next life, and the walls of their tombs were often used as a written biography of their worldly achievements and their expectations for the afterlife.

Because of these beliefs, they left us a wealth of material evidence and as a result we know more about the lives of individual ancient Egyptians than of the people from any other ancient civilization. Thanks to their obsessive, lively, and sophisticated documentation, we have the privilege of knowing these people and resurrecting them in our mind's eye. In this sense at least, the ancient Egyptians succeeded in their efforts to attain immortality.

THE BOOK OF CAVERNS *describes a vision of the underworld as a series of caverns or pits over which Ra sails in his solar boat. Its central theme concerns the rewards and punishments of the dead in the afterlife and describes the destruction of the enemies of Ra. A complete version is found in the tomb of Rameses VI.*

THE BOOK OF THE EARTH *dates from the Twentieth Dynasty. Its four parts narrate the sun's nightly journey through the underworld.*

THE BOOK OF GATES *is about the gates of the underworld as barriers and evil the serpent Apepi (Apophis), justice and time. The most complete texts are found in the tomb of Rameses VI and on the sarcophagus of Seti I.*

THE BOOK OF THE HEAVENS *is also known as The Book of the Day, The Book of the Night, and The Book of the Divine Cow. It is a collection of texts that date from the late New Kingdom and describes the sun's passage through the sky.*

(LEFT) AN IMAGE FROM THE BURIAL CHAMBER SHOWS THE DAMNED BEHEADED AND TURNED UPSIDE DOWN BY THEIR EXECUTIONERS. (BELOW) THE CEILING OF THE BURIAL CHAMBER IS PAINTED WITH SCENES FROM THE BOOK OF THE HEAVENS. IN THIS DETAIL THE GODDESS NUT SWALLOWS THE SETTING SUN GOD RA, WHO TRAVELS THROUGH HER BODY DURING THE NIGHT AND IS BORN AT THE DAWN OF EACH DAY.

THE DYNASTIES

Egyptian history is expressed in terms of ruling families or "dynasties."

I**N 300 BC, THE EGYPTIAN HISTORIAN MANETHO WROTE A HISTORY OF EGYPT CALLED *AEGYPTIACA*, WHICH PUT THE NUMBER OF DYNASTIES AT THIRTY.** ALTHOUGH HIS ORIGINAL BOOK DID NOT SURVIVE, WE KNOW OF IT FROM THE WORKS OF LATER HISTORIANS SUCH AS JOSEPHUS, WHO LIVED AROUND 70 AD AND QUOTED MANETHO IN HIS OWN WORKS. ALTHOUGH MANETHO'S HISTORY WAS BASED ON A MIXTURE OF NATIVE EGYPTIAN SOURCES AND MYTHOLOGY, IT IS STILL USED BY EGYPTOLOGISTS TO CONFIRM THE SUCCESSION OF KINGS WHEN THE ARCHAEOLOGICAL EVIDENCE IS INCONCLUSIVE.

The ancient Egyptians listed their kings in a continuous sequence beginning with the reign on Earth of the sun god, Ra. Events were recorded by the reigns of kings and not, as in our dating system, based on a universally agreed-upon calendar system. For that reason, exact dating of events in Egyptian history is unreliable.

Modern scholars have divided Manetho's thirty dynasties into "Kingdoms." During certain times, kingship was divided or the political and social conditions were disordered, and these eras are now called "Intermediate Periods." Today, we have agreed upon a chronology that is divided as follows, beginning from around 3100 BC:

The Archaic Period (414 years)
The Old Kingdom (505 years)
The First Intermediate Period (126 years)
The Middle Kingdom (405 years)
The Second Intermediate Period (100 years)
The New Kingdom (481 years)
The Third Intermediate Period (322 years)
The Late Period (415 years)
The Ptolemaic Period (302 years)

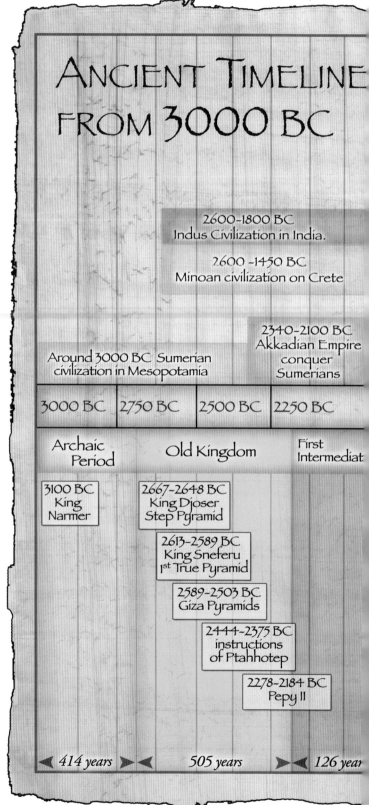

ANCIENT TIMELINE FROM 3000 BC

2600-1800 BC
Indus Civilization in India.

2600 -1450 BC
Minoan civilization on Crete

2340-2100 BC
Akkadian Empire conquer Sumerians

Around 3000 BC Sumerian civilization in Mesopotamia

3000 BC	2750 BC	2500 BC	2250 BC

Archaic Period	Old Kingdom	First Intermediat

3100 BC
King Narmer

2667-2648 BC
King Djoser Step Pyramid

2613-2589 BC
King Sneferu
1st True Pyramid

2589-2503 BC
Giza Pyramids

2444-2375 BC
instructions of Ptahhotep

2278-2184 BC
Pepy II

◄ 414 years ► ◄ 505 years ► ◄ 126 year

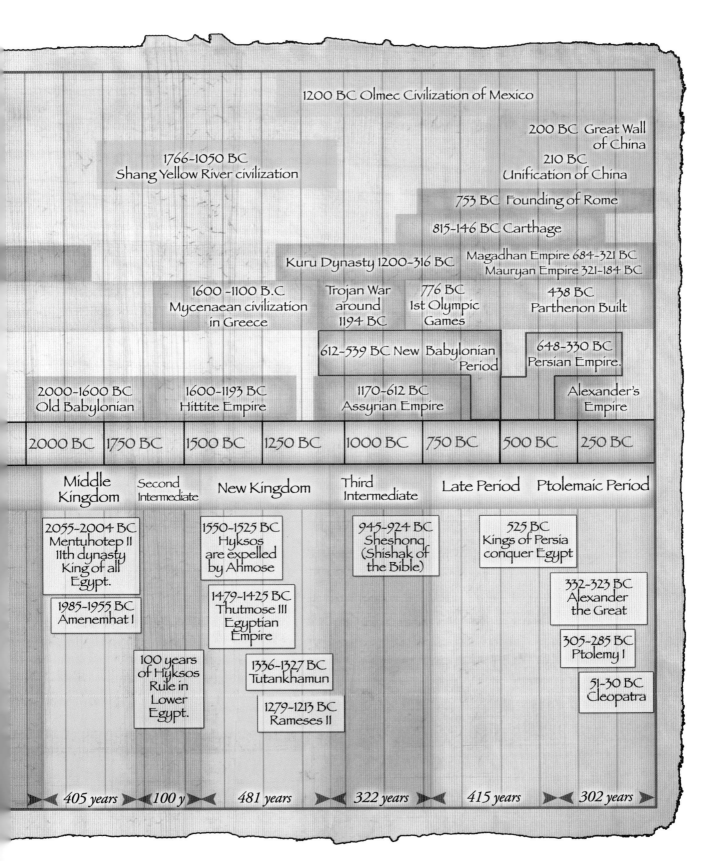

1200 BC Olmec Civilization of Mexico

200 BC Great Wall
of China

210 BC
Unification of China

1766-1050 BC
Shang Yellow River civilization

753 BC Founding of Rome

815-146 BC Carthage

Kuru Dynasty 1200-316 BC

Magadhan Empire 684-321 BC
Mauryan Empire 321-184 BC

1600 -1100 B.C
Mycenaean civilization
in Greece

Trojan War
around
1194 BC

776 BC
1st Olympic
Games

438 BC
Parthenon Built

612-539 BC New Babylonian
Period

648-330 BC
Persian Empire.

2000-1600 BC
Old Babylonian

1600-1193 BC
Hittite Empire

1170-612 BC
Assyrian Empire

Alexander's
Empire

2000 BC	1750 BC	1500 BC	1250 BC	1000 BC	750 BC	500 BC	250 BC

Middle
Kingdom

Second
Intermediate

New Kingdom

Third
Intermediate

Late Period   Ptolemaic Period

2055-2004 BC
Mentuhotep II
11th dynasty
King of all
Egypt.

1550-1525 BC
Hyksos
are expelled
by Ahmose

945-924 BC
Sheshonq
(Shishak of
the Bible)

525 BC
Kings of Persia
conquer Egypt

1985-1955 BC
Amenemhat I

1479-1425 BC
Thutmose III
Egyptian
Empire

332-323 BC
Alexander
the Great

305-285 BC
Ptolemy I

100 years
of Hyksos
Rule in
Lower
Egypt.

1336-1327 BC
Tutankhamun

51-30 BC
Cleopatra

1279-1213 BC
Rameses II

◀ 405 years ▶ ◀ 100 y ▶ ◀ 481 years ▶ ◀ 322 years ▶ ◀ 415 years ▶ ◀ 302 years ▶

First Dynasty, 3100 – 2890 BC

Narmer
Aha
Djer
Djet
Den
Anedjib
Semerkhet
Qaa

Before the First Dynasty, Egypt was in fact two lands. According to folk tales, the unifier of these lands was Menes, (also thought to be Narmer) the first mortal king of Egypt. The Greek historian Herodotus wrote in the fifth century BC that Menes founded the capital, Memphis, by damming the Nile to reclaim land for the city.

During this time, papyrus was invented and the written word became an important tool of government. The prosperity of the age can be seen in the magnificent artifacts that survive from this period.

(BACKGROUND) A DRAWING OF THE NARMER PALETTE SHOWS THE KING DEFEATING HIS ENEMIES.

Second Dynasty, 2890–2686 BC

Hetepsekhemwy
Raneb
Nynetjer
Peribsen
Khasekhem (Khasekhemwy)

A STATUE OF KING KHASEKHEM

At the end of the first dynasty there appears to have been rival claimants for the throne. The victor's Horus name, Hetepsekhemwy, translates as "peaceful in respect of the two powers." This may be a reference to the opposing gods Horus and Seth, or to an understanding reached between two rival factions. But the political rivalry was never fully resolved and in time the situation sank into conflict. The fourth pharaoh, Peribsen, took the title of Seth instead of Horus, and the last ruler of the dynasty, Khasekhemwy, took both titles, creating a Horus/Seth name meaning "arising in respect of the two powers" and "the two lords are at peace in him." Toward the end of this dynasty, however, disorder and possibly civil war set in.

THE SUMERIANS INVENT THE WHEEL.

THE SUMERIANS BEGIN TO FORM CITY-STATES RULED BY KINGS.

3600 BC

3500 BC

3400 BC

3300 BC

3200 BC

3100 BC

Old Kingdom 2686–2180 BC

Third Dynasty, 2686–2613 BC

Sanakht 2686–2667
Djoser 2667–2648
Sekhemkhet 2648–2640
Huni 2637–2613

This period was one of the landmarks in human history, a prosperous age during which Djoser created the world's first great monumental building, the Step Pyramid at Saqqara —the forerunner of later pyramids.

The artistic masterpieces discovered in the tombs of the nobles show the material wealth of this age.

A STATUE OF KING DJOSER AND A RECONSTRUCTION OF HIS STEP PYRAMID.

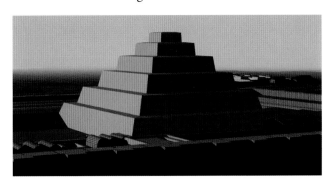

Fourth Dynasty, 2613–2494 BC

Sneferu 2613–2589
Khufu 2589–2566
Djedefra 2566–2558
Khafre 2558–2532
Menkaura 2532–2503
Shepseskaf 2503–2498

The Egyptians of the fourth dynasty accomplished one of the greatest feats in human history by building the Giza pyramids. There had been a long period of peace with no threats of invasion and the people's energies were spent cultivating art to its highest forms.

The rulers of the fourth dynasty came from Memphis and those of the fifth from Elephantine in the south, and the transition from one ruling family to another appears to have been peaceful.

RAHOTEP WAS THE KING'S PHYSICIAN. HE LIVED AT THE END OF THE THIRD AND THE BEGINNING OF THE FOURTH DYNASTY. (BELOW) A RECONSTRUCTION OF THE GIZA PYRAMIDS.

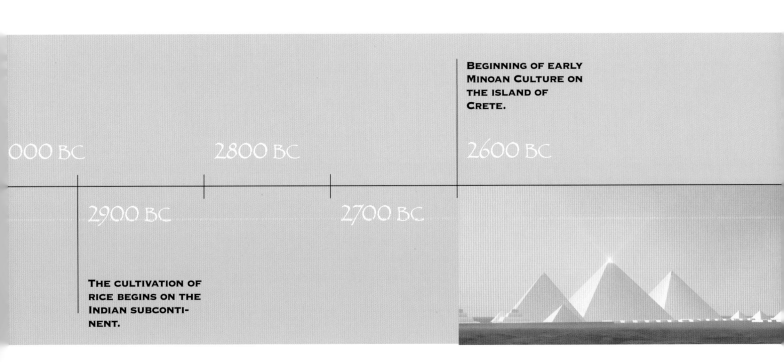

BEGINNING OF EARLY MINOAN CULTURE ON THE ISLAND OF CRETE.

3000 BC

2900 BC

2800 BC

2700 BC

2600 BC

THE CULTIVATION OF RICE BEGINS ON THE INDIAN SUBCONTINENT.

Fifth Dynasty, 2494–2345 BC

Userkaf 2494–2487
Sahura 2487–2475
Neferirkara Kakai 2475–2455
Shepseskara Isi 2455–2448
Raneferef 2448–2445
Nyuserra 2445–2421
Menkauhor 2421–2414
Djedkara Isesi 2414–2375
Unas 2375–2345

The first two kings of the fifth dynasty were sons of Lady Khentkaues, a member of the fourth-dynasty royal family. Institutions were created to handle the king's business and, for the first time, high officials were appointed from outside the royal family.

The pyramids of this period were smaller and less solidly constructed than those of the fourth dynasty, but the carvings from the mortuary temples are well preserved and of the highest quality.

The surviving papyri from this period, documenting the redistribution of goods among the royal residence, the temples, and state officials, demonstrate well-developed methods of accounting and recordkeeping.

Sixth Dynasty, 2345–2181 BC

Teti 2345–2323
Userkara 2323–2321
Pepy I 2321–2287
Merenra 2287–2278
Pepy II 2278–2184
Nitiqret 2184–2181

Many inscriptions survive from the sixth dynasty, including records of trading expeditions to the south from the reign of Pepy I. One of the most interesting is a letter written by Pepy II.

The pyramid of Pepy II at southern Saqqara is the last major monument of the Old Kingdom. None of the names of kings of the short-lived seventh dynasty are known, and the eighth dynasty shows signs of political decay.

THE FACE OF TI FROM A LIFE-SIZE STATUE. (BELOW) A DRAWING FROM THE MASTABA OF TI AT SAQQARA, SHOWING A HERD OF CATTLE FORDING A CANAL. TI WAS A HIGH-STATUS OFFICIAL DURING THE REIGN OF NYUSERRA.

SILKWORM CULTIVATION BEGINS IN AN AREA NOW KNOWN AS CHINA.

2500 BC

2400 BC

2300 BC

2200 BC

THE INDUS VALLEY CIVILIZATION BEGINS IN AN AREA OF WHAT IS NOW MODERN PAKISTAN AND NORTHEAST INDIA.

SECOND PHASE OF BUILDING AT STONEHENGE IN ENGLAND AROUND 2300 BC

About this time, Egypt simultaneously suffered political failure and environmental disaster and the Old Kingdom state collapsed. There was famine, civil disorder, and a rise in the death rate. The climate of northeast Africa was becoming drier, the Nile floods lower, and the cemeteries fuller. This was a dark time for Egypt. We know least about the years following the death of Pepy II. The only person from that era to have left an impression on posterity is a woman named Nitokris, who appears to have acted as king. There are no contemporary records but Herodotus wrote of her, "She killed hundreds of Egyptians to avenge the king, her brother, whom his subjects had killed. She did this by constructing a huge underground chamber and inviting all those she knew to be responsible for her brother's death to a banquet. When the banquet was underway, she let the river in on them through a concealed pipe. After this fearful revenge, she flung herself into a room filled with embers to escape her punishment."

Seventh & Eighth Dynasties, 2181–2125 BC

Wadjkara
Qakara Iby

Ninth & Tenth Dynasties, 2160–2025 BC

Khety Meryibra
Khety Wahkara
Merykara
Ity

The eighth dynasty was said to have had seventeen kings who left little evidence of their existence and we only know the names of two kings. The dynasty was short lived and for a time, petty warlords ruled the provinces.

Then, from the city of Herakleopolis, there emerged a ruling family led by Khety, who for a time held sway over the whole country. This did not last, though, and Egypt split into north and south. The north was ruled from Herakleopolis and the south from Thebes.

Manetho refers to a ruler of the ninth dynasty who was punished by the gods for his cruelty by being driven mad and then eaten by crocodiles.

Whereas the Theban dynasty was stable, kings succeeded one another rapidly at Herakleopolis. There was continual conflict between the two lands that would not be resolved until the eleventh dynasty.

The Admonitions of Ipuwer

IT'S NOT POSSIBLE TO GIVE A DATE FOR IPUWER. THE SURVIVING PAPYRUS OF HIS WORK IS A COPY MADE DURING THE NEW KINGDOM, BUT HE IS THOUGHT TO HAVE LIVED DURING THE MIDDLE KINGDOM. THE DOCUMENT DESCRIBES THE MANY CATASTROPHES AND PROBLEMS THAT PLAGUED EGYPT DURING THE FIRST INTERMEDIATE PERIOD, INCLUDING THE FOLLOWING:

"Wrongdoing is everywhere, and there is no man of yesterday."

"The land has knotted itself with criminals, and a man goes to plough with his shield."

"Scribes are killed, the laws of the council chamber are thrown out and the coward takes the brave man's property."

"The king has been deposed by the rabble."

"What the pyramid concealed has become empty and the possessors of tombs are ejected on to the high ground."

Middle Kingdom   2055–1650 BC

Eleventh Dynasty, 2125–1985 BC

Intef I 2125–2112
Intef II 2112–2063
Intef III 2063–2055
Mentuhotep I 2055–2004
Mentuhotep II 2004–1992
Mentuhotep III 1992–1985

The Middle Kingdom begins with the reunification of Egypt under Mentuhotep I, who ousted the kings of Herakleopolis. He assumed the Horus name "Divine of the White Crown," implicitly claiming all of Upper Egypt. This was later changed to "Uniter of the Two Lands."

His remarkable mortuary complex at Deir el-Bahri was the architectural inspiration for Hatshepsut's temple, built alongside it some five hundred years later.

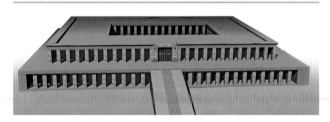

A RECONSTRUCTION OF MENTUHOTEP II'S FUNERARY TEMPLE AT DEIR EL-BAHARI.

Twelfth Dynasty, 1991–1782 BC

Amenemhet I 1985–1955
Sesostris I 1965–1920
Amenemhet II 1922–1878
Sesostris II 1880–1874
Sesostris III 1874–1855
Amenemhet III 1855–1808
Amenemhet IV 1808–1799
Queen Sobeknefru 1799–1795

During the twelfth dynasty Amenemhet I moved the capital back to Memphis and there was a revival of Old Kingdom artistic styles.

Amenemhet later took his son, Sesostris, as his coregent. During the ten years of joint rule, Sesostris undertook campaigns in Lower Nubia, which led to its conquest. Amenemhet was murdered during Sesostris's absence on a campaign in Libya, but Sesostris was able to maintain his hold on the throne and consolidate his father's achievements.

Sesostris III reorganized Egypt into four regions: the northern and southern halves of the Nile Valley and the eastern and western Delta. He and his successor, Amenemhet III, left a striking artistic legacy in the form of statuary depicting

THE REMAINS OF THE MUD-BRICK PYRAMID BUILT BY AMENEMHET III AT DAHSHUR.

THE ZIGGURAT OF UR IS MADE IN MESOPOTAMIA.

2100 BC   1900 BC   1700 BC

2000 BC   1800 BC

WORK BEGINS ON THE PALACE OF KNOSSOS, ON THE ISLAND OF CRETE.

THE BEGINNING OF CHINESE CALLIGRAPHY.

them as aging, careworn rulers. It was during this period that the written language was regularized into its classical form of "Middle Egyptian." The first body of literary texts was composed in this form, although several are ascribed to Old Kingdom authors. The most important of these is the "Instruction for Merikare," a discourse on kingship and moral responsibility.

Queen Sobeknefru, the first female monarch, marked the end of the dynastic line.

Thirteenth Dynasty, 1782–1650 BC

Wegaf
Intef IV
Hor
Sobekhotep II
Khendjer
Sobekhotep III
Neferhotep I
Sobekhotep IV Around 1725
Ay
Neferhotep II

The true chronology of the thirteenth dynasty is rather vague as there are few surviving monuments from this period. There were many kings who reigned for a short time, who were not of a single family, some of whom were born commoners. The last fifty years was a time of gradual decline. It seems that after the death of Ay the eastern Delta broke away under its own petty kings.

Fourteenth Dynasty

Lasted for around 57 years to about 1650 BC

Little is known about this dynasty, which was probably contemporary with the thirteenth dynasty. Asiatic immigration became widespread, and the northeastern Delta was settled by successive waves of nomadic people from Palestine.

Amenemhet I was murdered but Sesostris I was able to maintain his hold on the throne and consolidate his father's achievements.

Sinuhe

THE STORY OF SINUHE WAS ONE OF THE GREAT LITERARY ACHIEVEMENTS OF THE MIDDLE KINGDOM. IT BECAME A CLASSIC OF PROSE AND POETRY AND WAS COPIED AS AN EXERCISE BY SCHOOL BOYS FOR MANY HUNDREDS OF YEARS.

SINUHE WAS A COURT OFFICIAL DURING THE REIGN OF AMENEMHET I WHO FEARED THAT HE MIGHT BE DRAWN INTO A PLOT TO ASSASSINATE PHARAOH. TO AVOID BEING IMPLICATED HE FLED FROM EGYPT ACROSS THE SINAI DESERT, WHERE HE ALMOST DIED OF THIRST BUT WAS RESCUED BY BEDOUIN TRIBESMEN. AFTER MANY YEARS OF WANDERING SINUHE EVENTUALLY BECAME A TRIBAL CHIEFTAIN AND TRAVELED TO BYBLOS, ON THE SYRIAN COAST, WHERE HE MET THE PRINCE OF RETENU. THE PRINCE GAVE SINUHE THE HAND OF HIS DAUGHTER IN MARRIAGE, ALONG WITH SOME OF HIS LAND, AND SINUHE BECAME A WEALTHY MAN. BUT AS HE GREW OLD SINUHE LONGED TO RETURN TO EGYPT, WHERE HE WOULD BE BURIED WITH THE PROPER CEREMONIES TO ENSURE HIS ENTRY INTO THE AFTERLIFE. THE STORY ENDS HAPPILY WHEN THE NEW PHARAOH, SESOSTRIS I, ISSUES SINUHE A PARDON AND HE RETURNS HOME TO BE GREETED WITH GREAT HONOR BY THE KING.

THIS STORY TOUCHED THE EMOTIONS OF THE EGYPTIANS BECAUSE THEY CONSIDERED THEIR LAND A PARADISE, AND TO DIE IN A FOREIGN LAND WAS BELIEVED TO BE A PITIFUL FATE.

The Middle Kingdom fell because of the weakness of its later kings, which led to the invasion and settlement of Egypt by an Asiatic, desert people called the Hyksos.

These invaders eventually made themselves kings of Lower Egypt. The word Hyksos goes back to an Egyptian phrase meaning "ruler of foreign lands." The Jewish historian Josephus describes the Hyksos as sacrilegious invaders who despoiled the land but—with the exception of the title Hyksos—presented themselves as Egyptian kings and appear to have been accepted as such. They tolerated other lines of kings within the country, both those of the seventeenth dynasty and the various minor Hyksos who made up the sixteenth.

Fifteenth Dynasty, 1650–1550 BC

Sheshi
Yakubher
Khyan
Apepi I
Apepi II

Sixteenth Dynasty, 1650–1550 BC

Anather
Yakobaam

The Hyksos, sometimes referred to as the Shepherd Kings or Desert Princes, sacked the old capital of Memphis and built their capital at Avaris, in the Delta. The dynasty consisted of five or possibly six

kings, the best-known being Apepi I, who reigned for around forty years.

Their rule brought many technical innovations to Egypt, from bronze-working, pottery, and looms to new musical instruments and styles. New breeds of animals and crops were introduced. The most important changes were in the area of warfare: composite bows, new types of daggers and scimitars, and—most significant—the horse and chariot were introduced.

In many ways the Hyksos modernized Egypt and, ultimately, the civilization benefited from their rule.

Seventeenth Dynasty, 1650–1550 BC

Sobekemsaf
Intef VII
Tao I
Tao II Around 1560
Kamose 1555–1550

While the Hyksos ruled northern Egypt, a new line of native rulers was developing in Thebes. They controlled the area from Elephantine in the south to Abydos in the middle of the country. The early rulers made no attempt to challenge the Hyksos, though an uneasy truce existed between them. However, later rulers rose against the Hyksos and waged a number of battles. King Tao II, also know as Seqenenre, was probably killed in one of these battles—his mummy shows evidence of terrible head wounds. It was to be one of his sons, Ahmose, the founder of the eighteenth dynasty, who was to expel the Hyksos from Egypt.

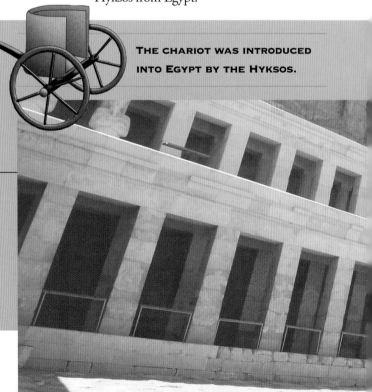

MINOAN CRETE REACHES THE PEAK OF ITS CIVILIZATION.

THE CHARIOT WAS INTRODUCED INTO EGYPT BY THE HYKSOS.

1600 BC

1550 BC

THE BUILDING OF STONEHENGE IN ENGLAND IS IN ITS FINAL PHASE.

Eighteenth Dynasty, 1550–1295 BC

Ahmose 1550–1525
Amenhotep I 1525–1504
Thutmose I 1504–1492
Thutmose II 1492–1479
Hatshepsut 1479–1425
Thutmose III 1473–1458
Amenhotep II 1427–1400
Thutmose IV 1400–1390
Amenhotep III 1390–1352
Amenhotep IV 1352–1336 (Akhenaten)
Smenkhkare 1338–1336
Tutankhamun 1336–1327
Ay 1327–1323
Horemheb 1323–1295

Egypt was reborn with the advent of the New Kingdom. The Theban kings expelled the Hyksos and the Egyptian army pushed beyond its traditional borders into Palestine and Syria. A huge empire was created that brought material wealth and new ideas into Egypt. The administration of the country and empire gradually changed from one of family succession to a more dynamic system of royal appointments: officials were now selected on merit.

The eighteenth dynasty marked the beginning of a period of unprecedented success in international affairs for Egypt. A succession of extraordinarily able kings and queens laid the foundations of a strong Egypt and bequeathed a prosperous economy to the kings of the nineteenth dynasty.

There was Ahmose, who expelled the Hyksos, followed by Thutmose I's conquest in the Near East and Nubia; Queen Hatshepsut and Tuthmose III, who made Egypt into the first super power; the magnificent Amenhotep III, who began an artistic revolution; Akhenaton and Nefertiti, who began a religious revolution by adopting the concept of one god; and finally, Tutankhamen, who has become so famous in our modern age.

(BACKGROUND AND LEFT) HATSHEPSUT'S TEMPLE AT DEIR EL-BAHARI, WITH A DETAIL FROM THE WALLS SHOWING WORKMEN TRANSPLANTING A TREE. (BELOW) A PORTRAIT OF THE HERETIC KING AKHENATEN AND A FIGURE OF THE BOY KING TUTANKHAMUN.

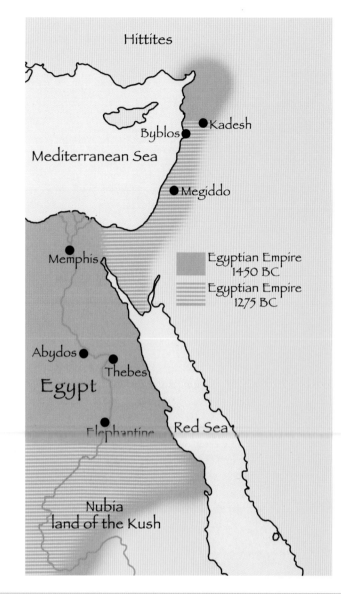

Hittites

Mediterranean Sea

Byblos ● ●Kadesh

●Megiddo

Memphis ●

Abydos ●
Egypt
Thebes ●

Elephantine ● Red Sea

Nubia
land of the Kush

Egyptian Empire
1450 BC

Egyptian Empire
1275 BC

Nineteenth Dynasty, 1295–1186 BC

Rameses I 1295–1294
Seti I 1294–1279
Rameses II 1279–1213
Merenptah 1213–1203
*Amenmessu
1203–1200*
Sety II 1200–1194
Saptah 1194–1188
Tausret 1188–1186

A COLOSSAL STATUE OF RAMESES II AT LUXOR TEMPLE.

Seti I looked to the mid-eighteenth dynasty as his model and ushered in a period of considerable prosperity. He restored countless monuments, and his temple at Abydos exhibits some of the finest carved wall reliefs.

His son, Rameses II, is the major figure of the dynasty. Around this time, the Hittites had become a dominant Asiatic power. An uneasy balance of power developed between the two kingdoms, prompting wars and treaties.

By this time Egypt was an ethnically pluralistic society, and this is reflected in its diversity of artistic expression. Unfortunately, the tide of history was turning and Rameses's son, Merenptah, had to struggle to maintain Egypt's prestige.

THE HINDU HYMNS KNOWN AS THE VEDAS ARE COMPOSED.

THE IRON AGE BEGINS IN EUROPE.

TIME OF THE TROJAN WAR.

1500 BC   1300 BC   1200 BC

1400 BC   1250 BC   1150 BC

THE LION GATE IS BUILT AT MYCENAE IN GREECE.

THE OLMEC PEOPLE OF MEXICO CARVE COLOSSAL STONE HEADS.

Twentieth Dynasty, 1186–1069 BC

Setnakht 1186–1184
Rameses III 1184–1153
Rameses IV 1153–1147
Rameses V 1147–1143
Rameses VI 1143–1136
Rameses VII 1136–1129
Rameses VIII 1129–1126
Rameses IX 1126–1108
Rameses X 1108–1099
Rameses XI 1099–1069

Setnakht ruled for only a few years but restored order after a period of chaos. His son, Rameses III, was the last great king. He gave Egypt a final moment of glory by defeating the Sea Peoples who had utterly destroyed the Hittite Empire and swept all before them on their march south.

A RELIGIOUS PROCESSION FROM THE WALL OF RAMESES III'S TEMPLE AT MEDINET HABU.

After Rameses III, Egypt began to suffer economic problems and a breakdown in the fabric of society. Egypt was unable to exploit the revolution of the Iron Age and there followed a succession of kings all called Rameses, perhaps in a vain attempt to recapture past glories.

Wenamun's Journey

THE EGYPTIANS DEFEATED THE SEA PEOPLES BUT THE VICTORY WAS COSTLY—IT LEFT THEM INCAPABLE OF DEFENDING THEIR EMPIRE IN THE EAST, WHICH WAS COLONIZED BY THE PHILISTINES AND SIDONITES. EGYPT'S PRESTIGE AS AN INTERNATIONAL POWER WAS DIMINISHED AND THE DISRESPECT FOR EGYPT'S AMBASSADORS IS DEMONSTRATED IN THE REPORT OF WENAMUN WHO LIVED DURING THE REIGN OF RAMESES XI. WENAMEN SAILED TO BYBLOS TO BUY TIMBER TO MAKE A SOLAR BARQUE FOR THE GOD AMUN. HE CARRIED A LETTER OF INTRODUCTION TO THE KING OF BYBLOS, A STATUE OF AMUN, AND A QUANTITY OF GOLD AND SILVER. HE DESCRIBED WHAT HAPPENED TO HIM LIKE THIS:

"I have been robbed in your harbor and you are the prince of this land. Search for my money for it belongs to Amun-Ra, king of the gods, and to the other great ones of Egypt."

He said to me: "Are you serious? I know nothing of this tale that you have told me."

Third Intermediate Period   1069–747 BC

From this point on Egypt is in steady decline as a great power. Others, including the Assyrians and the Babylonians, will determine events. Although Egypt has her moments of glory she is eventually conquered.

Twenty First Dynasty, 1069–945 BC

Smendes 1069–1043
Amenemnesu 1043–1039
Psusennes I 1039–991
Amenernipet 993–984
Osorkon 984–978
Siamun 978–959
Psusennes II 959–945

After the death of Rameses XI, Smendes proclaimed himself king and ruled from Tanis in the Delta.

Tanis was mostly rebuilt using monuments from the Middle and New Kingdoms. These structures were moved and relocated to Tanis. The city was known as "The city of obelisks."

The country was eventually divided between the kings and the high priests of Amun at Thebes. This era coincides with the biblical record of David of Israel's struggles against the Philistines.

THE GOLD FUNERARY MASK OF HIGH PRIEST AND ARMY GENERAL WENUDJEBAUENDJED FROM THE TWENTY-FIRST DYNASTY, REIGN OF PSUSENNES I, 1039-991 BC.

Twenty Second Dynasty, 945–715 BC

Shoshenk I 945–924
Osorkon I 924–889
Shoshenk II 890
Takelot I 889–874
Osorkon II 874–850
Takelot II 850–825
Shoshenk III 825–773
Pimay 773–767
Shoshenk V 767–730
Osorkon IV 730–715

Egypt was ruled for the next two hundred years by kings of Libyan origin.

Shoshenk (Shishak of the Bible) reunited the divided factions and the country.

Following the death of Solomon of Israel, Shoshenk moved against Jerusalem and defeated the kingdoms of Judah and Israel. He finally halted at Megiddo, the site of Thutmose III's victories some five hundred years before.

SAUL UNITES THE KINGDOM OF ISRAEL, WITH JERUSALEM AS ITS CAPITAL

962 BC

THE FOUNDING OF CARTHAGE.

800 BC

ROME IS FOUNDED.

753 BC

1000 BC

900 BC

776 BC

HOMER COMPOSES HIS TWO EPIC POEMS, THE ILIAD AND THE ODYSSEY.

THE OLYMPIC GAMES ARE HELD FOR THE FIRST TIME IN GREECE.

Twenty Third Dynasty, 818–715 BC

Kings at Leontopolis:
  Pedubast I 818–793
  Iuput I
  Shoshenk IV 780
  Osorkon III 777–749

During the reign of Shoshenk III, a prince called Pedubast proclaimed himself king in the central Delta at Leontopolis. Thus, there were two dynasties ruling at the same time: The twenty-second at Tanis and the twenty-third at Leontopolis.

The situation became even more confusing when yet a third man claimed to be king. In all, there was Iuput at Leontopolis, Peftjauabastet at Herakleopolis, and Nimlot at Hermopolis.

The weak government that resulted allowed the Nubians to exert a strong influence in southern Egypt.

Twenty Fourth Dynasty, 727–715 BC

  Tefnakht
  Bakenrenef

The Kings at Sais attempted to counter the Nubian threat by forming a coalition—but the endeavor eventually failed.

Twenty Fifth Dynasty, 780–656 BC

  Alara
  Kashta
  Piy 747–716
  Shabako 716–702
  Shabatka 702–690
  Taharka 690–664
  Tantarnani 644–656

The native princes of Kush (Nubia—modern Sudan) conquered a degenerate Egypt and established themselves as the twenty-fifth dynasty, restoring Egypt to its ancient customs and beliefs. They also contributed religious buildings at Thebes, had old texts recopied, and revived the custom of pyramid burials. Taharka supported Palestine's resistance against King Sennacherib of Assyria, but Sennacherib's son, Esarhaddon, defeated Taharka's army. Memphis was captured, along with its royal harem. On Esarhaddon's withdrawal from Egypt, Taharka returned from his refuge in Upper Egypt and massacred the Assyrian garrisons. He held control over Egypt until he was completely routed by Esarhaddon's son, Ashurbanipal, after which he fled south to Nubia, where he died and was buried in a large pyramid at Nuri.

After Solomon

AFTER THE DEATH OF SOLOMON IN 930 BC, HIS SON REHOBOAM RULED JUDAH WHILE ISRAEL WAS RULED BY JEROBOAM I, WHO HAD LED AN OPEN REBELLION AGAINST SOLOMON BEFORE HIS DEATH. THE TWO KINGDOMS WERE WEAKENED BY INTERNAL STRIFE AND IN 925 BC SHOSHENK I, KNOWN IN THE HEBREW BIBLE AS SHISHAK, DEFEATED THEM.

I KINGS 14: 25-26

"In the fifth year of king Rehoboam, Shishak, king of Egypt, attacked Jerusalem. He took everything including the treasures of the temple of the Lord and those of the royal palace, as well as all the gold shields made under Solomon."

706 BC

SANGON II'S PALACE AT KHORSABAD (IRAQ) IS BUILT. IT COVERS MORE THAN TWENTY-THREE ACRES (THR EE SQUARE KILOMETERS).

Twenty Sixth Dynasty, 664–525 BC

Neko I 672–664
Psamtek I 644–610
Neko II 610–595
Psamtek II 595–589
Apries 589–570
Amose II 570–526
Psamtek III 526–525

STATUE OF THE GODDESS TAWERET FROM THE SAITE PERIOD, TWENTY-SIXTH DYNASTY.

Psamtek I reunified Egypt, freed it from the Assyrians, and began the Saite dynasty. According to the Greek historian Herodotus, Psamtek I secured the aid of Greek mercenaries in order to become sole ruler. After an abortive rebellion by his vassals against the Assyrian ruler of Egypt in 663 BC, Psamtik was restored as governor of Athribis, a city of the Nile Delta, by the Assyrian king. Later rejecting his vassal status, he negotiated an alliance with Gyges, the king of Lydia, in Asia Minor, which enabled him to subdue the other Assyrian princes and vassals in the Delta. He reformed Egypt's government and removed the last vestiges of the rule of the kings of Kush.

Psamtek and Amose II carried out numerous building programs, including an enterprising scheme by Neko II to link the Red Sea and the Nile. Neko II defeated the army of Josiah of Judah but was later defeated by the Babylonian armies of Nebuchadnezzar.

Twenty Seventh Dynasty, 525–404 BC

Persian rulers of Egypt
Cambyses 525–522
Darius I 522–486
Xerxes 486–465
Artaxerxes I 465–424
Darius II 424–405
Artaxerxes II 405–359

In this period Cambyses II, the Achaemenid king of Persia, conquered Egypt. He received assistance from Polycrates of Samos, a Greek ally of Egypt. He was also helped by the Arabs, who provided water for his army to cross the Sinai Desert. Cambyses won the Battle of Pelusium (525 BC), in the Nile Delta, then captured Heliopolis and Memphis. After these defeats Egyptian resistance collapsed.

In 518 BC Darius I visited Egypt, which he listed as a rebel country, perhaps because of the insubordination of its governor Aryandes whom he put to death.

Twenty Eighth Dynasty, 404–399 BC

Amyrtaeus 404–399

For nearly a decade Amyrtacus led a rebellion against Persian rule. Upon the death of Darius II he declared himself king and once again established a native monarchy in Egypt. Little is known about him except that he set up his capital at Sais in the Delta and managed to assert his authority as far south as the old Egyptian border at Aswan.

He was the sole king of the twenty-eighth dynasty.

The Persian king Cambyses conquers Egypt

THE GREEK HISTORIAN HERODOTUS WROTE,

"After the surrender of Memphis, Cambyses took Psammenitus king of Egypt and confined him in the outer part of the city with other Egyptians, to insult him. He dressed the daughter of the king as a slave and sent her out with a pitcher to fetch water."

WEDJAHOR-RESNE WAS PHARAOH'S PERSONAL PHYSICIAN AND ALSO IN CHARGE OF THE ROYAL NAVY. IT IS POSSIBLE THAT HE BETRAYED HIS KING BECAUSE THERE IS NO MENTION OF A NAVAL ACTION, AND HE LATER RECEIVED HONORS AND GIFTS FROM CAMBYSES. HE WROTE,

"When the great King of all lands, Cambyses, came to Egypt he exercised sovereignty in the land in its entire extent. His Majesty conferred upon me the dignity of Chief San, and granted that I should be by him as Smer and Provost of the temple."

600 BC

Twenty Ninth Dynasty, 399–380 BC

Nepherites I 399–393
Hakor 393–380
Nepherites II 380

Egypt was now free of foreign rule and there was a period of consolidation and restoration.

After the death of Nepherites I there was a power struggle in which Hakor came out on top. During his fourteen-year rule, he carried out a great deal of building work. In 389 BC, he concluded a treaty with Athens against the Persians. With the help of Greek mercenaries he managed to repel several attacks by the Persians between 385 and 383 BC.

Thirtieth Dynasty, 380–343 BC

Nectanebo I 380–362
Takos 362–360
Nectanebo II 360–343

Nectanebo I reigned for eighteen years, and during this time Egypt was invaded by an army of Persians and Greeks. At first they were successful in overwhelming the Egyptians, but Nectanebo launched a counterattack and defeated the invaders.

His son Takos, with the support of Greek mercenaries, moved against the Persians in an attempt to gain Syria. Unfortunately, he made himself unpopular when he raised taxes to pay for this adventure.

Thirty First Dynasty, 343 – 332 BC

Second Persian Period:
Artaxerxes III 343–338
Arses 338–336
Darius III 336–332

Artaxerxes' first attempt to conquer Egypt, which had been independent since 404 BC, ended in failure. He tried again a few years later, using a great land and naval force and, at Pelusium in the Nile River delta, defeated the pharaoh Nectanebo II. The walls of Egypt's cities were destroyed, its temples were plundered, and Artaxerxes was said to have killed the Apis bull with his own hand.

Darius III was the last king of the Persian Empire.

Egypt's cities were destroyed, its temples were plundered, and Artaxerxes was said to have killed the Apis bull with his own hand.

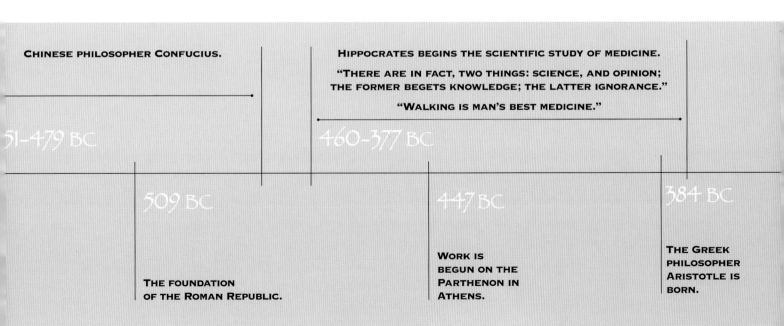

Alexander of Macedon (Alexander the Great), 332–323 BC

In November 332 BC, Alexander entered Egypt and the people welcomed him as their deliverer from the Persians. At Memphis he made a sacrifice to Apis, the sacred Egyptian bull, and was crowned with the traditional double crown of the pharaohs.

He founded the city of Alexandria, near the western arm of the Nile on a site between the sea and Lake Mareotis. From Alexandria he marched along the coast and then inland to visit the celebrated oracle of the god Amun in the oasis at Siwah. The priest gave him the traditional salutation of a pharaoh, as son of Amun. Alexander consulted the god on the success of his expedition but revealed the reply to no one.

The people welcomed Alexander as their deliverer.

(LEFT) A RECONSTRUCTION OF THE PHAROS LIGHTHOUSE AT ALEXANDRIA. TWO OF THE SEVEN WONDERS OF THE ANCIENT WORLD WERE EGYPTIAN: THE PYRAMIDS AT GIZA AND THE PHAROS LIGHTHOUSE. (OPPOSITE ABOVE) PTOLEMY III RECEIVES THE BLESSINGS OF GODDESSES REPRESENTING UPPER AND LOWER EGYPT.

Marriage contract between Heraclides and Demetria, 311 BC

HERACLIDES TAKES AS HIS LAWFUL WIFE DEMETRIA COAN, WHO BRINGS CLOTHING AND ORNAMENTS TO THE VALUE OF 1,000 DRACHMAE. HERACLIDES SHALL SUPPLY ALL THAT IS PROPER FOR A FREEBORN WIFE.

IF DEMETRIA IS DISCOVERED DOING ANY EVIL TO SHAME HER HUSBAND SHE SHALL BE DEPRIVED OF ALL SHE BROUGHT, BUT HERACLIDES MUST PROVE HIS ALLEGATIONS BEFORE THREE MEN WHOM THEY BOTH ACCEPT.

IT IS NOT LAWFUL FOR HERACLIDES TO BRING HOME ANOTHER WIFE NOR TO HAVE CHILDREN BY ANOTHER WOMAN NOR TO DO ANY EVIL AGAINST DEMETRIA ON ANY PRETEXT.

IF HERACLIDES IS DISCOVERED DOING ANY OF THESE THINGS AND DEMETRIA PROVES IT BEFORE THREE MEN WHOM THEY BOTH ACCEPT, HERACLIDES SHALL GIVE BACK THE DOWRY OF 1,000 DRACHMAE.

300 BC

Ptolemaic Period, 305–30 BC

Ptolemy I 305–285 (Soter I) General of Alexander
Ptolemy II 285–246 (Philadelphus)
Ptolemy III 246–221 (Euergetes I)
Ptolemy IV 221–205 (Philopator)
Ptolemy V 205–180 (Epiphanes)
Ptolemy VI 180–145 (Philometor)
Ptolemy VII 145 (Neos Philopator)
Ptolemy VIII 170–116 (Euergetes II)
Ptolemy IX 116–107 (Soter II)
Ptolemy X 107–88 (Alexander I)
Ptolemy XI 80 (Alexander II)
Ptolemy XII 80–51 (Neos Dionysos)
Cleopatra VII 51–30 (Philopator)
Ptolemy XV 44–30 (Caesarion)

Ptolemy I distinguished himself as a cautious and trustworthy troop commander under Alexander. During the council at Babylon that followed Alexander's death he proposed that the provinces of the huge empire should be divided among the generals. He became governor of Egypt and later its king.

With a defensive foreign policy he secured Egypt against external enemies and expanded its influence. He pursued a conciliatory policy toward the Egyptians and won them over through the restoration of the temples of the pharaohs, which had been destroyed by the Persians. He made gifts to the ancient Egyptian gods as well as to the Egyptian nobility and priesthood. In Memphis he established the Sarapis cult which combined the Egyptian and Greek religions.

Ptolemy I's other great achievement was the founding of the Museum (Mouseion), a common workplace for scholars and artists, and the establishment of the famous library at Alexandria. In the last few years of his life Ptolemy I wrote a reliable history of Alexander's campaigns that formed the basis of the works of later historians such as Arrian.

Ptolemy II was a prudent and enlightened ruler with great diplomatic ability and curiosity of mind. His most celebrated achievement was the construction of the famous lighthouse on the island of Pharos, off Alexandria. It was one of the seven wonders of the ancient world.

The last pharaoh was a woman—the famous Cleopatra VII Thea Philopator. Her attempts to maintain Egypt's independence and renew its glory were doomed. All the great civilizations of the ancient Mediterranean world had succumbed to the unassailable power of Rome.

It is not surprising that a country as rich and influential as Egypt could not maintain the liberty to pursue her own destiny. Her failed war against Rome made certain that Egypt would have no more pharaohs—and an Egypt without a pharaoh inevitably led to the end of ancient Egyptian civilization.

THE CARTHAGINIAN GENERAL HANNIBAL ATTACKS ROMAN TERRITORY.

218 BC

100 BC

211 BC

221 BC

QIN SHI HUANG UNIFIED CHINA AND DECLARED HIMSELF THE FIRST EMPEROR.

ARCHIMEDES, THE INVENTOR AND MATHEMATICIAN, IS KILLED DURING THE SIEGE OF SYRACUSE

Glossary

Here are some terms you need to know in order to explore and appreciate ancient Egypt.

A.D. abbreviation of the Latin words "Anno Domini," meaning "in the year of our Lord." A.D. refers to the measurement of time beginning with the year of Jesus Christ's birth. **B.C.** (Before Christ) refers to time measured *before* the birth of Christ. An alternative expression for A.D. is C.E. (Christian Era or Common Era); instead of B.C., some people say B.C.E. (Before the Christian or Common Era).

AKHET the season of inundation or flooding, running from mid-July to mid-November.

AKH the blessed dead, the ancestors. At times it is translated as "soul."

AMULET an object believed to provide good fortune and protection against evil.

ANKH a symbol of life resembling a looped cross. The ankh is widely used as an amulet.

BA an aspect of human personality. The Egyptians believed that it entered a person's body at birth and left at death.

BARQUE a boat sailed by the gods. The barque of Ra carried a host of deities across the sky each day.

BENU BIRD a manifestation of Atum, the solar god of Heliopolis, and later of Ra and Osiris.

BOOK OF AMDUAT "That which is in the Underworld," also called *The Book of the Secret Chambers.* It describes Ra's nightly journey from west to east, through the twelve regions of the underworld.

BOOK OF CAVERNS describes the journey of the sun god Ra through the six caverns of the underworld. It outlines the rewards and punishments of the afterlife.

BOOK OF THE DEAD a collection of magic spells and formulas, usually written on papyrus. It was considered an essential item for the dead to carry, to safely make their journey through the Underworld.

BOOK OF THE HEAVENS also known as *The Book of the Day, The Book of the Night,* and *The Book of the Divine Cow,* it is a collection of texts that describes the Sun's passage through the sky.

BOOK OF GATES describes the gates of the Underworld as barriers.

BIRTH HOUSE a smaller temple attached to the main temple of the Late and Greco-Roman periods.

BLUE CROWN also known as the khepresh, it is sometimes termed "the war crown."

CANOPIC JARS the four vessels that contained the mummified intestines, stomach, liver, and lungs of the deceased.

CARTOUCHE a French term referring to the ornamental oval frame that surrounded the name of a king, queen, or deity in inscriptions.

COFFIN a human-shaped or rectangular chest in which a mummified body was placed.

COFFIN TEXTS a collection of funerary spells usually written on the interior of wooden coffins during the Middle Kingdom (2008–1630 BC), intended for the use and protection of the deceased in the afterlife.

CONSORT a female companion other than a wife.

COPTIC from the Greek word *Aigyptos,* meaning "Egypt," the term refers to Egyptian art of the Roman and Byzantine period, after the introduction of Christianity in Egypt.

COLOSSUS A larger-then-life-size statue of a king, god, or person.

CATARACT from the Greek *kataraktes,* a term for a rapid or waterfall. The first Nile cataract was Egypt's southern border.

CUBIT an ancient Egyptian unit of length measurement the equivalent of approximately 1.7 feet (0.5231m).

CULT IMAGE a statue of a deity, sometimes made of precious metals, that served as the center of daily temple rituals.

DEMOTIC cursive script commonly used in the late dynastic and Greco-Roman periods.

DJED-PILLAR a representation of a reed column and the hieroglyph for the word "stability."

DOUBLE CROWN the two crowns associated with the kingship of Lower (northern) and Upper (southern) Egypt. Worn together, one inside the other, the double crown signified dominion over a united Egypt. *See also Red Crown and White Crown.*

DUAT the land of the dead, entered through the western horizon. Also called "Amduat."

ENNEAD   a group of nine gods.

ELECTRUM   an alloy of gold and silver.

FALSE DOOR   an imitation door carved or painted on a wall. It was believed that the ka (soul) of the deceased used this door to partake of funerary offerings.

HORUS NAME   one of the five royal names of the king.

HEB-SED FESTIVAL   a royal jubilee of rejuvenation celebrated by a king in the thirtieth year of his reign.

HEKA   magic.

HIERATIC   cursive writing of hieroglyphs.

HOUSE OF LIFE   a school within a temple.

KV   an abbreviation for the Valley of the Kings.

LITANY OF RA   a text found in New Kingdom royal tombs, showing the forms of the sun god Ra and his union with the king.

KA   an individual's vital life force, spirit, or soul.

KEMET   (kmt) the ancient name of Egypt, literally translated as the "black land," referring to the dark, fertile soil of the Nile flood plain.

KOHL   (from the Arabic kuhl) black eyeliner makeup.

KUSH   The Egyptian name given to ancient Nubia (modern Sudan).

LOTUS   a flowering water plant and a symbol of birth and dawn, thought to have been the cradle of the sun on the first morning of creation.

MASTABA   (from the Arabic mastaba, meaning "bench") an Old Kingdom underground tomb with an aboveground building.

MEMPHIS   (or Men-nefer) the ancient capital of Lower Egypt. Its ancient Egyptian name was Ineb Hedj, meaning "the White Walls."

NATRON   a naturally occurring salt used as a preservative and drying agent in mummification.

NAOS   a shrine in which a god's statue was kept.

NECROPOLIS   (from the Greek word meaning "city of the dead") cemetery.

NILOMETER   a staircase descending into the Nile and marked with levels for measuring and recording the depth of the Nile's inundation.

NOME   an administrative province of Egypt.

NOMARCH   The chief official of a nome.

OPET   an annual religious festival that took place in Thebes during the inundation.

PRAENOMEN   also called the Throne Name, a king's first cartouche name, adopted on his accession to the throne.

PYRAMID TEXTS   writings on the walls of burial chambers of the fifth through eighth dynasties.

RED CROWN   the crown of Lower (northern) Egypt. *See also Double Crown and White Crown.*

RELIEF   images carved into the surface of a wall.

SARCOPHAGUS   a stone outer container for a coffin.

SCARAB   an amulet in the shape of a beetle (the sun god Khepre). Its underside was often inscribed with text.

SHABTI   (also known as shawabti or ushabti) a mummy-form figurine inscribed with a magical spell empowering it to carry out agricultural work in the underworld on behalf of the deceased.

SHEN   a loop of rope that has no beginning and no end, symbolizing eternity.

SISTRUM   a sacred percussion instrument used in the cult of Hathor.

STELA   a stone slab, sometimes made of wood and decorated with texts commemorating an event (plural: stelae).

TRIAD   a term used to refer to a group of three gods.

THEBAN TRIAD   the gods Amun, his wife Mut, and their son Khons.

URAEUS   a goddess in the form of a cobra whose image was often mounted on the royal headgear.

VIZIER   the prime minister, the highest official of the royal court, responsible for the day-to-day governing of Egypt.

WASET   the New Kingdom capital of Egypt commonly known as Thebes and the site of modern-day Luxor.

WEDJAT-EYE   the eye of Horus symbolizing health, rejuvenation, and prosperity.

WHITE CROWN   the crown of Upper (southern) Egypt. *See also Double Crown and Red Crown.*

WADI   an Arabic term for a water-cut ravine or valley, now dry.

Index

Italics indicate illustrations.